ABOUT THE AUTHOR

TREVOR HORN is a multi-million-selling producer, song-writer, musician and record-label boss, who has won multiple BRITs, Grammys and Ivor Novello Awards across his 45-year career. In 2011, he was awarded a CBE for services to music.

ADVENTURES IN MODERN RECORDING

From ABC to ZTT

TREVOR HORN

NINE
EIGHT
BOOKS

NINE
EIGHT
BOOKS

NEB 011 PB

First published in the UK in hardback in 2022
This paperback edition published in 2023 by Nine Eight Books
An imprint of Black & White Publishing Group
A Bonnier Books UK company
4th Floor, Victoria House, Bloomsbury Square, London, WC1B 4DA
Owned by Bonnier Books, Sveavägen 56, Stockholm, Sweden

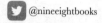 @nineeightbooks

 @nineeightbooks

Paperback ISBN: 978-1-7887-0606-3
eBook ISBN: 978-1-7887-0604-9
Audio ISBN: 978-1-7887-0605-6

Publishing director: Pete Selby
Senior editor: Melissa Bond

Cover design by Lora Findlay
All images in the plate section courtesy of the author
Typeset by IDSUK (Data Connection) Ltd
Printed and bound in Great Britain by Clays Ltd, Elcograf S.p.A

3 5 7 9 10 8 6 4

Nine Eight Books is an imprint of Bonnier Books UK
www.bonnierbooks.co.uk

I would like to dedicate this book to my late wife, Jill Sinclair.
Without her, none of this would have happened.

CONTENTS

Introduction

Produced by Trevor Horn (Prince's Trust) Concert at Wembley Arena (2004) – Part 1

In which I draw together the strings of my career so far

A lot happened in the period following this Prince's Trust concert. Things that I prefer not to think about, much less to discuss: my wife Jill's accident, losing my mother and then my father – all events that happened within three years of one another. It's one of the reasons that this account stops in 2004.

Another is that the concert became an opportunity to mark my work up to that point, a celebration of the artists involved in all the stages of my career. I was uncomfortable with the idea that it was all about me. I was worried that it might come across like some massive ego trip. But it ended up being among the best nights of my life.

Like many – most? – things in my career up to that point, it was something that Jill came up with. Her idea was for both a *Produced by Trevor Horn* compilation album and an accompanying concert. Deciding to do the gig in aid of the Prince's Trust came next. I'd done things for them before, and I always really liked Prince Charles and his work. That was the easy part.

I made a wishlist of the artists I wanted: the Buggles, Seal, Grace Jones, Pet Shop Boys, Lisa Stansfield, t.A.T.u., Dollar, ABC, Art of Noise, Propaganda, Belle and Sebastian, Yes, and Frankie Goes to Hollywood. Of those, the Frankies would of course prove most challenging. Could we get them back together?

We knew that during the previous year they had participated in aVH1 show, *Bands Reunited*, except that Holly and Nasher had bailed out and the planned reunion never actually happened. Hoping for a different response, we contacted them, but while the other members of the band were happy to share a stage, again it was Nash and Holly who declined to take part. Fair enough. We asked the original guitarist, Jed – Mark's brother – to cover for Nash and held auditions for a new singer.

The auditions made national headlines. Through them we recruited a singer called Ryan Molloy, who was a hell of a good frontman. That was our Frankie for the evening. Phew!

Similarly, Propaganda had a hiccough or two. I had asked Claudia and Susanne if they'd perform 'Dr Mabuse' as Propaganda, but Ralf and Michael from the original band objected. When it became apparent that they couldn't stop the performance going ahead, they insisted on appearing, so ultimately, we had to have them posing on stage behind keyboards that weren't plugged in.

Add to those headaches the usual problems of having to corral a dozen or so bands to play a major concert and, as you might imagine, it was a busy and stressful scene. There were meetings. Lots of meetings. By now I'd persuaded Steve Lipson to help me put the gig together, and in my office at SARM West we'd pore over numerous diagrams showing who was playing what and when, who was rehearsing when and where, who needed this, who needed that. All the bands were playing for free, but I had to cover their costs, which in some cases were fairly astronomical (flying Yes over from the States, for example). On the plus side, a production company, Clear Channel, were pitching in to film the concert for a DVD release, so at least we had a budget of sorts.

Meanwhile, there was a Grace situation. Of course, there was. I wanted her to do 'Slave to the Rhythm' but Clear Channel weren't keen. Why? I suppose you could say that Grace had a certain diva-like reputation at the time. People heard the name and right away, their foreheads got shiny with nerves. I'd had a similar reaction when I was working on the 2000 film *Coyote Ugly* and mentioned Whitney Houston. Two or three people visibly flinched and put their hands in their hair. But I stuck to my guns. I wanted 'Slave to the Rhythm' live at Wembley Arena. Which meant we had to have Grace.

'Well, all right,' they said, 'but you're going to have to go and talk to her.' So I did. I went to meet her at her apartment by the side of the Thames, where she sat drinking red wine. I declined and drank rice milk instead. 'I'm doing this show at Wembley Arena,' I told her. 'We'll have a big band on stage, as well as an orchestra. I'd love you to do "Slave to the Rhythm".'

She looked at me, lip curling. 'You didn't return my calls,' she wailed, which was true, I hadn't returned all her calls. 'And I came to Canada to do that song for you,' she continued. This was a thing she'd done for me on the 1992 *Toys* fantasy comedy soundtrack.

'But, Grace, you did get a lot of money for that song,' I pointed out.

At the end of the rant, I said to her, 'I'm sorry about all of that, but I can't change it. Now will you do the show or not?'

'I'll do it,' she purred, 'but it's going to cost you.'

I said, 'Is it going to cost me from my spirit or from my wallet?'

'Both,' she said.

We laughed our heads off at that. And by the time I left, we were buddies again.

I lost weight during the rehearsals, purely from the physical effort that I wasn't used to putting in. I spent most of that period rehearsing the band and orchestra: fourteen string players and ten brass players. I had three keyboard players, three on guitar.

As it got closer to the big day – Thursday 11 November 2004 – we discovered that Seal wouldn't be turning up until the afternoon rehearsal before the show. Nick Ingman, who was doing all the orchestral arranging, had given me a great bit of advice, saying, 'We won't be able to play the songs as they were recorded. We need to go online and see how the artists do them live.'

As if to prove his point, Seal submitted a live version of 'Crazy' and it was indeed different from the record version, i.e. the 'Crazy' we'd started rehearsing. Building that into those early rehearsals certainly helped from a technical point of view, even if it didn't do much to soothe my already tattered nerves. Don't forget I hadn't done any live work for a while at that time. I wasn't exactly what you'd call match fit. Not only that, but there were mutterings about making me compère. I'm a producer. The musical equivalent of a mole. I don't *do* on-stage announcements at Wembley Arena.

On the Sunday, with just four days to go before the gig, we had the first real dress rehearsal with everybody apart from Seal and Grace there. Forty people in the room. We were at the Music Bank in Bermondsey on the top floor, and I suddenly realised that there was no food available. Sure, there was coffee, Hobnobs and whatnot, but nothing substantial with which to feed forty musicians and technicians. I called the SARM chef, a lovely guy called Marco – he's Madonna's chef now. I said, 'I've got forty people, can you do food for forty?'

At about 3 p.m., people were coming up to me and saying, 'Where do we go to get some food?'

'Just give it half an hour,' I said, swallowing hard, until at about 4 p.m. Marco showed up with two guys and mountains of gorgeous food. It's such an important thing, feeding musicians. I think of it as part of the job when you hire them. If you want them to perform to the best of their abilities, you must look after them.

Although we were due to have a full dress rehearsal on the afternoon of the gig, with all the artists present, neither we nor Grace's people thought it would be a good idea to have Grace hanging around, getting bored and possibly being volatile. Instead, we'd had a special rehearsal for her on the Wednesday night, minus the orchestra.

Grace arrived at an otherwise deserted Wembley Arena, clutching a bottle of red wine. 'Do it exactly like the record,' we told her, and off we went.

As we played, I found myself looking across at the musicians, the guitarist Phil Palmer had a look of absolute bliss on his face, as though to say, *It doesn't get better than this, playing 'Slave to the Rhythm' with Grace Jones*. I could relate. What a vibe it was. Just us in that great big empty space with the music blasting out. As I said, I'd had all kinds of reservations about the show; it was hard work putting it together and I was nervous as hell. But seeing that expression on Phil's face made me think it would all be worth it.

It made me think something else, too. That if twenty-five years in the game had been leading to anything, then maybe it was this gig.

1

'The Parade of the Tin Soldiers', Leon Jessel (1897)

In which I discover music

Music first came into my life at five years old when I heard 'The Parade of the Tin Soldiers' on our family gramophone at home in Stonebridge, just outside Durham. Back then, the Horns consisted of: Dad, John; Mum, Elizabeth; my older sister, Janet (now living in Canada); a younger sister, Marj (who writes novels as M. M. DeLuca); and then much later – a whole nine years after me – a younger brother, Ken, who's now a TV producer, with *Line of Duty* among his credits. We were all pretty musical, in one way or another, and, for me, that was where it started.

'The Parade of the Tin Soldiers' is a jaunty tune, made famous by its use in Betty Boop and Disney cartoons. I distinctly remember the effect that the music had on me. The feeling of excitement it produced. It made me want to run around. The feeling was profound and, in many ways, has never left me. I'm lucky to have had a few musical epiphanies in my life. Hearing Seal sing for the first time. Playing with Anne Dudley for the first time.

Hearing 'Video Killed the Radio Star' on the radio for the first time. But 'Tin Soldiers' was the first. Arguably, it was also the most important.

From that moment onwards, I was drawn to the gramophone and radio. There was so much big band music around at that time. Artie Shaw. Benny Goodman. Not only was this the stuff I grew up with, but it was also the reason that I didn't love rock 'n' roll when it first came along, years later. To me, rock 'n' roll seemed like folk music: it only had three chords and you could hear them coming a mile off. Of course, I soon realised that it's all about execution, atmosphere and intent, but back then I didn't appreciate that – I just thought it was a bit rudimentary.

Meanwhile, as a newly minted music fan, I would listen on Sunday lunchtimes to Edmundo Ros, a Latin-American band leader whose music reached across the airwaves and spoke to me in a way that I'd never been spoken to before – so much so that I'd arm myself with wooden spoons and bash out a rhythm during his show. Sundays were a happy time.

Mondays, not so much. School had been purgatory from the moment I first stepped inside the gates. I remember returning home after my first day and my mother saying, 'How was it, Trevor?'

'It was okay, Mam,' I told her, 'but I'm glad it's over. I don't want to do it again.'

She broke the news gently: 'You've got to go back tomorrow.'

'Oh no, Mam,' I said, 'not a whole second day. . .'

Part of the problem was that I wore glasses. 'Brains' was what the other kids used to call me, and not in an admiring or affectionate way, more in a 'you're gonna get your head kicked in' way. I had been wearing them since the age of four, when I was diagnosed with astigmatism, which is basically deformed corneas from my mother having rickets when she was pregnant with me. But as a little pre-schooler, wearing glasses was just something I did. I thought nothing of it. Starting primary school, I realised that wearing glasses wasn't just a small and insignificant part of me. It *was* me. And like it or not (not), I was to be defined by them.

At primary school we were given recorders and told to go home and practise. For me, it was a revelation, another sort of musical epiphany, and over the weekend I learned how to play a rudimentary tune. Perhaps more importantly, I also began to understand the mechanics of reading music. Prior to that I had always been a noise- and sound-orientated person. For reasons that might have had to do with my poor eyesight, I had instead concentrated my senses on hearing. Now, though, I was beginning to appreciate how music made its way from the head of its composer onto the page and subsequently into the fingers of the musicians. I was experimenting with music, trying things on to see what would fit, and soon my attention went to my dad's double bass.

Dad was playing four or five evenings a week with the Joe Clark band at the Astoria in Durham, just outside our hometown of Stonebridge. It was a sweet musical relief from his days spent as a maintenance engineer for the Milk Marketing Board dairy that we lived next door to. He would take the bass with him at nights, of course, but there it sat during the day.

What had inspired him to take up the double bass? I don't know; he'd started off playing the banjo in a trad band but then for some reason moved to double bass. One thing I do know is that he never really had any designs on going professional.

He didn't think that being a professional musician was a particularly good job, for the simple reason that professionals tended to play all the time in the same place and play stuff they didn't like. What begins as a calling – a noble calling, come to that – ends up being just another job where you must play music you don't like just for the money. If you're an amateur you don't have to do that; you can do whatever you want. You can just enjoy your music without that kind of pressure.

Most of the time what Dad did was called busking, in the sense that he played without music. He knew all the standards but when he was playing with a big band he could sight-read. Some of those old tunes have got very complicated harmonic structures. So anyway, I finally bugged him enough to show me something on the double bass, we sat down, and he played a vintage minstrel song, 'Old Folks at Home', also known as 'Swanee River'.

He sang, 'Way down upon a Swanee River. . .', and then stopped. 'You're going to play the root notes of the chords.'

'What's a chord?' I asked.

'A chord's like a triad.'

'What's a triad?'

'It's three notes,' he said.

For a while he did his best to show me the basics, before ending the lesson: 'I've got a gig to get to. Have a go yourself, Trevor.' And off he went, leaving me with some written bass music and a burning desire to learn. Not long after that, I took up the guitar. After dinner I'd skulk off and spend hours plonking away at it, trying to figure it out.

And there it was, another piece of the jigsaw falling into place. I was putting my experience playing the recorder to good use in order to figure out how to play the bass. I said to myself, 'It's just like the recorder, only in a different place, and instead of a *bah, bah, bah* sound, it's a *bam, bam, bam* sound.'

What intrigued me was the chords. Dad had impressed as much upon me, the need to learn chords, even to appreciate the inversions of chords. And that's what I was doing then. The tin soldiers were marching in my head and from that moment on, I was playing music.

———

Dear old Uncle Robert had moved out – or should I say *had been* moved out – by the time my music addiction took hold. He'd been living with us for a while. For me, that meant I could move my centre of operations into his old room, which, as Uncle was a musician himself, already had its own piano. Now I had my music room, and I would go in there every evening to practise for hours.

Looking back, I think I would have done a lot better had I been taught formally instead of just fiddling around for myself. Ask me now and I'd recommend any budding musician gets a teacher. It's much quicker and you don't run the risk – or at least you mitigate the risk – of picking up terrible habits.

Meanwhile, our house now had a record player – a record player as distinct from a gramophone. It belonged to Janet, who had been given it for Christmas, along with an actual record, 'Multiplication' by Bobby Darin, which came out in 1961. Whenever I'm asked in interviews, 'What was the first record you bought?', that's my answer, but, in fact, it was all down to Janet, who, as the family's first teenager, was very much the musical tastemaker in our house. What I remember is being fascinated by the mechanics of it; I'd listen to that record and ask myself, 'What's happening here? How can I work out how to reproduce this sort of music?'

And then, as the 1960s made their presence felt, so, too, did the Beatles. I had first heard 'Love Me Do' on Radio Luxembourg and I thought it was okay. Only okay, though. I mean, I didn't *love* the Beatles right away, not until I heard them on *Easy Beat*.

In those days, the way that you heard music was totally different. You had the radio, just the radio, which was limited mainly to Radio Luxembourg, or the BBC Home Service and the BBC Light Programme. On the Home Service was what you might call the 'serious' stuff. Any music they played was either classical or old-style blues. It was eventually replaced by Radio 4.

The BBC Light Programme, on the other hand, was a national radio station, which in 1967 was replaced by Radio 1 and 2. It was on the Light Programme that you'd hear all the popular stuff. They had the *Billy Cotton Band Show*, which went out on a Sunday lunchtime and included Alan Breeze, Kathie Kay, Russ Conway and Mrs Mills. Terry Jones and Michael Palin both cut their teeth on the *Billy Cotton Band Show*. The Light Programme also broadcast *Family Favourites* and *Easy Beat*, and it was on those that you'd hear pop music. I'm pretty sure that it was on *Easy Beat* that I first heard 'Please Please Me'. And if we're talking 'moments' – that was one. Prior to that, I'd liked Cliff Richard & the Shadows, but once the Beatles came along, Cliff & the Shads were old news.

(Having said that, I used to love hearing 'Apache' on Radio Luxembourg late at night just before sleep, when listening to music would be an experience similar to the way being stoned is now, how you're a little bit out-of-body, the signal fading in and out. That phasing sound on 'Itchycoo Park' by the Small Faces? I swear they got that from listening to Radio Luxembourg in the wee small hours.)

My father had a four-string guitar he let me play. I'd started to teach myself the chords and triads. I still play a couple of chords in a weird way because I never had a book to show me the right way. Around the same time, I was given a double bass at grammar school, as well as a bow to play it with, and a place in the school orchestra. I was totally crap, but at least I was scraping away and making a noise. My Uncle Tommy had given me a tape recorder, and I can't think exactly when that was, but I had it in January 1963 when 'Please Please Me' was released because, having heard and loved the song, I set myself the task of trying to record my own version. Just me, the little four-string guitar and the tape recorder.

Decades later, an interviewer asked me, 'When did you first realise you were a musical genius?'

My reply? 'It's the wrong question. The question should be, "When did I realise I *wasn't* a musical genius?"' And that was when I learnt 'Please Please Me' on my little four-string guitar, recorded into my tape recorder and listened to it back. It was bloody awful. I sounded terrible. Back in those days I had a broad Geordie accent, very little skill as a singer and only slightly more as a guitar player. I compared the Beatles' record with my tape-recorded version of it and in many ways that experience has informed my musical life from thereon in. I've never been convinced that I'm particularly good at music. I've done it all my life, so I can't be that bad, but I've never had that arrogance of thinking I'm great, or that just because *I* did it then it must be good. I always think back to that first attempt at 'Please Please Me', and how utterly shit it was. Everything I've done since? At least it's an improvement on that.

I remember being at the bus stop and seeing the girl from down the road, Jan Bell, there. 'What are you thinking about?' I said, or words to that effect.

'The only thing I can think about at the moment is John,' she replied dreamily.

'John who?'

'John Lennon.'

I said, 'You like the Beatles?'

'Oh, I *love* the Beatles,' she said.

Now that may sound like the most mundane and prosaic of conversations, but it's symbolic of what the Beatles meant to our generation. It was all about how they brought us together; how they were all-consuming; how you went from being a person who had never heard of them to someone who *loved* them and could think of nothing else but John Lennon.

For me of course, it all coincided with puberty. Years earlier and I wouldn't even have been talking to Jan Bell because she was, *ugh*, a girl. Now she was, *wow*, a girl. My musical awakening went hand in hand with my sexual awakening.

At home I found myself comparing the Beatles 'live' (as in, on the telly, because that was the other thing about the Beatles: you got to see them on the telly) with the sound they made on the record. It sounded different. Better? I'm not sure I would have put it that way then, and, of course, the Beatles were such an incredibly tight live outfit that they sounded phenomenal live anyway. To me, it wasn't necessarily a question of one version being superior to another, more a simple case of the two versions having a different sound: the immediacy of the live performance versus the ability to play the record repeatedly.

The Beatles were followed by the Rolling Stones, and I loved the Stones but never quite as much. Their material was all three-chord stuff. It was simple. Same with the Kinks. The Beatles, on the other hand, had passing chords. They could play slow Spanish-sounding romantic numbers like 'Till There Was You'. It was as though they were drawing together the strings of everything that had fascinated me musically up till then. I was obsessed by them, fascinated by them. After seeing the Beatles, I wanted to be in a band. I could think of no higher calling.

As for that four-string guitar, I left it propped up against a chair, only for another member of the family to knock it over, breaking the head off. My parents couldn't afford to buy me another, so my father fixed it, but it was never quite the same. I still have it. It still has that repair on it. A similar thing happened with the double bass. The bow for the double bass was in a long cloth bag, and one time getting off the bus, the bow got stuck through a grab handle and snapped. I was distraught because the school couldn't afford to buy me another one, so my father fixed that, too, but that, also, was never quite the same again. To this day, one of the things that I'm obsessive about in the studio is that when you finish with a guitar you put it on a stand, you don't just leave it hanging around, on the floor or on a sofa. It all goes back to that four-string.

2

'The Lonesome Death of Hattie Carroll', Bob Dylan (1963)

In which I realise I have a love for lyrics

Musically, things started moving quickly for me in my early teens. In no particular order, then. Number one: I began 'depping' for my dad, by which I mean that there were some nights when he'd be too busy at the dairy and so I would take his place, maybe for the first set or so. I'd learned to sight-read bass music (to be honest, it wasn't all that difficult because back then double-bass parts were either walking crotchets or a plonk on one and three) and I could busk some of the old tunes and it would get me through.

My dad was playing fewer nights by then anyway, a change in circumstance that was indicative of the way music was evolving society-wide. By the time I was twelve, he was playing a regular gig at Durham Town Hall on a Saturday night. There was my dad's band plus the beat group. That was how it used to break down back then, 'bands' and 'beat groups', and the bands didn't like the beat groups at all.

The thing was that to play big band dance-band music you had to be able to read music. Most of the new beat groups didn't and so the old musicians despised them for it. 'Two frets up from shake rattle and roll' would be the kind of comment they would make. They also hated the way that the beat groups would play too loud and overshadow the singer. My dad used to say, 'When you're playing with a singer, listen for the singer. If you can't hear him, you're playing too loud – the singer is the main thing.'

He was right. Think of rock music, for example, where some of the most distinctive and memorable vocalists are those with a high voice that cuts through the cacophony from behind: Robert Plant, Freddie Mercury, Jon Anderson of Yes. Mick Jagger is a great example of a vocalist who simply has an exceptionally loud (and excellent) voice and manages to cut through that way.

Never a problem for the Beatles, of course. They always had dynamics. Again, it's that dance-band background. That unconscious smushing together of two worlds.

I loved depping for my dad. I loved playing 'Let's Twist Again' on the double bass. Sometimes I'd go down there just to be with him anyway. It was a way of spending time with him, too. He'd pack me off with money for the bus home before it got too late (although I'd spend it on fish and chips), but I was there long enough to see grown-ups getting a little bit drunk, which is an exciting thing when you're eleven and twelve. I loved the smell of the cigarette smoke, the perfume and alcohol.

Number two: the youth orchestra. I played double bass in the school orchestra and the youth orchestra both at senior and junior levels. I was by far the best double bass player in the county. There wasn't another double bass player in the area that could hold a candle to me.

Okay, fair enough: I was the best double bass player in the area by virtue of the fact that I was the *only* double bass player in the area, and even if my playing wasn't always as technically proficient as it might have been, I still really enjoyed it. We were rehearsing Tchaikovsky's Symphony No. 1 (*Winter Revels*), which is still one of my favourite pieces of music. I remember the conductor stopping everything. 'There's something wrong in the bottom end,' he said, finger held aloft. 'Let me hear the cellos.'

The cello players played. The conductor decided it wasn't the cellos.

'The bass. The double bass, let's hear the double bass.'

The double bass player played. That was me.

He stopped me: 'I think you're misreading it,' he said.

'I'm not misreading it,' I told him. 'I just can't play it.'

This got a laugh from the others and from then on, I was a bit of an orchestra comedian. But it didn't matter to me back then; I was there for the music. Music, music, music – that's what it was all about. I'd become aware of Burt Bacharach. The Cilla Black version of 'Anyone Who Had a Heart' was the first record I heard where the voice was mixed really close-up. I don't know what George Martin was up to (and of course at that age had no concept of George Martin 'producing' it anyway), but that record just did something to me, the way the voice was used. The sentiment, too. I've always had an affinity with sad, intimate songs. I liked the sad songs in the Beatles' catalogue – for example, 'No Reply' or 'Every Little Thing'. I like songs where the protagonist has a pathetic, slightly tragic quality. Somebody said, '"Anyone Who Had a Heart" isn't Cilla's originally, that's an American singer, Dionne Warwick,' after which I was listening out for Dionne Warwick and then I heard 'Walk on By', another Bacharach classic, and one of the saddest songs ever.

I remember being away with the youth orchestra, someone had a copy of it, and I kept playing it over and over. I could get like that with records. Everyone around me seemed to like the music of the time. I certainly wasn't alone in that respect but for me, it went further. Everyone else liked music. I *loved* it. To me, it was like seeing emotions. Like visualising a place. A place that you can't quite put into words.

Number three in the way things were moving musically was my band. When I was about the age of thirteen, and seeing that I was hopelessly hooked on music, my parents gave me a guitar to replace the four-string one that got broken. It was a proper six-string job, which they bought on hire purchase.

I can tell you from experience that it is difficult to go from a four-string to a six-string guitar, but I practised hard. And I wouldn't say that I mastered it, but I got there, and having got that far, I decided to start a band. Well, that was one of the reasons. The other reason was the bullying. My big mistake had come sometime in the second year. This horrible kid whose name I can't remember was showing everybody a picture of a penis in a vagina, which of course was an object of great fascination for us, except muggins here made the mistake of saying to the horrible kid, 'Is this your mum and dad?'

It was just something I blurted out. Clearly, though, it counted as an egregious insult, one for which recompense would be required, reparations in the form of my physical suffering. Thus, for the rest of the year, the horrible kid and his mates would chase me around, trying to beat me up with varying degrees of success.

Now, this bullying was by no means the reason that I started the band. The reason I started the band was more to do with my six-string guitar than my sick sense of humour, but I will say this: it turned things around for me, for the simple reason that I suddenly had a little gang of my own. I was the lead guitar player and we had a guy called Hemmings on drums, while a bloke called John Kell was the bass player. This was swiftly followed by the appearance of Robin Batie, who wanted to be the singer and had two very important things going for him: firstly, he was pretty good-looking; secondly, he was one of the toughest kids around. The fact that he played harmonica was a bonus. He told the bullies that I was now under his protection.

So that was us: the Outer Limits. I had named us after the TV show, of which I was very fond and if it sounds as though we were a little bit sci-fi and psychedelic, well, nothing could be further from the truth. Our genre wasn't psychedelic, our genre was more . . . crap. Still, we tried. That basic three-chord stuff I was occasionally prone to looking down my nose at suddenly looked a far more attractive proposition when it came to trying to play it for myself. Our speciality was rudimentary R&B nicked from the Stones and the Kinks.

The Outer Limits performed one of our first gigs in a place called Meadowfield. During the gig I discovered that if I turned the amplifier up very loud it did a strange thing – a strange thing I would later come to know as distortion.

There were a couple of Teds in the audience and despite having quite a benign and dapper reputation these days, Teddy Boys were a properly fearsome tribe at the time. These two had been giving us the evil eye right up until the moment when I cranked up the guitar. We were playing 'Walking the Dog' at the time. Next, I was distorting the guitar and the two previously unfriendly Teds suddenly both thought I was God's gift to rock 'n' roll. Wanting to play to the crowd (of course), I started really laying into it, only to find that after about three songs my set-up had mysteriously conked out.

What I understand now – now that I've been doing it for fifty or sixty years – was that the way to distort your guitar correctly is to distort the preamp stage. My guitar rig consisted of my six-string and electric pick-up, as well as an old public-address amplifier and speaker in a box. What I was doing was distorting the speaker, driving it too hard and eventually blowing it. That's what I'd done. And suddenly it literally wouldn't play any more.

I'd love to make out that I was like Pete Townshend or something, but I wasn't. Back then a loudspeaker cost something like £20, which was a week's wages for my father. To put it into perspective, I never saw a whole pound until I was at least seventeen. We just didn't have the kind of money to replace a speaker like that.

The fact was that after the Meadowfield youth club gig, the Outer Limits was virtually a thing of the past. Not because of 'creative differences', a huge financial rift or sexual jealousy but for the simple reason that my speaker was blown. At the same time, my world was changing in even more profound ways. My dad had got a job at the Co-op dairy in Leicester, which meant that the family had to move, and because I was still doing my GCEs at home, the solution was to leave me with my grandparents while the rest of the family upped sticks to the East Midlands.

Staying with my grandparents meant moving to Hetton, Durham's mining heartland. I would have to get on the 137 bus to go home. The 137 was renowned for being the one the feared

Hetton lads used, and the first time I boarded that bus I did so as unobtrusively as I could, taking a seat at the front and desperately trying not to catch the attention of the Teds who were sitting in the back three rows. Hetton Teds. The scariest kind. They made my Meadowfield Teds look like Girl Scouts.

Back in those days, all the kids our age decorated combat jackets from the Army & Navy Store with the names of bands they liked. The Beatles, the Stones, something like that. Me, I had Arthur Askey, Ken Dodd and Vera Lynn written on my jacket. One of those sarcastic, clever-clever things that seemed like a good idea at the time – right until the moment that you step on the bus bound for Hetton and the only other people on it are a bunch of angry-looking Teddy Boys.

'Oi, you!' came a shout from the back.

I shrank into my seat. Perhaps they were talking to somebody else.

'Oi, you! Four eyes!'

They were being insistent – so insistent that I had no choice but to join them at the back of the bus.

They wanted to know who I was. After all, I was a stranger on the bus. *Their bus*. They also wanted to know what I was wearing. Sorry, *what the fuck* I was wearing, because not only was I failing to sport regulation Teddy-Boy gear, but I was trying to be ironic into the bargain.

Big mistake.

'I'm staying with my grandmother on Coalbank Terrace,' I told them, fully expecting my payment for this information to be a bunch of fives.

'Wait a minute, are you Betty Lambton's lad?' said one of them. 'It's Betty Lambton's lad, sit down.' So I did, and whenever

I got on the bus from that point onwards, I would head straight for the back and sit with the Teds. 'Anybody says owt to you, you tell them the Hetton lads will fucking kill them,' I was informed. *Where were you at school?*

I had never been part of a gang or even a community up to that point because our house was quite isolated. For a tubby bespectacled kid it was like being protected by the Mafia.

Coalbank Terrace was a typical northern street in a mining village: two sets of terraced houses divided by a road, except that you entered your house from the rear. (Visiting Beamish open-air museum about ten years ago, I came upon a house identical to that of my grandma. When I walked into the dining room, I unexpectedly burst into tears.)

Me being there wasn't great for my grandmother. At that time, my grandfather was living in the back bedroom, suffering from silicosis, which is coal dust on the lung, and there wasn't a lot left of him. It meant there was hardly any space in the house, so I pretty much had to wave goodbye to any privacy I'd enjoyed previously. I shared a bed with my Uncle John, who was a big man, twenty stone, so not the most comfortable arrangement but he and I got along fine. There was no bath, barely a sink to wash in, so I'd find myself getting dirty and smelly. I remember reading that Frank Sinatra showered twice a day, but I had yet to experience so much as a single shower, unless you counted the rain.

The loss of my speaker had clearly tweaked my grandparents' heartstrings, though. 'Your grandfather's got a surprise for you,' said my grandmother upon my return home from school one day.

'Look under the bed,' he told me when I went to visit him in the back bedroom.

Underneath was a brand-new 12-inch Fane loudspeaker.

'Is that what you wanted?' he asked me. 'Because I didn't really know which one you would. . .'

'Oh no, it's perfect, it's absolutely perfect.'

And it was. Not just because it was the right speaker and a great replacement, but because my grandparents, who didn't have a lot of money, had bought it for me. At that age, and especially at that time in society, there was a huge gulf between parents and children, so you can imagine the divide that existed between me and them. We might as well have been on different planets. But I wonder if by buying me the speaker, my grandparents were waving goodbye to any hope that I might possibly follow my relatives down the mines. My grandmother used to say to me, 'It was good enough for your granddad, it should be good enough for you,' but I think that by then they'd realised my interests lay in a different sphere. As much as anything else, their gift was an acknowledgement of that fact.

Charlie looked at me, tubby with glasses and my silly combat jacket: 'Why, I diven't knar,' was all he said.

If I was there now I'd say, 'I diven't knar either, Charlie.'

It was while living at Coalbank Terrace that I first heard Bob Dylan. I remember the occasion well. We were having dinner with the BBC News on, and although I'd already heard some Bob Dylan, I suppose that I hadn't really listened properly, or not with the right ears, for on this occasion, when the newscaster finished reading the news and said, 'We've got something very special for you tonight, a young man called Bob Dylan is going to sing you a couple of songs.' When Dylan appeared, complete with guitar and harmonica, to play 'Mr Tambourine Man' and 'With God on My Side', my life changed.

Perhaps I was particularly susceptible, living in an over-crowded house with my grandparents, and feeling like my life was in a state of suspended animation, but hearing 'Mr Tambourine Man' had the effect of broadening my horizons. I didn't fully understand the lyrics, but I instinctively picked up on the idea of Dylan following his muse, being taken to another, better, place. Not only that but watching him made me feel like *I can do this*.

My dad was always trying to talk me out of being a musician. 'You're not good enough,' he would say, which was probably true at the time. 'It's not a good life. It's all right when you're young, but it's awful as you get older. Unless you're a real genius, you end up playing music you don't like and hating it.'

Point being that seeing Bob Dylan instantly made me discount his reservations. I thought, *I'm going to do something. I don't know what it is, but I know it's out there.*

It was Bob and the Beatles who were to blame for the fact that at night, when my grandmother thought I was revising for my GCEs, I was in fact listening to music on my headphones.

I left Coalbank the day after sitting my O levels and went on a tour of Germany with the youth orchestra, playing Rossini at various concert halls along the Rhine. I remember being surprised at how affluent Germany was, a real contrast to Durham.

Next stop was Leicester to join my family, where my father was keen that I should have a profession, something you could rely on. Because I was good at maths, accountancy seemed the best way to go and I had an interview with an account-ancy practice who said they'd take me on as an articled clerk, provided I got six O levels.

My results came, and I had only passed two, maths and English literature. My parents were distraught. They blamed themselves for moving away but I knew it was my fault.

I was enrolled at college in order to try to get those missing four O levels. Meantime, I began to get to grips with my new living environment, which was pretty much my first glimpse of a modern, multi-cultural city and a million miles away from life in the north-east, where I'd only ever met a black person once. (That was when a black engineer had come up from London to show my dad how to work a new machine and was subsequently invited to dinner.) In Leicester, I was surrounded by people of all ethnicities, which was as exotic to me as having a shower.

Mind you, we still didn't have one of those. We lived in a flat above a Co-op in a place called Brent Knowle Gardens, where I had to sleep on a sofa. In a bid to help me get used to my new environment, my mother enrolled me at a local youth club at which I took guitar classes. This was the first time I'd ever had a lesson and was also where I began to learn the technique of fingerpicking.

Meanwhile, what I found was that Leicester had lots of coffee bars and folk clubs, and I started taking myself along to them, singing Paul Simon songs. I also played three or four songs in the interval of a Christmas concert at my college – the Charles Keene College of Further Education – and though I wasn't in any way trying to emulate the look of Bob Dylan – he had a craggy face and not an ounce of fat on him, whereas I was a chubby teenager in spectacles – I was trying to sound like him. When, in 1966, I heard that he was coming to the De Montfort Hall, I was practically beside myself with excitement. I mean, this was peak Dylan for me. I was so into him. Totally into his lyricism. I was learning all the songs at that point, so I paid closer attention than most, and the lyrical content used to blow my tiny mind. 'The Lonesome Death of Hattie Carroll', for example, in which he tells the story of a man who in 1963 beat an African-American barmaid to death and got just six months for it. 'Masters of War', which was his protest song about the nuclear arms race of the early 1960s. 'Desolation Row', with its interlinking character-driven stories. Lyrically, he was on a different plane.

The gig at De Montfort Hall (Sunday 15 May 1966) was part of a tour during which he played a first half of just him, his harmonica and an acoustic guitar, and a second half of him and a band, his 'electric' set. This was the same tour that culminated with a gig at Manchester's Free Trade Hall, during which somebody shouted 'Judas' as he commenced the electric portion of his set; also the same tour at which he was accompanied by the filmmaker D. A. Pennebaker, who was making the film that later became *Don't Look Back*. I actually witnessed Pennebaker in action, filming the queue outside the De Montfort. Inside, meanwhile, I was rewarded by a brilliant first half, while the second, electric, half was noteworthy for different reasons. Very loud and raucous and punctuated by hecklers yelling things like, 'Can we have a folk song?' Bob's band were too loud and his voice got a little hoarse as the show went on.

'This is a folk song,' Dylan replied. 'It's called "Yes, I See You've Got Your Brand-New Leopard-Skin Pill-Box Hat",' which, when he played it, didn't sound like much of a folk song to me. It just sounded like rock 'n' roll but great. 'Play an old one, play an old one,' went another cry.

'Here's an old one called "One Too Many Mornings",' he spat. By the end of the gig he was clearly pissed off, to the extent that he practically shouted the lyrics to 'Like a Rolling Stone', then threw the microphone on the floor, knocked the stand over, and stalked off.

So Dylan was pissed off. Most of the audience seemed pissed off, too. Me? I was happy as Larry. I'd bought 'Like a Rolling Stone' the week that it came out. I don't think I've ever played a single as much as I played that one, before or since. Plus I loved the fact that he did 'Desolation Row', which I also knew so well. And still do. Years later, I helped Seal do a guide vocal for a Bob Dylan covers album, *Chimes of Freedom: The Songs of Bob Dylan*, to which he was contributing, which involved playing 'Like a Rolling Stone' on guitar, and even though I'd never played it before, I knew it note for note, as did Seal.

One take.

3

'Do Your Own Thing' by the Blokes at Yates's Wine Lodge (1969)

In which I'm bitten by the production bug

Looking back now, I can see that being in Leicester broadened my horizons considerably. It opened me up. Moving to the city had coincided with my growing interest in technology and recorded music in general. I had various part-time jobs: I worked at Woolworths and Lewis's department store, but the best was working in the electrical section of the Co-op selling stereos and stuff, which suited me down to the ground.

Meanwhile, another thing that had struck me about seeing Dylan at the De Montfort Hall – one of the many things – was the quality of the sound. This was the first time I had ever seen in action a speaker that I'd heard about, the American JBL. Dylan had obviously brought them over from the States: big, beautiful bits of kit with no grill on the front so you could see the diaphragms vibrate. Any picture of somebody wearing headphones in a recording studio, I'd snip out and keep, while at the same time I was turning my attention to what I could do for myself.

I still had the two-track tape recorder that my Uncle Tommy had given me, and somehow picked up two tape-recorder microphones. My father had shown me how to solder, so I made myself a crude mixer, enabling me to plug two microphones into the recorder at the same time. Having seen Dylan play, I knew that he always had one microphone on the guitar and another on his voice, and I was keen to do the same. And, having no mic stands, I had been forced to improvise by taping my adapted microphones onto broom handles before placing them the Bob Dylan way, one on my acoustic guitar and another for my voice.

By this point I'd also started writing my own songs, so I started making recordings of them. My father, seeing that I was serious about the whole music-making thing, hearing a couple of the songs I'd recorded and deciding that maybe they weren't too bad, made me an offer I couldn't refuse: three hours in a proper recording studio.

The studio was Shield Recording Studios in nearby Kettering, owned by a guy called Derek Tompkins, and the idea was for me to record a particular song I'd written called 'This Side of Paradise'. I'd nicked the title from the F. Scott Fitzgerald book of the same name, which I'd read not as part of my English studies (God forbid!), but because I'd heard Dylan mention Fitzgerald in 'Ballad of a Thin Man', after which, being the Dylan acolyte that I was, I'd promptly read all of Fitzgerald's novels. So anyway, I'd written this song and recorded it in Shield, where Derek, who would later go on to record Bauhaus and the Barron Knights among many others, said to me, 'Would you like to overdub it?'

I looked at him askance. 'What do you mean, "overdub"?'

'Well, you can play something on top of it,' he said.

'Really?' My thoughts went to my bass guitar. Now we were talking. I did the overdub, listened back. Just me, an acoustic guitar and, now, the bass. 'What else could I play?' I asked him.

'Well, there's a piano out there. . .'

I could play piano. Just about. In a rudimentary fashion. So yeah, great, I overdubbed a piano part. And then I double-tracked my voice. And all of a sudden, the song that I'd written in my bedroom was sounding like a proper record.

I left Shield pleased as punch with a demo that I would listen to over and over again. It probably wasn't very good, but I loved it. My mother really liked it, too, and insisted I send it along to Radio Leicester.

Next you thing you know, I'm getting a letter back. Would I like to come in to do a session? Of course, I would. And, after a rocky courtship that involved me turning up to do my session, waiting for an hour, nobody turning up, phoning the producer, losing my temper and telling him to fuck off, and then my mum insisting I call back and apologise, I recorded my session: five or six songs which they would often play on Radio Leicester, my first ever radio airplay. All of which was very exciting but completely overshadowed any schoolwork I was supposed to be doing. And at the end of the year, when I should have passed my four O levels easily, I only got one of them: English language.

My abject exam failure meant that a career in accountancy was out of the question. Actually, it meant that any kind of proper 'career' was pretty much out of the question; instead, I would have to settle for a job, a job-job, a means of bringing in the bacon and paying my way. After a series of false starts, I ended up at the John Bull Rubber Company, working in the costing offices.

You know that hose between the radiator and the cylinder block in a car? There was a time when I could have told you all about that hose. I could have talked about extrusion and compound. I might even have produced a slide rule in order to tell you exactly how much the hose would cost. That, back then, was my life at the John Bull Rubber Company. Bored stiff and gazing around at my colleagues, some of whom had been there for thirty years or more, thinking, *God, is this it? Forty hours a week, fifty weeks a year, 8.30 in the morning until five in the evening.* Literally the only glimmer of light was the fact that I was working three nights a week, Wednesdays, Fridays and Saturdays, playing bass guitar with the Eric Upton Band in Coalville, places like the Coalville Grand, and various working men's clubs in the area. At seventeen, I was the youngest person in the band, which put me more in touch with some of the music we used to play.

Playing with the Eric Upton Band was the first time I ever actually sang through a microphone without playing acoustic guitar, the reason being that the regular singer thought the words to 'A Whiter Shade of Pale' were terrible and refused to perform the song on principle. I loved the words, still do, and was more than happy to sing it. Later, I sang 'Daydream Believer' and then 'Hey Jude'. The first time you sing on a live mic with a band is a breath-taking but also humbling experience. Your voice sounds big and strong and, if you're not careful, very off-key. Mainly, though, we performed old-style dancing and dinner music, which is the worst thing to play. People are having dinner, so nobody pays you a blind bit of notice. You sit there, bored out of your skull, tweaking away, thinking only of the fiver per gig you're getting, good money in those days.

There were highlights, though. For example, we supported the Who. Their equipment was set up so that I had to read my music off Keith Moon's purple drums. An even bigger thrill was bumping into lead singer Roger Daltrey backstage. 'Alright, mate?' he said to me, and I looked at him, realising that he was the first man I'd ever met who had dyed hair. To the young Trevor Horn, Roger Daltrey's two main attributes were his friendliness and his dyed hair.

Then they went on. And although I already knew that they were going to be special live – I'd seen them six months earlier at the Leicester Arts Ball – they knocked it out of the park that night. Even some of the crusty old players in the Eric Upton Band were impressed. Which reminds me: it was at the Coalville Grand that I saw the Bee Gees for the first time. This was around the time of 'New York Mining Disaster 1941', their debut single, which came out in 1967. I loved the harmonies, and I remember being especially impressed by their bass player, Maurice Gibb, who looked great and, better still, was loud.

But as bands like the Who, the Bee Gees and then the Move became more popular, not to mention louder (no coincidence, perhaps), so it seemed the days were numbered for bands like the Eric Upton Band. Technology was moving, driven by society, or was it the other way around? I was starting to answer ads in the *Melody Maker*, wanting to move on. At the same time, my tenure at the John Bull Rubber Company was soon to end. Because I hated it so much, I'd started bunking off. I'd go to the cinema instead of the accounting classes I was supposed to attend, until one night, feeling particularly fed up, I woke up my parents and told them, 'I want to be a professional musician,' only for my dad to give me a different version of the same old talk, making me promise to give regular work one more try.

And so I left the John Bull Rubber Company and moved to a plastic-bag factory, J&B Plastics, as a progress chaser, a job which was just as bad as it sounds. I loathed every second of it until one day I kept the British Sugar Corporation waiting on the phone for forty minutes and got fired. They gave me two weeks' wages and I walked out of the building on air.

'What are you doing home?' asked my mother, her face falling. 'Oh no, you haven't been fired, have you?'

My father arrived home that night. 'What are you going to do? You think you're just going to walk into a professional musician job?'

It was a Wednesday. 'I'm going to get the *Melody Maker* tomorrow, and have a look through the ads,' I told him.

They despaired. They tried to persuade me to get another job, even waiting tables just in the interim, but I was adamant: I wanted to be a professional musician. Something would turn up.

And it did.

The next morning. I went to buy the *Melody Maker* then took it back home to read over breakfast when there came a knock on the door.

I opened it and there was Johnny Wollaston.

———

I had first heard about Johnny Wollaston back at the John Bull Rubber Company, when one of my colleagues announced that somebody new had moved into his village: 'It's a guy called Johnny. He's the bandleader at the Top Rank.'

I perked up. 'Oh, really?'

'Yeah, and I told him about you.'

Everyone knew that I played bass guitar. I'd started with Eric Upton by then and used to do the odd appearance at one of Leicester's many coffee bars as a proto-folkie, hence was John Bull's resident muso.

To cut a long story short, I ended up bowling down to the Top Rank Suite just by the clock tower in Leicester city centre, where I met Johnny Wollaston, not actually in the Top Rank, but in a pub just around the corner. 'I want you to come and see my band play,' he told me.

So I watched his band – and particularly the bass player. I had enough of an eye to work out that he was an old double bass player. He played the bass guitar like it was a double bass, which is fine on the old stuff, but at the time there was a new song out called 'Everlasting Love' which had a difficult bass part. If you played it with your fingers like an old double bass player, it would sound a bit of a mess, whereas if you played it with a pick, as I did, it wasn't so difficult. This chap made a dog's dinner of it.

'Can you play that?' said Johnny Wollaston after the set. 'Can you play the dance stuff?'

'Yeah, I can do that.'

'Can you read?'

'Yes.'

'I'll be in touch,' he told me.

Except he wasn't. Well, he was, eventually. Nine months later. That Thursday morning, as I was contemplating my future over a copy of the *Melody Maker*, along came Johnny, who said he wanted me to join his band and offered me five nights a week at the Top Rank for £24 a week, which was great money in those days. I told him he hadn't heard me play. He said he didn't care, he just wanted me to sign a contract to start in a month's time: 'You can come in during the day and work your way through the bass pad.'

Johnny Wollaston was about forty-one or forty-two at the time. A big guy with a bit of American jazz trombonist Tommy Dorsey look about him, lots of hair and a pair of small round glasses. He was a keyboard and trumpet player and he arranged as well. I remember that a lot of his arrangements would start with him playing the keyboard and then end up with him playing the trumpet. Dad was gobsmacked: 'You'd better start practising because you're not good enough yet, I'm surprised he gave you the job without hearing you play.' So was I.

As I came on board it became clear that the rest of the band hated him. Not for any single good reason. Just there seemed to be a general antipathy towards him. It could have been because he had sacked one of their mates, or because he took all the best bits of the arrangements, or perhaps because he was a little bit up himself. Either way, they hated him. Me, I was slightly bemused by him. I didn't feel one way or the other about him. He was just my boss and he'd given me my first professional job.

In less than twenty-four hours, I had gone from being the guy who hated his job at J&B Plastics to a professional musician. The only person more astounded than me was my dad. In those days he was playing double bass at the Grand Hotel in Leicester, working during the day as an engineer at the Co-op dairy. You might wonder if he was jealous, but he just wasn't built like that. Besides, he still didn't have any designs on being a professional musician.

Meanwhile, I settled into my new life and, boy, did I like it. I rehearsed like mad for a few weeks and did my first night, and from then on I was happy not having to get up in the morning and clock in, left to my own devices during the day when everyone was at work, kicking back and relaxing until it came time to grab my bass and make my way to the Top Rank. I would sit in coffee bars reading and everywhere would be quiet because everyone but me was at work. Next thing you know, I was moving out of my parents' flat, lying to the landlord of my new place on London Road that I was a married man in order to take on a one-bedroom flat on the ground floor of a house (and at one point having to pass off one of the Top Rank barmaids as my wife).

No doubt my bandmates' dislike for Johnny Wollaston was vindicated when he suddenly announced that the band was moving from Leicester to Blackpool. Not the whole band, however, just three of them: Johnny, the drummer, Arty . . . and me. Everybody else was told to sling their hook.

When it came to going to Blackpool, my dad drove me. It was a rainy day, January 1969. He took me to lunch in Woolworths, which was right on the seafront. I had steak and kidney pie and chips then we went to the door, shook hands and he said to me, 'Well, you're on your own now, son, you just watch it,' and then left.

And I guess you could say that a new phase of my life began.

———

The advantage of arriving in Blackpool during the winter, and thus off-season, was that you could get a flat for buttons. I had left my London Road abode in Leicester and rented a place on the seafront, not far from the Savoy Hotel, which was to be my workplace with the slimmed-down Johnny Wollaston band. The same night that my father bade me farewell, I took myself off to the cinema and met two girls in the queue who ended up staying with me for a fortnight. My tiny flat had two fold-down beds so there was plenty of room. When they left, they nicked all my money, but we had a great time in that fortnight. I had no regrets.

Not long into my time in Blackpool – March 1969, to be precise – I saw Pink Floyd at the Winter Gardens, where it struck me that the keyboard player – Rick Wright – had the same keyboard as Max the keyboard player in the Eric Upton Band. A Farfisa Compact Duo, which is a very specific kind of organ. The difference was that Rick Wright played his through a Binson Echorec platter echo, which is an echo unit with converging lights. He made the Farfisa sound like a mystical space flute. I was hooked.

Floyd played 'Set the Controls for the Heart of the Sun', which I loved. Now, of course, it's recognised as an early-Pink Floyd classic, but I had never heard it before and stood in awe, amazed that people in the crowd were booing them. People booing Pink Floyd because they weren't playing rock 'n' roll.

The very next day, I went out and bought the album *Saucerful of Secrets*. I'd bought it because I'd heard them play live but to my ears the version of 'Set the Controls for the Heart of the Sun' on the album wasn't a patch on the live incarnation. Live, it had given me the feeling of being on a spaceship about to crash into the sun. I've made up for it since, but apart from alcohol, I'd never taken drugs at that point. Never even smoked a cigarette.

But watching Floyd, it was as though I was experiencing the same trip as the band on stage. It was one of those moments that made me realise what you could do with music, where you could go. Plus it made me evaluate myself, how I was playing with two old guys in a dance-music band. At that point, I went from somebody who was pleased to have realised his immediate ambition of becoming a professional musician to someone who wanted to stretch his musical wings.

But how?

Blackpool has a lengthy summer season, and so it was that around the same time as I saw Floyd at the Winter Gardens, I was priced out of my flat on the seafront and ended up flat sharing with a guy called Mick Taylor (no, not that Mick Taylor), who had a beautiful flat on the seafront in Fleetwood (no, not that Fleetwood) just opposite the tram stop, which meant I could pop on a tram and go straight down to the Savoy.

Mick was something of an idol in my eyes. Good-looking. Well-dressed. One day, I tried on his Levi jeans while he was at work. I couldn't fit into them so I decided to put myself on a diet. True, I did become constipated on a menu of eggs and steak and kidney pie – not something I would recommend – but I got results, going down from 13 stone to 9.5 stone, so skinny compared to my former self that my mother burst into tears the next time she saw me.

The Savoy was and still is a beautiful hotel, and there were certainly worse places to work. On the plus side, I got to sing certain songs such as 'By the Time I Get to Phoenix' and 'The Fool on the Hill', but the trouble was that they were arranged in a very dinner-dance fashion. David Bowie was on my radar by then. The Beatles had released *Abbey Road*. Even my dad was saying to me, 'Trevor, you're doing an old man's job.' He wanted me to resume the songwriting I'd started in Leicester. He was so keen, in fact, that he offered to pay for a second studio session. And so, with that thought ahead of me, like a carrot and stick on a Blackpool beach donkey ride, I set to work writing more songs.

I used the session to record a demo of a new song I'd written called 'The Blackpool Astronaut' and another song called 'Heavy Stone'. I had acetates made and one midweek took the bus to London, a six- or eight-hour journey – but much cheaper than the train – where I spent two days tramping around various record labels with my demo.

I almost got a bite. One of the label workers liked it and took me to a guy he said was a music publisher in Oxford Street, who turned out to be Muff Winwood, who I'd heard of from his time with his younger brother Steve as a member of the Spencer Davis Group. I played him the demo and Muff spent most of the time while my music was playing on the phone talking about a party he'd been to, but still said afterwards, 'We'll publish it if you put it out,' to the guy I had come in with.

He didn't.

I didn't really understand at the time, and anyway, nothing ever came of it.

Better still, I also got to meet Chris Blackwell of Island at Basing Street Studios.

Basing Street Studios has a special place in this story. We'll get to the details later, but for the time being, let's just say that it was a recently converted church, also known as Island Studios, where over the years Blackwell would record the likes of Bob Marley, Robert Palmer, Nick Drake and King Crimson. The year after my visit, for example, Led Zeppelin's *Led Zeppelin IV* and Jethro Tull's *Aqualung* were both recorded there, to name but two. Jill and I later ended up buying the studio, re-christening it SARM West, and then just SARM, and would even make an album as the Producers, *Made in Basing Street*, all of which are tales for a later date. For the time being, that's where I found myself, having called up and cajoled the person on the other end of the phone into letting me come in with my stuff.

Arriving, the receptionist said, 'Chris Blackwell's upstairs if you want to go up there. But don't say that I said you could go up.'

Strange, I thought, and still puzzling over the need for secrecy went upstairs, only to find Chris in a room that would later become a studio for SARM West, but back then was an office, sitting on the sofa with a girl. Fortunately, everybody involved was fully clothed. Even so it was clear that I had interrupted something.

'What do you want?' snapped the long-haired, flared-jean-wearing founder of Island Records.

At that time, Island were known mainly as a folk label, with John Martyn, Cat Stevens and Fairport Convention on their books, although more rock-orientated artists like Free and King Crimson were also coming through. Blackwell would shortly sign Toots and the Maytals and, perhaps even more significantly, Bob Marley.

'I've got a track to play you,' I said.

'Why should I listen to your stuff?'

'Well, it might be good, you never know,' I replied, full of the arrogance of youth.

Nobody can accuse Chris Blackwell of having a closed mind because to his credit he did indeed listen to 'The Blackpool

Astronaut' and even liked one of the changes in it. In fact, he was good enough to talk for quite some time about that one bit in 'The Blackpool Astronaut' that he had liked. We went on to talk about Cat Stevens – 'What are you doing with Cat Stevens? I didn't like his last record, a bit too Norrie Paramor,' I told him, forgetting myself somewhat. 'You've got to stop using an orchestra with him.'

But he agreed with me. 'That's exactly it. We're not going to use an orchestra next time.'

If this had been a film, he would have snapped his fingers and told me that my Cat Stevens' observation made me *exactly* the kind of person he wanted onboard and when could I start? But it was real life, and so he wrapped up the meeting: 'Write another four songs like this and then come and see me again,' he told me.

These days I know that it's the oldest brush-off in the book, and I've used it myself. But it's a brush-off employed with solid reason, because you can't sign somebody on the strength of one song, especially if it's not a hit song. And 'The Blackpool Astronaut', even with that solid change, was not a hit song.

I left, and it wouldn't be until a lot later that I realised how my audience with Chris Blackwell had been a complete fluke, just a case of being in the right place at the right time with the right receptionist in the right mood. When I met him years later, he didn't even remember me.

And so, at the end of my short London sojourn, I returned to Blackpool, a little disheartened but not necessarily discouraged. For some reason it popped into my head that it would probably take ten years for me to make it in the music business. My dad thought that it was time for me to move on . . .

Fortunately, and though I didn't realise it quite yet, I was to get a taste of another discipline. I was about to take on what would turn out to be my first-ever production job.

Mick and I would go out at weekends when I didn't have to play at the Savoy. One of our favourite haunts was Yates's Wine Lodge, partly because the booze was cheap, and partly because it had a carvery, allowing you to slice a bit of roast beef and make a sandwich on the spot, which was very nice (although, incidentally, I'm a vegetarian these days. Haven't eaten any kind of meat since 1988).

There was a group who often played in the main bar. I say 'group', but there were just two of them: a drummer and a Hammond-organ player. They were very popular in Blackpool because they could both sing well, were young and did excellent versions of Four Seasons songs featuring all the high castrato stuff. Mike and the newly slim me would always go to see them play. One night, I was talking to them after the show and they asked me how to go about making a record. They'd written a song called 'Do Your Own Thing'. It was terrible.

'I know a guy in Kettering,' I told them, thinking of Derek Tompkins at Shield. Not long later that's exactly where we were in order to record the track. I played bass as well as helping with the arrangement, and looking back, that was probably the first time that I was ever an actual, proper 'record producer'.

The thing about being a record producer is that when all is said and done, you're the person responsible for delivering the record to whoever is paying you. That's the task. A band or an artist comes to you wanting to make a record, and by the time you all wave goodbye, they have one. How you accomplish that varies from one producer to another, but that's the bones of it. Meanwhile, you have engineers, who are different from producers again. It's the job of an engineer to record the music. I tried my hand at engineering, but I couldn't get on with it – I was always more interested in the emotional impact of what was going on and my attention would wander.

However it happens, the net result is the same: it's up to the producer to midwife the record. To take a song from being notes on a piece of paper or an idea in somebody's head and turn it into a track. And, although I certainly didn't think it at the time, this was probably what I had done with my Yates's Wine Lodge duo. The record ended up being sold on the bar at Yates's, and it didn't have my name on it. But even so.

Meanwhile, I was bored playing with Johnny Wollaston and decided to take another job in Sheffield, only to return with my tail between my legs and find that there was no longer a job for me with Johnny. Next, I took a job in Preston and lived there for five or six months. Then I returned to Leicester, playing with the Ivor Kenney Sound at the Palais, before moving back to Blackpool, until one morning at 3 a.m. I got a call from a bloke called Johnny Joseph, who wanted me to move to London and join his band, Joseph's Colours, who had a residency at the Hammersmith Palais.

Was I interested? Yes, I bloody well was. I went to London, auditioned and got the job.

I'd made it to London.

In Joseph's Colours were me, Johnny, a keyboard player called Dereck and a guitar player called Jocelyn Pitchen, who was the first truly brilliant musician I'd ever encountered, somebody far better than I was and, crucially, willing to pass on his knowledge. Thinking back, so much stuff starts with him.

I lived in the same building as Jocelyn, a place in Earl's Court. I shared a bedsit with my girlfriend at the time, Yvonne, who painted a multi-coloured stripe around the room and then left when I was a prat. The guy who lived next door to Jocelyn was Turkish and he showed me how to make Turkish coffee; another neighbour became an early-hours chess partner. We even had a drug dealer living in the building – not that I ever partook. At that stage.

I was only with Joseph's Colours for a year. One of the things that hastened my departure was an incident when we were playing the Top Rank in East Croydon. There, we would often get a bunch of skinheads doing a terrible synchronised dance to 'Hi Ho Silver Lining', and on this particular occasion, I was singing when one guy came up, got hold of the microphone and pinged it back so that it hit me in the mouth and bust my lip. Without thinking, I kicked him hard in the side of the head and sent him flying, at which point he and three of his buddies jumped on stage. I took off my bass and held it like a club, ready to defend myself, before the bouncers descended upon us and turfed the skinheads out.

But that wasn't the end of it. By the end of the night, there was a shaven-headed mob outside the Top Rank baying for my blood. The organisers had called the police, who arrived just as the skinheads were using paving stones that they'd pulled up in order to try to smash their way in. They ended up having to smuggle me out of the building, with Top Rank making it clear that they didn't want to see me again.

Truth was, I was getting pretty fed up by that point anyway. All those Mecca ballrooms full of people who weren't allowed to wear jeans, which I've always thought is the dumbest thing. Top Rank was the same. I'd turn up in my jeans: 'You can't come in here.'

'I'm in the band, I've got a band outfit to put on. Give me a break.'

Years later, when I was in my mid-thirties and a famous record producer, I got a call from Shirley Bassey's manager: would I be interested in producing Shirley Bassey?

'Yeah, sure, let me come and see her play live.'

She was playing at the Circus Tavern in Purfleet, and so on Friday night, just after dinner, Jill and I got into a limo sent by her management and went down there, a journey during which I suddenly realised that I was wearing jeans. Jill waved away my concerns: 'If they tell you, you can't go in with jeans, you tell Shirley Bassey that the deal is off.'

Well, they let me in, but every time I stood up in order to go anywhere – the toilet, say – half-a-dozen bouncers would descend, escorting me to the loo in order that nobody else in the club might have their vision scarred and their sense of propriety blemished by my offending jeans.

It was while with Joseph's Colours that I experienced what you might say was a 'proper' recording studio for the first time. Back then, the BBC had to abide by something known as 'needle time' restrictions, which meant they could only play up to five hours of commercial gramophone music per day, with the rest being specially recorded cover versions by bands like ours. Thus, Joseph's Colours would record versions of popular hits at the BBC studios at Maida Vale and Wigmore Street.

Much as I loved it, Shield studios was Heath Robinson compared to what the Beeb had. I remember being knocked out by the playback, the sound in the control room and studios, the fact that we were recording our songs on eight-track or sixteen-track, much the same way that the Beatles had started out. The studio even had a red 'recording' light.

It was also while with Johnny Joseph that I tried LSD for the first time. Two guys from Blackpool were the suppliers and we did the acid in my bedsit one night. They were really into Black Sabbath, a band I'd never been especially fond of prior to that evening. I thought they sounded like farm labourers, but on LSD they suddenly acquired a new depth: I finally 'got' Sabbath.

I remember following my drug mates around the bedsit, tidying up after them. 'Man, you're so uptight,' they told me. 'No, I'm not,' I retorted. 'I just want to keep my flat tidy,' and made a mental note that on the next occasion I took LSD, I'd do it alone.

Sure enough, a week after that first experience, I did it for a second time, again in my bedsit, only this time alone, and I took the opportunity to go through my entire record collection in order to experience it all in this heightened state. When I was done, I organised my records into the ones that I liked and the ones that I now realised were dogshit. In that second pile, the dogshit pile, went the easy-listening albums, the coffee-table jazz and soft classical albums – records where instead of playing music, the musicians were merely reading it.

Becoming aware of this difference between *reading* and *playing* naturally influenced the way that I viewed my own musical endeavours. This, again, was something else that hastened my departure from Joseph's Colours. Jocelyn had introduced me to Miles Davis, and I'd never heard anything like it before. I bought *Miles Ahead*, *Sketches of Spain*, *Porgy and Bess*, and for a while those albums were rarely off my turntable. He and I would have the occasional fall-out about music – a difference of opinion about Miles Davis's *Bitches Brew* being one memorable example – but we stayed mates until eventually life got in the way. Joycelyn realised that being self-taught, I had many bad habits, so he showed me how to use my left hand properly, which really helped my playing; necessary because bass parts were becoming more fluid and James Jamerson, the bass player for Motown, was changing the landscape.

In the end, the music I was listening to was so different to the music that I was playing that I had to leave Johnny Joseph, I had to try something different. Which is how I relocated to Margate and joined a band called the Canterbury Tales.

I quickly realised that the Canterbury Tales had a limited shelf life, but what killed it off was a thirty-date Norwegian tour where on the first night in Bergen, I had to have stitches in my face after getting into an altercation with a bloke over his wife. Another night, a bunch of guys tried to set fire to the guitar player's bellbottoms, while that same evening I narrowly avoided getting beaten up in the toilet. And then, to add insult to injury, I realised that I'd gone from earning £25 a week with Johnny Joseph to £5 with the Canterbury Tales – if I was lucky.

My life after that was a revolving door of bands and relocations and ads in the *Melody Maker* until I ended up in Tottenham, at a pub supposedly owned by the Kray twins, where, after auditioning for the house band, I met a lady called Jan Butler who sang with Ray McVay. She told me they needed a bass player. Was I interested?

Yes. Yes, I was.

Everybody who did the shit gigs like me had heard of Ray McVay because of all the shit gigs, Ray McVay and His Orchestra was the top shit gig. He made albums, did radio broadcasts, went on TV. Jan had told me that Ray was playing a gig at the Leicester Square Empire the following day and maybe I should go there and see if he'd give me an audition.

So I showed up and Ray McVay said, 'Can you read?'

'Yeah, I can read.'

'Yes, but can you *really* read?'

'Yes, I can really read.'

I played a one-hour set.

'How's that?' I said to Ray McVay.

'Play the next set,' he told me.

I played it. A set that included 'Shaft'. Big bass part. I was being watched to see if I'd make a mistake, and I didn't.

'Play the last set.'

Towards the end of that third set, Ray McVay called out a number, as he had been doing the whole gig, and I felt all eyes on me. I looked through the book and found it, a special arrangement of 'MacArthur Park', a really long one, like three, four pages long. If you're sight-reading, one of the things you always do if you've got ten seconds spare is use that time in order to scan ahead to see what's coming up. Try to get ahead of the game.

I looked and saw there were a couple of 5/4 bars, and I knew that's what they were going to catch me out on. Sure enough, they did. I played it all perfectly until I got to that section where, for some reason, the arranger had put a 5/4 bar in, and then a 6/4 bar in, and I played a wrong note.

That was it. My only mistake during the whole try-out.

'You fucked up "MacArthur Park",' said Ray McVay sourly.

'Sorry,' I told him.

'Make sure I've got your number,' was all he said.

The next morning, he phoned to offer me the job and that was it, five nights a week every week with Ray McVay. Back to dance bands, albeit one of the country's top dance bands.

He wasn't easy, Ray McVay. After being with the band about a week, he sidled over. I thought he was going to say something nice: 'You're too fucking loud. If you don't turn down, I'll find somebody who will,' he told me.

I was so angry I just switched off, stood there and played silently for the next three minutes. A couple of other players looked over, but Ray McVay came over: 'That's better,' he said.

It was my first experience of a real recording session, a thirty-piece big band in the BBC studios in Maida Vale. A big red light when you were recording, as if you weren't paranoid enough already. Top and tail it (play the start and check the finish), then record it generally in one take. You couldn't make a mistake, or should I say you weren't supposed to. On one of the first sessions I stopped a take because I got lost on the part. When the lead trumpet player saw that I had stopped every-one, he yelled at me, 'You don't make mistakes! *We* make the mistakes!'

It was on either *Ray McVay's Party Hits* or *Ray McVay's Big Band Swing Time* where we were playing the 'Hokey Cokey', and when the key was supposed to change from C to B-flat, I hit an A by mistake. I didn't stop the take. When I bought the record later and played it back, there it was, my A.

I used to have to do some singing. The dreaded 'Hi Ho Silver Lining' was one, again because no one else wanted to sing it.

'Long-Haired Lover from Liverpool', what a stinker that was! Meanwhile, the first song I ever sung at Wembley Arena was 'The Pushbike Song' by the Mixtures. One time we were doing the World Ballroom Championships broadcast live from the Albert Hall on the BBC, playing the *Paso Doble*. We rehearsed from 5 until 5.30 p.m. and were then told that we wouldn't be needed until 9.50 p.m. Ray's brother Archie, the band's tour manager and comedy trombone player, was begging us not to go to the pub, 'Don't go lads, please,' but of course that's exactly where we went, only to bump into the brass section of the London Philharmonic. Everybody got talking and we were having a laugh and moaning about Handel until after what only seemed like five minutes of drinking and chatting, somebody shouted, 'It's 9.45,' and we had to sprint back.

As we started playing our *Paso Doble*, we were all busting for a leak, none more so than the drummer, who wore a genuinely pained look. Sure enough, I saw piss begin to gush out of his trouser leg and flood down the stage. The only people allowed to take fluid on stage were the horn players, and so the trombonist 'accidentally' kicked over his glass of water in order to take responsibility for the lake of piss on the stage. Very noble but sadly ineffective. Ray had spotted the culprit and the drummer was sacked.

I survived that episode. Not that it was any great cause for celebration. The trouble was that I had quickly grown sick of the band. I was sick of sight-reading. I was sick of the music we played – I used to call it 'the cavalcade of crap' – but most of all, I was sick of the lifestyle. Hours and hours of travelling on coaches with the same musicians telling the same old jokes. 'Two drunks on a train, one says, "Is this the train to Wembley?" The other one says, "No, it's Thursday." The first one says, "So am I, let's have a drink."'

I can't tell you how many times I heard that joke. And no amount of pranks and even a great relationship I had with Jan was enough to counterbalance the boredom.

The job's one saving grace was that it was well paid. And, for once in my life, I'd been using my money wisely. I had decided that I wanted to turn my short periods in recording studios into much longer ones and concluded the best way to do that, or at least one of the ways to do that, was to assemble my own studio. Thus, I put my ill-gotten gains to good use, purchasing a Revox tape recorder, as well as a six-channel mixer, and when I eventually returned to Leicester, taking a job in a nightclub in order to tide myself over, my luggage consisted mainly of those two bits of kit. By then, Leicester's Top Rank Suite was called Bailey's, and I had had some great times playing in the house band there; we were called Brass Foundry. I was there for a year, playing every evening, seven nights a week. On one memorable occasion, I was shouted out by Tommy Cooper for not laughing at his jokes. Suzi Quatro played, as did Neil Sedaka, Gene Pitney, Tiny Tim and Lonnie Donegan. I even witnessed the beginnings of Showaddywaddy.

While working at Bailey's during the evening, I was keeping busy in the day building my recording studio. Literally *building*. For this project, I had a partner in crime. His name was Gary Osborne, who, as well as being a good singer in a band at the Mecca, went by the nickname 'Mr Aggro' on account of his terrible temper. That aside, he was a good bloke and, more to the point, as interested in building a studio as I was.

We had a building. An old stable behind a musical equipment shop called Drumbeat Music on Leicester's Loughborough

Road. Starting at 9 a.m. every day until it was time to go to our evening jobs, we basically rebuilt the place: we cladded it, built the skin inside, bricked up the doors, put in the ceiling. It took us a year. A year of building and blagging and back-breaking work. And when that year was over, and Drumbeat Studios was built and open for business, we settled back and waited for the work to come rolling in.

Reader, the work didn't come rolling in.

We swallowed hard and hit on the idea of advertising. And wouldn't you know it, but the very first job that we got was for Leicester City Football Club. There was this guy called Ivan Slack, who was a Leicester City super fan who'd written a song, called 'This Is the Season' as well as another song, 'The Tank', which was the nickname of the City player Graham Cross, who was having his testimonial. Ivan had interest from Decca and his plan was to record 'The Tank'/'This Is the Season' and put it out.

They came to us, so I assembled a band to play it, just guys from bands I knew around the city, and we got the Leicester team into the studio. Trouble was, they were crap, they just couldn't sing at all, so me and my buddies did most of the singing, recorded it all on our Revoxes, made the single and sent it to Decca, who printed up 5,000 copies.

And that was that. It wasn't credited to me as producer and I didn't really think of myself as having produced it at all, even though it does fit precisely the remit of a producer as I've described. Just that I never thought of it that way. All the local musos would come into Bailey's when they finished their gigs because the bar was open until 2 a.m. One night, a guy called Coleman, who I really respected as a musician, said to me, 'You know what you've done is be a record producer.'

'Really?'

'Yeah, you got the musicians together, you sorted the song out.'

'Sorted the song out?'

'Well, the song was a bit duff, wasn't it? You changed a few chords, didn't you? That's being a record producer.' He paused, as though about to deliver an uncomfortable truth, which I suppose, in retrospect, he was. 'But you know what? You can't be a bass player *and* a record producer, because if you're a record producer, you've got to use the best bass player you can, because the record's your main responsibility.'

The passage of time has taught me that strictly speaking, this is not true and I have played bass on plenty of the records I've produced, mainly because I'm cheap. But what he was really saying was, 'Don't limit the kind of record you could make by your own playing. It's a different job.'

I took the guy's words to heart.

Still, although Drumbeat Studios had been responsible for the Leicester City track, it didn't prompt a deluge of new business. I began to worry that we'd spent a year building our studio in the wrong place, until eventually, probably about a year after the Leicester City single – a year that was punctuated by dribs and drabs of business, none of it especially inspiring – I upped sticks yet again, this time moving back to London, back to the same bedsit in Earl's Court, still with the stripe, and joined a band called Nick North and the Northern Lights.

It was while in Nick North and the Northern Lights that I met Tina Charles, the singer. In short order I'd meet Geoff Downes and Bruce Woolley and Rod Thompson, and life was about to take a sharp and very interesting turn indeed.

4

'Baby Blue', Dusty Springfield (1979)

In which I discover that having a hit is not all it's cracked up to be

I didn't produce 'Baby Blue', I co-wrote it. But it's here not just because it's the first proper 'hit' that I was involved with, but because it marked the high point – or at least one of the high points – of a period up to and including 1979, when not only did I begin to learn my trade but I met some like-minded fellow travellers along the way, many of whom I'm still working with today.

Anne Dudley, for example. She and I first met when I was playing with a trio called Coldwater Morning, a proper rent-paying job that I'd often 'dep out', which was the practice of giving your regular paying gig to another musician, usually while you went and played a more lucrative one.

I wasn't the only one in the habit of depping out. The keyboard player did it, too, and one night, this girl came in who was about twice as good as the guy she was depping for. She brought the band to life, her playing was so bold and confident.

'Have you ever done any sessions?' I asked her in the interval. I wasn't coming on to her, but I got the impression she thought I was, so she was rather evasive, mumbling something about having done some work on *Play School* for the BBC. (As it later turned out, she had also studied at the Royal College of Music, where she'd been given the B.Mus prize for the highest marks in her year, then King's College.) By then, my own recording experience had broadened somewhat. Not only had I appeared on a couple of those *Top of the Pops* records where they used to re-record the hits of the day and knock them out cheap in Woolworths – this when I was playing with Nick North – but I'd also fronted and produced a single called 'Caribbean Air Control' by Big A. As luck would have it, they happened to play the record during the evening and so I was able to use that as my bona fide when I told Anne, 'I'm a producer and one day I'm going to get you to play on my records.'

I took her number that night, but it wasn't until slightly later that I actually got to work with her for the first time, on a project called Chromium. She'd also appear on the second Buggles album and would become a mainstay of the ZTT team in the 1980s.

But I'm getting slightly ahead of myself. Prior to meeting Anne, I already had a relationship with perhaps the musician I've known the longest, a guy called Luis Jardim. Luis was introduced to me by Jocelyn: 'You've got to meet this guy. He's from Portugal. He's a brilliant player,' he said and he was dead right. If Jocelyn was the first truly brilliant musician I ever met, then Luis was the second. Born into a wealthy family, he'd come over to England supposedly to study medicine, except that instead of going to university he'd been playing bass in a nightclub and driving around in a red Cortina.

He was and still is a brilliant bassist, an outstanding drummer and an amazing percussionist. I mean, I had a certain technique, but my skill lay in the fact that I could sight-read. I was never good in the way that Luis was good.

I still see him to this day. Just about every record I ever made, Luis has played at least percussion on, and it's his first wife, Linda, who appears on 'Video Killed the Radio Star'. She's the one who sings, 'You are . . . a radio star-ah-ah-ah.'

Another of my friends from Leicester was a singer, guitar player called Rod Thompson. Rod came from the family of an industrialist who lived in Rearsby, a small village just outside of Leicester. Loads of people had been telling me about him – 'There's this guy, a lot like you, who lives in a big house in the country, you should meet him.' And then one day this guy in a stripy T-shirt turned up and, what do you know? He did look a bit like me, albeit it a blond, better-looking version. What's more, he was totally into music and wanted to be in a band. We became friends immediately and still are to this day.

Whenever I went back to Leicester after that, I'd stay with Rod at his magical crumbling mansion in Rearsby, listening to records till the early hours. My mother would complain that she never saw me. Rod was ultimately responsible for getting me my first production job, though.

It was through Rod that I met Bruce Woolley, another Leicester lad. The two of them, Rod and Bruce, were like a Simon & Garfunkel act, playing pubs and clubs and working men's clubs. When I first met Bruce, I'd been warned that he was a little bit eccentric – he was – but as well as being a good songwriter, he had a really lovely voice.

Rod and Bruce were signed to a publishing company, Ever-blue, run by a guy called Alex Everitt. When Rod and Bruce did their deal they needed a producer and by that time I had put a band together for Tina Charles. I ended up going into the studio with them as a duo called R.B. Zipper, although it all went wrong because I spent too much money and made Bruce sing an opening line for four hours, which is something I'd never do now. These days I know you never get anything good by being rough on the band, especially the singer, but back then I was still learning, and I used to go into what Rod and Bruce called 'lead helmet mode'. If something happened that I didn't like, I wouldn't say something but would radiate discomfort in a way that used to upset people.

Tina was a brilliant singer. She could be challenging on occasion, but there you have it: great talent often goes with slightly outlandish behaviour. Like most musicians, she wore several hats and had been releasing singles under her own name since 1969, while in 1975 she had a hit with 'I'm on Fire' as part of 5000 Volts. Trouble was, although Tina had provided the vocals for 'I'm on Fire', the group were using an actress, Luan Peters, for their public appearances. If it wasn't the final nail in the coffin, it was certainly one of them and Tina went solo again, only this time with the backing of a disco producer called Biddu.

I remember hearing the early fruits of her labours with Biddu and being really impressed. Not so much with Tina – I already knew she was good – more with Biddu: the way he was using his musicians. The stuff he was doing in the studio.

Some guy involved with 5000 Volts came over with a suitcase full of cash and tried to persuade Tina to rejoin the band. 'But that song Biddu's got for you is really good,' I told her. 'It's far better than you'll get in 5000 Volts.'

I had a cassette of Biddu's backing track for Tina's new record, and I must have worn it out, I listened to it so many times. Spot on, it was the first time I heard a backing track of what was to be a number-one record. It was simple and clear in a way that I wanted to copy.

The song was 'I Love to Love (But My Baby Loves to Dance)', and in 1976 it became a number-one hit for Tina. Other than that bit of advice, I had nothing to do with it, but for the first time in my life, I was around a number-one record. I got to visit the *Top of the Pops* studio and hang around behind the scenes. I met the head of CBS, had dinner with him and Agnetha Fältskog from Abba. Half the time I was pinching myself because I was just some oik from Durham by way of Leicester, and the other half I was thinking, *I want this. I want a hit record of my own.* The next few years would be a time of broadened horizons and shifting aspirations. *I'd love to get in the studio.* You get in the studio. *I'd love to get a record out.* You get a record out. *I'd love to have a chart hit.* You have a chart hit. *I'd love to have a big hit.* You . . . etc., etc.

Tina and I were in a personal as well as professional partnership, but in both respects things were up and down between us. At that time I was playing with a band that would later become Shakatak, chasing the muso jazz-rock dream.

'I don't know why you bother with jazz rock,' Tina told me. 'Why don't you just try playing simple things properly?'

I was pretty hurt at the time, but looking back, she was right. I was already feeling that my true calling lay in recording music rather than playing it. Even so, when it came to me and Tina, the writing was on the wall and sure enough, she ended up dumping me. However, she kept me on as her bandleader: 'I want to go out live,' she told me and gave me the job of assembling a band. I decided to put a six-piece together: keyboards, bass, drums, two guitarists, percussionist. First order of business: I needed a really good keyboard player.

I advertised. Poacher-turned-gamekeeper. Either way, seventeen or eighteen keyboard players turned up, and one of them was a bloke called Geoff Downes. First impression, I liked the way he was dressed. I wasn't accustomed to auditioning people and I tended to find it a bit off-putting if they came on too strong, trying to schmooze me into getting the gig, but Geoffrey wasn't like that. You can sometimes just feel it with people, and with him, I could feel it. He could also play two synths at the same time, which I have to admit was always an impressive feat.

———

It was during this period that I began working for Tina's publisher, Stuart Reed, on Denmark Street, producing demos for him. At night, I played with Tony Evans at the Hammersmith Palais and during the day I'd go into the studio, knocking out demos as well as the occasional master. Over the next couple of years, I'd produce singles for Nola Fontaine ('Love You Tonight'), Allan Stewart ('Heaven Above'), Lips ('Say Hello to My Girl'), John Howard ('I Can Breathe Again'), as well as dozens of demos, some more successful than others.

My work with Rod and Bruce and Everblue, aborted though it was, led to the band Big A and the 'Caribbean Air Control' single, and my first experience of being played on the nation's favourite, Radio 1. Although it failed to chart, it became the song with which I was able to convince Anne Dudley that I wasn't trying to chat her up.

Big A morphed into a sci-fi disco project called Chromium, another early production outing for me. Making that record, I found myself listening to a lot of American dance records, especially the Bee Gees, now well into their disco phase, and Chic. I wasn't really aware of Nile Rodgers as the driving force of Chic, but I loved the sound.

Bruce, meanwhile, had been turning me on to Giorgio Moroder, especially 'I Feel Love' by Donna Summer, and Kraftwerk, in particular 'The Man-Machine', as well as 'Warm Leatherette' by the Normal.

As far as Chromium were concerned, I'll be honest and say that I thought that the whole thing was fairly cringeworthy. There were some great people involved – Anne and Geoff, to name but two – but the material wasn't there. Not only that, but our sci-fi theme was done better by Sarah Brightman's 'I Lost My Heart to a Starship Trooper' single, which came out around the same time. Still, the important thing as far as I was concerned was that I was spending time in the studio learning my craft, gaining experience. In order to get more and better work, that's what I needed – experience. Back then, you had to pay for studios by the hour, and who was going to pay through the nose to have a wet-behind-the-ears producer at the helm?

As a process it was not without its pitfalls. For example, on the strength of a demo I'd made, a duo called Gardner & Boult, who saw themselves as a bit of an English Hall & Oates, got a deal with Gem Records, who hired me to do the master. It's all part of the learning curve, but I messed it up. For a start, I committed the error of dressing up to go to the studio. When I was making demos, I'd just wear what I wanted and get out of my head, but on the master, I stayed straight and dressed up in my Sunday best for the session.

Looking back, I don't quite know what came over me, sitting there at the board in a pair of smart black shoes like I was off to church. It was no great surprise then that the session went badly and the masters I produced didn't sound nearly as good as the demos. I would like to apologise to Gardner & Boult for that. I still tried really hard.

Apart from leaving the smart black shoes at home, the lesson there was that whatever magic you have on the demo, you must try to keep on the master. Don't get clever and second-guess yourself. If the demo's great, then just copy that. At which point I'm often asked, 'So why not just make the demo the master?' and the answer is that most demos were recorded on fairly basic equipment. With the Gardner & Boult stuff, the demos were made on eight-track, whereas a master was being recorded on 24-track. On the second Seal album (*Seal II*, 1994), Seal went off to make some demos with Wendy & Lisa so I lent them my 24-track, 2-inch Otari recorder and said, 'For God's sake, do the demos on this, and then we'll be able to use them instead of recording them on some shitty four-track.' Rarely do you have that luxury.

Even though I wasn't enamoured of Chromium, I wasn't going to pass up the opportunity to go to America – my first time there – where Geoff and I met a studio bigshot called Eddie Germano, owner of the Hit Factory in New York: 'Your stuff doesn't sound like anything I've heard before,' he told me. Together, we finished off a bunch of songs for the Chromium album *Star to Star*, which Eddie then mixed, a process that turned out to be something of an education for me.

To explain about mixing. In the 1960s, mixing a track meant balancing out the instruments. So when, say, the Beatles made their first album, *Please Please Me* in 1963, what you hear is them playing straight to quarter-inch tape. There's a possibility that, having recorded the first three or four songs, producer George Martin used a two-track to put all the backing onto one track and all the vocals onto another track, so he had a little bit of leeway in how he was balancing the vocals against the backing track, but otherwise, that was pretty much it. Back then, there was a certain amount you could do after people finished playing, but not a whole lot. Mostly the sound of the record was the sound of the band. That all changed completely when you got to the era of eight- and sixteen-track recording. Recording to sixteen tracks meant that one would be the bass guitar, three of them would be the drums, left, right and kick drum, et cetera, et cetera. Mixing was a case of putting all of those sixteen tracks through the board, balancing them and making a stereo imprint. Once you go up to sixteen-track, you can do a lot in the mix. But – and it's a big but – what a lot of people do is to make the mistake of thinking that you can do everything in the mix:

'Don't worry, we'll do that in the mix.'

'Never fear, we'll fix that in the mix.'

What I learned fairly early on was that it was always better to record effects rather than try to add them in the mix. So, for example, if you have an echo effect, a guy singing, 'I love you, you, you, you, you. . .', it's better to record that to tape during the recording process than leave it to the mix. That way you always have that effect, even if something happens with, say, your echo unit – it breaks down the night of the deadline, or, as happened to me before, it was a borrowed unit and somebody needed it back, or you simply run out of time. Never, ever, leave anything to the mix. All of this production advice is from a different age.

When it came to Eddie Germano and his mixes on the Chromium album, I was both impressed and horrified. Horrified because he'd left a lot of stuff out but impressed because, by doing that, he'd also made it much more succinct. Plus I loved the way he'd used EQ to boost the brightness. All of which were lessons that I would take to heart later, when it came to mixing 'Video Killed the Radio Star'.

As well as these production lessons, I was learning about myself. There were some great records around at the time, brilliant productions from the likes of Queen or Elton John. To go into a studio and make a record that sounded as good as they did takes real skill and experience, and that might have been something to aspire to. At the same time, I was learning that I couldn't do that – however hard I tried, I couldn't sound like anybody else. Around that time, musicians would criticise me for making them play things that they didn't want to play, making them play simple bass drum patterns or making them play in time. They wouldn't like it, but at the same time nobody was telling me not to do it, and the sounds I was producing were unusual: I was finding my way and finding my voice.

Still, as 1978 came and went, I didn't feel that I'd made a record that really lived up to the sound in my head. I hadn't yet been involved in something about which I could say, 'Yes, I'm really proud of that.' It was all very well fixing up other people's songs, but I wanted something of my own. I realised that for the first time in an age, I should maybe write something. I had always been into war comics and was struck by how the hero would often run through volleys of gunfire without so much as a scratch. From that thought came the lyrics to 'Clean, Clean'.

As a sidenote, it's funny, because although I'm often thought of as being a producer with a sonic imprint, more often than not it's lyrics to which I'm most attracted. To me, back then, the music was often quite boring. What differentiated one song from the other was the lyrics. How the music had to be made to fit the lyrics fascinated me.

I loved Joni Mitchell. I listened to *Court and Spark*, *Blue* and *Ladies of the Canyon* in the car all the time and to me, they were the height of lyric writing – the more you heard them, the better they got.

With 'Clean, Clean', I showed the lyric to Bruce, who put a tune to it straight away. I liked his voice, I liked the way that it added a certain legitimacy to my lyrics. After 'Clean, Clean' I would spend so much time with Bruce at his flat in East Sheen that Tessa his girlfriend (now wife) was convinced that he and I were having some kind of gay scene. Ironically, given her concerns, we were doing poppers the night we wrote 'Baby Blue'. Myself, Bruce and Geoff had found ourselves in the kitchen at a party – now there's a song I wish I'd written – and we were throwing a bunch of daft lyrical (me) and melodic (them) ideas around, turning it into the song that became 'Baby Blue'.

History tells us that the song was then recorded by Dusty Springfield, but I'm struggling to remember exactly how she got involved. It was probably to do with Bruce, who was still signed to Everblue. He had designs on being a solo artist and, indeed, would soon strike off in that direction, forming Bruce Woolley and the Camera Club. What I do recall is that Geoff and I signed our publishing in what was no doubt a 50:50 split to some guy who had an office close to Hyde Park Corner, whose name was Terry something or other. Nowadays, I would never sign over half the publishing like that – but back then we were just thrilled that somebody of Dusty's stature wanted to do our song. It still works that way these days. You sign your publishing to somebody with access to an artist who will cover the song, because the song, however good, is nothing unless somebody sings it. As for the finished product, we thought we'd made a good demo of it and of course were excited to see what Dusty might do with it. Until, that is, we heard her version, and . . .

Well, it was pretty average. And sure enough, when it eventually came out it wasn't much of a hit – it got to number sixty-one.

———

Somewhere among all of this general end-of-decade excitement, I had met the woman who would turn out to be the love of my life. At the time I was playing for Tony Evans at the Hammersmith Palais and on the other side of the revolving stage was a small beat group led by the bass player. I think he liked my thumb slapping on the bass. One Saturday night he invited me to a party at his house in Clapham and there I bumped into Jill Sinclair. It wasn't my first sighting of her. About six months earlier I was working on a R. B. Zipper record called 'Come Back Marianne' in a studio called SARM in the East End. I remember arriving to find that it was a bit of a pokey place but good because it had TV meals in the freezer and a microwave. You took the packet out of the freezer, popped it in the microwave for two minutes, and lo and behold, you had a whole meal. Kip's house didn't have a microwave, none of my pads had a microwave: a microwave was exotic.

As was Jill. I first clapped eyes on her during that session, my attention arrested by the fact that she wore a T-shirt that went down to her knees. I remember sharp attractive angles and jet-black hair.

'Who's that?' I said to the engineer.

'No chance, mate. That's the owner's daughter. Plus she's got a boyfriend.'

So I left well alone. Didn't even say hello. And almost – almost – forgot about her, until I walked into John's party that day, when she was literally the first person I met coming through the front door.

'I was in your studio a couple of months back,' I said.

SARM was a family-owned place, and during the period between my session and the party, Jill had taken over the running of it. As a result, she was full-on, giving it the big sell to me as a producer, and we talked for about ten minutes. I liked her. A lot. She was nice. There was a warmth about her. Trouble was that she left the party early, departing in her Porsche 911. And that was that – or so I thought at the time.

It turned out that John's house was huge and had a large basement. 'I don't suppose you've ever thought of renting this out?' I said at one point.

'Who'd want to live in here? There's no windows?'

'I don't mind no windows.'

And that was it. He offered me a reduced rent provided I taught him how to thumb slap on the bass. Although I ended up living in that basement for quite a while, I never did teach him to thumb slap.

My housemates were John and three other people, who all worked during the day, so I rarely saw them. When I got up in the morning, they'd all be at work. When I came back from gigs at 1 a.m., they were all asleep. Subsequently, I moved rooms and an Australian bloke moved into the basement. He didn't work at all and spent all day playing dub reggae really loud. It rubbed off on me. Sometimes I used to go down and listen to it with him. I loved how it was so brutal. How the producer would break down the sound, strip it to its raw elements. How everything would go through an echo unit and clank between the speakers. Most of my ideas for the 12-inch remixes I used to make in the 1980s came from those records. Or should I say they came from my recollections of those records, which is an important distinction.

I was living in that house right up until 'Video Killed the Radio Star' in 1979. And it's funny because the year before it came out, I was chatting to one of the girls who lived there, Edie, and she said, 'What are you doing with your life?'

'What do you mean?'

'Well, look at you, you're nearly thirty. You don't own a house. You don't do a regular job, you drive around in a beat-up old car. What do you think's going to happen to you?'

And I said to her, 'I'll tell you what's happening: I'm pulling the handle of a slot machine and I'm going to keep pulling it until it pays out the jackpot. And it will.'

I had no idea.

5

'Video Killed the Radio Star', The Buggles (1979)

In which everything changes

For me, plenty of things happened in the late 1970s. There was my work with Chromium. With Gardner & Boult. With Tina. Projects that overlap chronologically, as well as in my recollections, but ultimately funnel into the two events which would shape and define my life from then on. Firstly, Jill. Secondly, the Buggles.

I was living in the dub house when I met Jill for the third time. It was 1978, and I had arrived home in the early hours to find her there with John, the homeowner. They'd been on a date, but it was clear to me there was no chemistry between them. However, something happened between Jill and me as the two of us got talking that night.

At the same time, Bruce and I were both into J. G. Ballard and Kraftwerk and found ourselves thinking along the same sci-fi lines. To us, the future was techno, and we had this idea for a band that had been invented by a record company using computers in a basement. We called it the Buggles, a riff on the

Beatles, and we had this line, 'I heard you on the wireless back in '52', which we liked for the way it combined our love of sci-fi with our fondness for the 1950s radio comedy we had loved growing up, especially *The Goon Show* and *Educating Archie*. So we chucked the line around without it really going anywhere, until one day we were out walking, and I came up with, 'Lying awake intently tuning in on you. If I was young, it didn't stop you coming through.'

The whole next bit was taken straight from Ballard's short story, *The Sound-Sweep*, about a future where music is obsolete: 'They took the credit for your second symphony. . .' Then I think maybe Bruce suggested, 'What did you tell them?' After which I came up with, 'Video killed the radio star. . .'

Bruce said, 'We can't use that. What about Snips?'

The band Snips had released an album called *Video King* (1978). Bruce also pointed out that there was a band called the Radiostars, but I told him they'd be history by the time our song came out.

And then I heard the Dusty Springfield version of 'Baby Blue', and that made my mind up. The rough demo that me, Bruce and Geoff had made of 'Baby Blue' was a prototype Buggles record using a drum machine on top of which we'd added all kinds of crazy gags, like hitting telephone directories with wooden spoons and putting it through a fuzzbox to make an interesting rhythm track. The Dusty track was bland and pedestrian by comparison.

'I've got a feeling that we need to do this ourselves,' I told Bruce. 'Nobody else is going to do it the way we want it.'

I've already mentioned that Bruce struck out by himself, and it was around this time that while on one of our lengthy walks around Richmond Park he made his big announcement. He was leaving our band. He didn't think that the songs that he, Geoff and I were writing were commercial enough. Mike Hurst at CBS had showed interest in him. Bruce had an opportunity to go off and perhaps realise his commercial potential.

I made up my mind that if Bruce wasn't going to do those songs we'd written then I would. Meanwhile, I was still working with Tina. We embarked on a tour of the Far East, which was six gigs in Thailand and another few in Singapore. It wasn't the financial windfall I'd hoped for, and although I still had some irons in the fire – Chromium, various bits of production work, songs I'd been writing with Geoff and Bruce – I still spent a miserable Christmas worrying about money. But Tina had some cash and wanted to invest it in a musical project.

'Well,' I told her, 'I've got a project.'

'What's it called?'

'Video Killed the Radio Star.'

'Really? You're not going to sing it, are you?' said Tina.

You'd have to say that Tina was not one of life's confidence builders. She'd always been derisive about my voice, calling it my 'little wibble'.

'I think Bruce might sing it,' I said, which, since Bruce was by far the best singer of us all, seemed to put her mind at rest. I put aside any lingering feelings of betrayal I felt, called Bruce and asked him if he'd be in on the session. He agreed.

We had a day in a sixteen-track studio in order to record a demo. I've done plenty of sessions in my time. Some are good, some are bad. The first session for 'Video Killed the Radio Star' was by far the best session I'd ever done up to that point. Not that it was all plain sailing. I asked the engineer to set up the drums with three mics in the system used by Glyn Johns (which I had read about in *Melody Maker*) instead of the normal five or six. Then and throughout my career I was always trying to get the drums to sound better, and if you're going to learn from anyone, you learn from the experts.

The drummer we used was a guy called Paul Robinson. Paul used to drum with Nina Simone and one of his great skills as a musician was his ability to remember arrangements and play in time. Which is kind of a basic requirement for a drummer. In demo sessions it's essential to get somebody who can remember arrangements because you're putting together what we call a 'head arrangement', not writing anything down. 'Video Killed the Radio Star' has a clever arrangement, one that reflected everything that Geoff and I had learned up to that point – and given by now we were both in our late twenties, that was a fair bit.

On that particular session we were putting the arrangement together on the fly – the drums coming in after the first eight bars, then another eight bars and then the bass – and because it was one of those magical sessions, it worked really well. The verse had sounded a bit like 'Hang on Sloopy' but Geoff came up with a piano part that transformed it. The keyboards on 'Video' are exceptional largely due to Geoff's use of the Solina, Minimoog and Polymoog synths. Nothing was programmed because we didn't have that technology, but we would use echoes and repeats to emulate that sort of sound.

Bruce and Tina sang the chorus, but I was to sing the verse. Geoff suggested I sing it as though my voice was coming through a radio speaker, and we achieved the effect by having me singing into a handheld mic through an old Vox C30 amp. The chorus took slightly more work. Bruce and Tina sounded a little dull at first.

'Why don't you try singing it in American?' I suggested. Which they did, to great effect, repeating the trick with the *oh-ah, oh-ah* bit. I got Tina to exaggerate that bit, as though she was doing it in a 1960s style, and again it worked brilliantly as a counterpoint to the vocal on the verse. An idea that worked.

We had ourselves a demo of the song, and for the first time – and I'd been in the business a while by now – I had something in my hand that I really, *really* thought would be a hit.

———

I had bumped into Jill at the launch party for Infinity Records. I was there because their first release was going to be 'Fly on UFO' by Chromium, produced by yours truly. I met Jill on the way out and she invited me down to SARM the next day as they were shooting a video for her brother's band. I told her about 'Video Killed the Radio Star' and said I'd come to SARM and play it to her the following week.

Jill was impressed with 'Video Killed the Radio Star', so much so that she offered us a free day in her studio, SARM in east London, in order to record another track. ('Kid Dynamo', which would eventually end up on the B-side of 'Video Killed the Radio Star'.) It was quite a canny move on her part. It meant that we got precious studio time for free while she would be able to confirm that the Buggles really were the people who made the song. It's not unheard of for groups to present a demo as all their own work when nothing is further from the truth.

Meanwhile, we started playing 'Video Killed the Radio Star' to record labels. It was just a demo. Any deal would involve us having to make the record properly. But it was a good demo.

We'd sit in offices where executives would put their feet on the table, pretend to listen intently, then turn it down and fling our well-worn cassette tape back across the desk at us. Courtesy? Forget it. Constructive criticism? No. It was just a summary dismissal.

I don't get it.

Not for us.

Barbara, would you show these two gentleman out.

This was, and probably still is, the thing about record labels. They run very hot or very cold. They either love you or they treat you like dog shit on their shoe. And when it's the former they expect you to forget it was ever the latter.

At the same time, Jill was starting to push a bit. She really wanted to sign us. We kept having meetings (and the more meetings we had, the more I liked her) and she was beginning to look like the best bet. The trouble was that she could only afford to pay us a small advance. Geoffrey and I were poor at the time, and we were sure that 'Video Killed the Radio Star' was worth more than that, but it was the only offer on the horizon.

I had grown closer to Jill over this period. I'd spent time with her over the weekends and had even stayed overnight at her house, where she immediately dispelled any romantic intentions I might have had by telling me, 'I don't mix business and pleasure.' I'd never met anybody like her. She was funny, assertive and very, very clever, all of which was an intoxicating combination.

One time she dropped me off at Baker Street, and as I got out of the car, she looked at me and said, 'You're not going to give me a goodbye kiss?'

'I thought you didn't mix business and pleasure,' I said.

'I'm just talking about a goodbye kiss.'

So I gave her a goodbye kiss, and although there wasn't any-thing particularly passionate about it, I remember thinking, *Right, she's not quite the fortress of rectitude that she's pretending to be.*

And then, just as the Buggles were on the verge of signing with her and making the record, Geoff got a call from Island, saying that they really wanted to see us again.

I called someone there. 'Why do you want to see us again? I'm not coming to play the track again.'

'No, we're really interested. We want to sign you.'

Subsequently I found out what had happened. A guy called Lionel Conway, who had managed Elton John and now ran Chris Blackwell's Island Publishing Company, had heard the demo. I don't know how he heard it, but he did, and he liked it and even though it wasn't Island style, he wanted to sign it.

So we went into Island for a second time. Lionel Conway was there, and we were at last treated to the experience of somebody at a major record label being enthusiastic about our record. Not only did they want to sign it, but they were also prepared to give us what amounted to £15,000 each, which at the time, and given that we were both broke, was an incred-ible amount of money. My total earnings for the previous year were £2,500. But still, there was Jill. We'd been about to sign and were even booked into SARM the following day in order to make the record.

I was trying to get to her in order to deliver the news, trying and failing until about 2 a.m. when I finally managed to speak to her. She was of course disappointed but suggested that we went into the studio anyway. Why? Two reasons. Firstly, if we didn't go in, then it would be downtime for the studio and no studio wants that. Secondly, since we were signing to Island she could bill them for the studio time. Even though she lost out on the Buggles, she at least got a tiny slice of the pie. So that's what we did. We went into SARM the following day and started making the proper record.

That night she called me. 'Well, we're not doing business together, are we? And if we're not doing business together then what are you doing on Saturday night?'

It was 2 June 1979, which was a Saturday. A year later, Jill and I were married and in all we were together for the next twenty-seven years. Until Jill had a tragic accident that ultimately took her from us. With the feelings of our children paramount in my mind, it's not something I'll be discussing here.

Meanwhile, it came to making 'Video Killed the Radio Star'. We had the demo on cassette but we didn't have a multi-track, but that was no problem, we'd just do it again. Except it *was* a problem. And after a fortnight of hard labour, with nothing quite gelling and the fact that we were using a different drummer being just one of our problems, we listened back to what we had.

'It's good, it's good, it's good,' we said, trying to convince each other what we both knew, which was that there was something missing. It just wasn't the same.

There was a silence. An awkward, uncomfortable silence. 'Start again?'

'Yeah, let's start again.'

So we scrapped two weeks' worth of work and went back to square one. The problem was that we had made too many changes to the demo and in doing so had lost the magic. First job was to rehire the drummer, Paul Robinson, while the next thing we did was move from SARM to Nomis studios.

At some point Hans Zimmer came on board. This is the same Hans Zimmer who later went on to compose soundtracks for *Gladiator, The Lion King, Inception*, etc., but back then was a 23-year-old budding keyboard genius who came with his very own Prophet-5, which was a five-note polyphonic keyboard.

The Prophet-5 was something of a revelation. Prior to that we'd been using our old Polymoog synth, which as well as being a bit temperamental, lacked the ability to 'remember' sounds. The Prophet-5 allowed you to program a sound and then save it to patch memory, meaning you could recall your programmed sound at the touch of a button.

Hans was charming, good fun to be around, and an excellent programmer. Gradually he became part of the band and his Prophet-5 was integral to the sound that we came up with.

I'd never edited a multi-track tape at this point. I'd heard you could do it, and in principle it was fine, but I was too chicken to have a go myself. In essence, we weren't experienced enough to know how to redo anything, so if we made a mistake we had to stop and start again. So, say for example the first three things you lay down are the piano, bass and drums. If you make a mistake on the piano but the drums and bass are fine, you ought to be able to send your drummer and bassist home, and redo the piano track. Not us. We lacked the experience and confidence to do that, so instead the whole lot had to be played through perfectly, and you try playing four minutes of music absolutely perfectly. It's hard. As an aside, I should say that it's a perfectly legitimate way of recording, and doing it that way focuses the band, keeps them tight. Years later I met Blink-182, who claimed that they had been exhausted working with a producer who made them do exactly that. I knew and liked the album they were talking about. 'It paid dividends,' I told them.

Still, we'd ended up working until the early hours, urging Paul, 'Please, one more time,' before offering him double rate and then triple rate. Finally we got it right. I remember Hans' voice coming down the talkback – 'I don't think you've got it yet' – and Geoff and I looking at one another, thinking, *What the hell is he talking about?*

'No, that's the one.'

The next thing we had to try to find was the AC30 amp that I'd used for singing on the demo. I'd sold it to a guy called Alvin, who struck a hard bargain for its release, but I had no choice. We'd tried other amplifiers and even a bullhorn, but it just wasn't the same.

Getting the vocal right took a long time and was eventually achieved one Saturday morning. I don't normally smoke anything in the mornings, but on this occasion I did, and needed a lift from Jill to the studio. I recorded the vocal holding the hand-mic into the AC30, which was a bit dodgy. In fact, if you listen to the finished product, you can hear the amplifier making a static sound. I'd be singing, 'I heard you on the wireless back in '52,' *kicking the amp*. Who knows? Perhaps it even enhanced the sound.

Months had passed by the time we had a finished song. Island were becoming increasingly alarmed: 'You've spent nearly the whole budget and you don't have the song yet.'

'Well,' we told them, 'we finished it, sort of, but we thought it was only good enough to get to number thirty, and we want to get to number one, so we started again.'

Give them their due, they shut up and didn't bother us again. And somehow, we got the bloody thing done.

———————

During work on 'Video Killed the Radio Star', I went along to see Bruce play a gig in Covent Garden, and blow me down if he wasn't doing 'Video Killed the Radio Star'. He sang a line that wasn't in our version, a line I liked so much that the next day I put it in. I figured I had every right to do that. After all, he would be credited on our version. 'Put the blame on VCR.'

What eventually happened was that Bruce Woolley and the Camera Club, his band at the time, aided by Thomas Dolby, were in fact the first to appear with a recorded version of 'Video Killed the Radio Star', which appeared on his album, *English Garden*. Listen to it now – it's widely available – and you'll see that it's quite different from the Buggles' version. Bruce had a band and was hoping to have a career as a singer-songwriter, so his version is a 'band' kind of version, not especially 'produced'-sounding, whereas the Buggles were going for a hit single. I would think it fair to say that back then neither of us was enamoured with the other's version of the song. Time (and money) is a great healer.

Just as we were about to release our version, Sony started making noises about stopping it on the grounds that Bruce was a co-writer, and there was a week or so when things were look-ing decidedly dicey on that front. In the end, both versions came out, ours just slightly behind his. However, ours was the one with the most heat. Right from the early promotional stages there was a huge PR buzz surrounding it. Hans was still in the band, but it was Geoff and I who became the focus of most attention. We had initially thought of ourselves as being a faceless group, an abstract construct, but then as now the media needs a focus, and we were it.

We found ourselves on Radio Oxford being interviewed by Timmy Mallett.

'This is going to be a big hit,' Mr Mallett told us. 'I reckon it'll go to number one.'

'You know that the record's not even out yet, right?'

'Don't worry,' he said confidently, 'just talk as if it's out and as though it's a big hit.'

'But it isn't out. And it isn't a big hit.'

'Trust me,' he said, 'the record is going to be a hit.'

The next thing we knew, 'Video Killed the Radio Star' was racing up the radio play chart in *Music Week*. Capital Radio played it. The idea was that they would showcase five new songs for listeners to phone in and vote for their favourite. There was some pretty stiff competition that week. Madness had 'My Girl', and they had a following; they had credibility.

We didn't win the public vote – Madness, maybe, can't remember – but I do remember the presenter saying, 'You know what? I think that Buggles record is the one for me. I think that's the one I'm going to play again.'

I began to worry that there was a mistake on the record. When Linda Jardim comes in singing, 'You are . . . a radio star-ah-ah-ah. . .', she's ever so slightly out of time. Just a millisecond or so behind the beat, if that. But then I heard it on the radio and I realised that in actual fact it works to our advantage. Somehow it exaggerated the effect of her being in the distance. That's the kind of luck we were riding on 'Video

Killed the Radio Star' – the kind where even a record's flaws end up enhancing it.

Being suddenly thrust into the limelight, Geoff and I had to consider our 'look' as a band. We bought silver, metal-looking suits, so that was a good start, especially when Island told us not only that we had to make a video but also that we had to come up with ideas for a screen treatment. Having abandoned an idea where we would perform on a bandstand in Clapham, we agreed that the best course of action was to leave it to the professionals and instead employed a director, Russell Mulcahy, who would later go on to make the *Highlander* films and more exotic promo videos for Duran Duran. He immediately proved that he knew what he was doing by booking us a soundstage close to Wormwood Scrubs.

I bought some new spectacles especially for the occasion. Big, over-the-top things, they were.

'You're going to be wearing those from now on, then?' said Geoff when he saw them.

'Yeah,' I said, 'I'm a Buggle now.'

They became my trademark glasses, and practically their first outing – before we shot the cover for the single, even – was making that video, which was mainly a case of hanging around and taking instruction from Russell. 'All right, stand on this mark. Hold this microphone. Hold the microphone stand. Lean into the light. Lip-sync the opening.' We had a day of doing that, hearing from Russell how we were easier to deal with than Howard Devoto of Magazine, who apparently refused to do what was asked of him, and then four days later, hey presto, our video appeared.

I didn't like it. I mean, I liked the opening minute or so, but after that I couldn't really bear to watch it. Though not by any means the first music video to be made, it ended up being the first to be played on MTV in 1981 when it prompted a new and slightly belated wave of interest in us.

Meanwhile, advance word on 'Video Killed the Radio Star' was going crazy. Radio play had taken us to the top of the *Music Week* chart and the record wasn't even out yet. At some point it was released, of course, going in at number fifty-seven on 9 September 1979, rising to number twenty-four the following week, number six the week after, number two on 13 October and number one the week after that.

It was the same story abroad. 'Video Killed the Radio Star' raced up every chart it met, home and away. Up to that point, I hadn't had a proper hit. I'd had records played on the radio but nothing that really set the world alight. 'Video Killed the Radio Star' would end up going to number one in sixteen countries, selling around 12 million. It was insane.

At one of our earliest promo appearances, in France, we were told to mime.

'I'm not miming it,' I insisted. 'I've never mimed. I wouldn't even know how to mime.'

The radio person took me to one side, a look on his face as though addressing an especially slow child. 'Just mime, Trevor. If you don't mime, they will stop playing your record.'

So mime we did. I stood there lip-syncing, my right leg shaking with nerves, and Geoffrey behind me, pretending to play the keyboard. And after that, of course, we mimed.

Back home, we did *Tiswas*, the anarchic Saturday-morning TV show. I think it was there that Chris Blackwell collared me: 'I thought you weren't going to appear anywhere. I thought you could be completely anonymous.'

'Try telling that to the PR department. They weren't interested in us turning all these TV shows down.'

Back on a plane and we flew to Germany, where we appeared on the same show as Roxy Music. As a new boy the old guard normally look at you askance, probably hoping you'll have one hit then die a death and stay out of their hair for good. Not Bryan Ferry. He came over and said hello and complimented us on the record. What a lovely man.

On and off planes we jumped. Spain, Germany, France again, miming on countless TV shows, both standing stock-still. Whatever Geoff and I were trying to do, Pet Shop Boys did it so much better a few years later. Somehow they managed to pull off the two-grumpy-blokes' look in a way that Geoff and I never could.

It sours you, as in *makes* you sour.

In Spain we did forty interviews in two days. Can you imagine trying to do forty interviews in two days? You do your interview. You say the same things. You get up on stage and mime to 'Video Killed the Radio Star'. Another time, also in Spain, there was so much dry ice that the two cameras collided trying to find us. Everywhere we went, we'd have to have dinner with the label when we just wanted to go to bed. We'd keep crossing paths with other bands. We learned to our delight that AC/DC – then with their original singer Bon Scott – were a bunch of great people. We had to put up with Madness insisting on referring to us as 'grandad', because we were so much older than they were.

And if it sounds like I'm complaining, I'm not. The one truism of the music industry is that you must promote your record. If you don't promote, nothing will happen. Just occasionally that promotion takes the form of controversy, and I would certainly have my fair share of that in the years to come. Most of the time, though, it's the tried-and-tested path of interviews, TV appearances ad infinitum. For music fans, part of the appeal of their favourite band is that the group look like they love what they're doing. From the Beatles to the Stones to Frankie, you picture those groups and, for the most part, they look like they're having the time of their lives and that forms part of their attraction. Fans can tell when two approaching-middle-age blokes really aren't into it, and the truth was, we weren't.

In downtime, though there wasn't too much of it, we were recording the album that would become *The Age of Plastic*. Writing the album was fun and not too taxing. These were the days when you only had eight songs on an album, and we already had 'Video Killed the Radio Star', 'Living in the Plastic Age', 'Kid Dynamo' and 'Clean, Clean' up our sleeves, so that was half the battle won.

Our album came out on 10 January 1980, just a few days ahead of our second single, 'Living in the Plastic Age'. I didn't think that 'Living in the Plastic Age' would do anywhere near as well as 'Video Killed the Radio Star'; it just wasn't as strong, and I was proved correct when it peaked at number sixteen. I remember it being on *Jukebox Jury*. Ian Anderson from Jethro Tull was on the judging panel, his scathing reaction based on it being music that he didn't understand. He meant of course that it was electronic music, but, even so, it was a telling comment. The strength of 'Video Killed the Radio Star' was that it crossed those divides. Rock or synth, people liked that song. Builders whistled it. The rest of the stuff we did just didn't have that appeal. That's the problem with having a huge hit right out of the box: you haven't built up a following or reputation. I liked 'Living in the Plastic Age', and I really liked 'Elstree', but the problem is that it's very hard to follow a record as big as 'Video Killed the Radio Star'.

Plenty of water had flowed under the bridge by the time it came to album number two, *Adventures in Modern Recording*. Not only had I been on an adventure with Yes but Geoff had left to join Asia, and so I ended up producing it with my long-term engineer, Gary Langan, who had done so much mixing work on 'Video Killed the Radio Star' and *The Age of Plastic*.

As a piece of work, I like the second album better, despite the fact that its only hit was a track called 'Lenny', which reached the giddy heights of number seventeen in the Netherlands. By this time I had a different take on arranging, thanks to my work with Yes, and as a result the album became something of a template for how I would later produce. Yes songs unfolded more slowly than Buggles songs, thus the arrangement was longer and slower. The first Buggles album was all about radio play. It was about hooks and brevity. Yes was the opposite, and I took that on board for the second Buggles album, where I worked hard on the arrangements, partly – I fully admit – to cover the fact that the material just wasn't as strong this time around – but partly because that's where my head was at by then. There was a song called 'Inner City', for example, which was based on a drum loop using synthetic drums. Claude Carrère who ran Carrère Records, the label that had picked us up after Island, loved it. He loved the production. Being French, he didn't click that the lyrics were a bit naff, which was lucky, because the fact was that I had begun to lose interest in the Buggles. Where once upon a time I had been happy and even proud to be a Buggle, now even the name had begun to annoy me. Orchestral Manoeuvres in the Dark – now that's a good name. The Buggles is not. Not to mention that fact that, to me, the studio just seemed like a more exciting place to be.

We never played live with the Buggles. We never did a single gig. And what's so strange is that we could so easily have played live. Geoff and I were at least as good as most of the musicians around at the time, and I've since performed 'Video Killed the Radio Star' live plenty of times. Just that we never did as the Buggles. Perhaps we instinctively realised that we were creatures of the studio.

So it felt like the second Buggles album was the end of that project. The prospect of being a producer was far more attractive. In the event, I wouldn't sing or produce myself for thirty or forty years after that. I always thought that the artists I was producing were far better than the artist I was myself. I was a bigger act as a producer than I was as a singer, and whatever magic I had as a producer, I could only make a little bit of it work on myself. I suppose it gave me a bad impression of myself as an artist, that second Buggles album. It made me not want to return to that spot again. Even so, I had an enormous amount to be grateful for when it came to 'Video Killed the Radio Star'. The thing about the music business is that you're aiming at a target that you can't see until you hit it. With 'Video Killed the Radio Star' it was like we hit the bullseye and the target caught fire. It was that extreme. It all felt a bit surreal. But in the end it gave me financial stability, which allowed me to keep abreast of changes in musical technology and explore creative production techniques. It gave me a massive financial leg-up and therefore an advantage over many other producers. It meant I was able to afford the technology. I was able to take creative risks. Indirectly, it also led to perhaps the strangest detour of my career, when I ended up joining my favourite-ever band . . .

6

'Tempus Fugit', Yes (1980)

In which my microphone stand falls to bits

Of all the bands in all the world, it was Yes that I really loved growing up. For years I would play them in the car. Wherever I was going and whatever shabby vehicle I was driving to get there, I'd have my bass on the back seat and Yes on the car stereo. When my brother and I went to see them at Leicester De Montfort Hall, it was one of the best musical experiences of my life up to that point, and probably still is. I never had a very soulful voice, but then neither did Jon Anderson and yet it worked in the context of Yes. But the bass player was the real game changer. I had never heard anybody play the bass like Chris Squire. He made the bass into a lead instrument in a way I had never thought possible. Together, they really did create something very, very special indeed.

Fast-forward to 1980 when Geoff and I, reluctant pop stars, employed a manager to handle our Buggles stuff. The less said about this manager, the better. Let's just say that . . . actually, let's not say *anything* about this manager. We'll leave it that the only good thing about this guy was that he also managed Yes, which right from the outset meant that at some point I was surely going to meet my heroes.

And so it came to pass. Geoff and I encountered Chris Squire in the offices of our manager, where it turned out that Chris had heard our track 'Living in the Plastic Age' and really liked it, especially the production. He invited us to his rockstar pad in Virginia Water, where upon arrival, it turned out that his kids had asked if they could stay up late in order to meet the famous Buggles, the irony of which slightly blew our minds.

That night, we sat and talked, a conversation that culminated in me picking up an acoustic guitar and playing him a song we'd written called 'Fly from Here'. Seeing a bunch of de-commissioned airliners in Israel in 1979 had given me the opening line, 'Along the edge of this airfield, the old prop shaft airliners stand.'

'You sound a bit like Jon Anderson,' Chris told me when I'd finished. 'Why don't you come down to rehearsals and do this with us?'

'Is Jon going to be there?' I asked.

'No, no, Jon won't be there.'

'Will Rick be there?' asked Geoffrey. As a fellow keyboard maestro, Geoff felt about Rick Wakeman the way I felt about Chris Squire.

'No, no, Rick won't be there,' came the reply. 'But they'll show up at some point.'

Fine, fine. Not long later, we found ourselves in rehearsal rooms in Bayswater, where we got to witness Chris Squire, Alan White and Steve Howe actually play. Up close and in the wild they were incredible: consummate musicians, capable of playing the paint off the walls. The only slight dampener was the absence of Jon and Rick.

We started fooling around with 'Fly from Here'. I was under the impression that we were just routining it, perhaps to hand to Jon at a later date. Asking Chris where he and Rick had got to, I kept getting the same slightly evasive answers. In the end it took a full week of stonewalling about the missing two members before Chris came clean: Yes had fallen out. Jon and Rick had left the band. Oh, and hey, would Geoff and I like to replace them?

By now I had already established that the group were planning an album followed by a huge 44-date tour, including three consecutive nights at Madison Square Garden. So did they mean . . .? Yes, they did mean: you'll be the frontman for the tour.

'I can't do it,' I told Jill, but in a subsequent meeting, Chris expertly applied the thumbscrews. 'Haven't you got the bottle, Trev?' he said, and that bit of needle, not to mention the fact that I'd tasted success and this in turn had boosted my confidence, got my dander up. So I went into a meeting determined to say that although I was more than happy to help write and even produce the next Yes album, no way was I going to embark on the tour, and certainly not as frontman, but came out of it having agreed to do so.

The album, *Drama*, was due for release in August of that year, the tour commencing shortly afterwards, going all the way through to December. Jill wasn't best pleased; we were due to get married that June, and as everybody knows, huge rock tours aren't exactly the foundation for a successful and stable marriage.

Meanwhile, the music world was horrified at the very notion of the Buggles joining Yes. The news even made that fortnight's edition of *Smash Hits*. The audience would still come, of that we could be sure, but with what expectations? What assumptions? I had visions of being barracked at concerts. My nights were spent in a cold sweat of indecision and anxiety until the only way I could get a grip on my fear was by putting it into perspective. *It's only music*, I told myself. *When doctors make mistakes, people die; when musicians make mistakes, people either don't notice or they think it's funny. But nobody dies.*

Anyway, I'd been a frontman for the Buggles; that genie was out of the bottle, so I might as well be frontman for Yes, who as well as being my favourite-ever group were a proper band. No more tapes and miming. This was standing up on a stage with brilliant, brilliant musicians. I've subsequently been lucky enough to do that enough times in my career to safely say that it is one of the better experiences in life.

First, though, the album. I wrote most of the lyrics for *Drama*, and I developed a really good system for doing it: I smoked a load of pot and then wrote down the first thing that came into my head. For me, it felt like a relatively easy thing to do, but it seemed like nobody else could do that, so obviously my system had some value.

Work began and was pretty intense, to the extent that mine and Jill's proposed honeymoon in Miami Beach transmogrified into a few days in Bournemouth, while the wedding itself was squeezed in between sessions on the album. As a kid, I couldn't possibly have imagined Yes being at my wedding, but here they were, treating me like a member of the Yes family.

But I was still wrestling with my fear. One minute I'd be quite confident, telling myself, what's the worst that could happen?

The next moment I'd be completely bricking it. Two weeks of rehearsal in Pennsylvania, a torrid period during which we never seemed to get through an entire set without something going wrong, did nothing to put my mind at rest. To the other blokes from Yes, this was meat and drink; they'd been gigging together for a decade. But to me and Geoff, the vastness of the enterprise, starting with the huge revolving stage and carrying right through to the floating drum set, the sheer theatrics of the whole enterprise just seemed like another world.

Two nights before our opening gig at the Maple Leaf Gardens in Toronto, I went with the tour manager to watch Chuck Berry. 'Is our stadium as big as this one?' I asked her.

'Oh no, this is only little. It's much bigger tomorrow.'

I felt my stomach go clink. I was getting more and more jumpy, especially since we never got through the entire set successfully.

At the following day's soundcheck, I said, 'Who does the talking in between songs?'

They looked at me: 'The lead singer does that.'

'But I'm the lead singer.'

'Well done, Trev.'

By this point, I was past caring.

The way we used to arrive on stage was quite something. Our stage was a circular set-up shaped like a gargantuan tiered wedding cake in the middle of the arena. At 8.15 p.m., which was stage time, we'd be anxiously awaiting the arrival of Chris, who was always late – late for everything. He had this thing about rock stars never being on time – 'No such thing as a punctual rock star,' he'd say. At last, the call would go up. 'Fish is in the building. He is *in* the building,' which was our cue to assemble by a huge set of doors at one side of the arena. The intro music would start – *The Young Person's Guide to the Orchestra*, of course – and at the same time all the lights would swing to illuminate a set of doors on the opposite side of the arena, so that the audience were all craning to look in that direction. With their attention sufficiently diverted, we'd run on through a different door on the other side of the stadium, surrounded by a phalanx of security guys, and dive underneath the stage, where there were a load of aircraft seats dangling from the underside of the lowest portion of the wedding cake. This is where the crew used to sit as well as being used to house all the outboard equipment for the guitar effects. On top of the wedding cake was a small riser. At a certain point in the music a curtain would come down from the rigging and enclose this little circular riser. There was a trapdoor in the floor of the riser and we would each clamber up a small wooden ladder and stand in a tight circle on the riser, all looking outwards. As the intro music reached a climax, the curtain would lift, revealing us to the ecstatic fans. The band would run to their places and join in with the opening tape then into the opening song as I threw my tambourine in the air (my only rockstar move) and launched into the opener, 'Does It Really Happen?'.

It was a spectacular opening, the biggest I've been involved with before or since. The stage would constantly revolve – there were crew members on their hands and knees pushing the stage around for an hour and a half – and, at one point, Alan White's drums lifted into the air and spun around 360 degrees. Talk about a drum riser.

The first night, ripping through 'Does It Really Happen?', I had a revelation. I thought, *Yeah, this is all right. I can do this. This is no different from the Hammersmith Palais with the Tony Evans band.* What's more, I didn't even have to play the bass.

It proved to be a false dawn. For starters, I had trouble with my voice. For the first few shows we did, it was battered at the end of two hours. I found that as the show went on my voice would get better but would then take a dive. There were a couple of songs that I simply couldn't sing – I didn't have the stamina or the technique. One number in the setlist was 'Parallels', which was one of Chris's songs that he really wanted us to do. I sang it twice but then refused on the grounds that it was too hard, and for years afterwards, I had a recurring nightmare that I was in a taxi with Chris, who was insisting on doing 'Parallels', with me begging him not to do it.

That dream didn't come true, but my pre-tour visions of audience heckles did. There were times that we'd finish a song, there would be some applause, and somebody would fill the silence afterwards by shouting 'Fuck off, Trevor,' or maybe, if they were a Rick Wakeman fan, 'Fuck off, Geoff.' Some of them held up signs saying, 'What's a Buggle?' Thankfully, they were in the minority. Most Yes fans knew that if it was a choice between no Yes or Yes with me and Geoff instead of Jon and Rick, then they would prefer the latter. I did become a little bit aware of the criticism, though, and found that I would avoid looking at members of the audience during the show. At the same time, I had stopped speaking in order to try to preserve my voice, which added to a preconception of me as being a bit standoffish.

Each member of Yes had their own roadie. The Yes road crew were a loyal bunch, and as I was new, mine was what you might charitably call 'inexperienced'. One night I picked up my guitar to play the intro to a song called 'I Am a Camera' and realised that he had tuned every string to the same note. He told me later that he had broken a lot of strings in the process. Another time, I picked up the mic stand in a rare moment of showmanship and the bottom dropped off it. If you're in front of 20,000 people, you pick up a mic stand and the bottom falls off it, every single one of those 20,000 people is thinking, *How the hell is he going to get the bottom back on that mic stand without looking like a tit?* And the answer is that there is no way. What you must do is keep hold of that mic stand until such time as either a roadie runs on to sort it out for you, or you can sort it out for yourself.

In this instance, since my roadie was probably off incorrectly tuning a guitar, I had to handle it myself. Fortunately, the music of Yes is suited to quick repairs of this nature because there are long instrumental-only passages and on this occasion, I used one of those to my advantage. I wasn't so lucky with my tambourine, which literally disintegrated in my hand that very same night.

By the end of the American leg of the tour, I could feel people starting to lose faith in me because my voice wasn't standing up to the pressure. There were financial problems, too, that I can't go into here. Even so, we embarked on the UK leg, finally taking the whole thing home to two nights at the Hammersmith Apollo, where we finished the tour in a blaze of, not glory, but relief. That was it, the tour was over. I remember getting home, making a cup of tea, sitting in the kitchen and feeling very, very strange, decompressing from being on tour, feeling at home but also . . . not. And then Yes did what all bands do when they want to get rid of a member. They didn't tell me; they left me to find out by a process of joining the dots and reaching what could be the only conclusion: I'd been sacked.

Geoff and I went into the studio to start work on new Buggles' material, but by that point Steve Howe was talking about starting a supergroup called Asia and, needing a keyboard player, invited Geoff along for the ride. Being cut from the same non-confrontational cloth as Yes, Geoff didn't tell me. He just stopped showing up and I read about Asia in the music press. I didn't blame him, though. As a keyboard player, Geoff needed a frontman, and in that regard, I had certain deficiencies. I lacked that sense of showmanship or onstage charisma that people like Jon Anderson and John Wetton, the Asia singer, seemed to have in spades.

We must have been about two months into the album when Geoff left. By then, I didn't really need him to help me produce, so I finished it with Gary Langan at the desk, but the day I found out about Geoff leaving, I said to Jill, 'Now that Geoff's gone, you can manage me.'

'Well, if I'm going to manage you, then I think you should forget about being an artist and concentrate on being a producer,' she said wryly. 'As an artist, you'll always be second division, whereas if you go into production, you can become the best producer in the world.'

7

'Mirror Mirror', Dollar (1981)

In which the Fairlight comes into my life

If memory serves, Jill's exact words were, 'I've found the perfect band for you to produce.'

'Who?'

'Dollar.'

Dollar were a duo who had started off in a group, Guys 'n' Dolls, with whom they had hits like 'There's a Whole Lot of Loving' and 'You Don't Have to Say You Love Me'. After becoming an item, Thereza Bazar and David Van Day went on to form Dollar in 1977. More hits followed and their debut album, *Shooting Stars* (1979), did well, but the second album, *The Paris Collection* in 1980, not so much. Around this time, even though they stayed together as a duo and maintained the illusion of being a happy couple, their romantic relationship fell apart.

In other words, there were lots of stories when it came to Dollar. Plenty of history.

Even so, I wasn't sure about them. They seemed a little bit throwaway to me but Jill, being Jill, had a way of selling it. 'All you have to do is make a Buggles record, just with Dollar singing it,' she said, and she must have put the idea in Dollar's head, too, because when I met them in a Japanese restaurant, they looked across the table at me with 'give us another "Video Killed the Radio Star"' written all over their faces.

In the old days, whichever producer was working with, say, Cliff Richard and the Shadows, would never have seen Cliff or the Shadows in the control room. The band did its bit and left the producing to the producer. Did the Ronettes chip in during the making of 'Be My Baby'? It's safe to say they left the writing, producing and arrangement to Phil Spector and his team.

It was the Beatles who changed all of that. George Martin remained the producer, but the four members of the band were having their say. Nowadays it depends on the band as much as it does the producer as to who has most input, but I dare say that most producers would prefer it the old way, and here was a band practically begging me to take the reins.

Lovely though they both were, there was no denying the aroma of cruise liner that hung around Dollar. But they were nice and fun to be with. I liked the fact that they were like two dolls, living in a techno pop world, and what's more I liked their backstory: the divorced couple who had to remain together in the public eye. I thought to myself, who could help me to write songs to fit this dynamic? And the answer was Bruce Woolley.

Mind you, there was a sticky moment when we all got together for a meal. It was me and Jill, and Bruce and his wife Tessa, and just as we were sitting down to eat, Jill said, 'Bruce, I'm going to eat dinner with you, but I must tell you that I think you're a total c*nt. What you did over "Video Killed the Radio Star" was unforgiveable.' All things considered, Bruce took it well.

After that, Bruce and myself would meet at his house and draw up our plans.

We talked through our impressions of David and Thereza and together we came up with something that we hoped captured the fleetingness of relationships. I came up with a line about a photograph: 'Handheld in black and white'. On the same afternoon, I had this idea of them looking at each other and being reflections of each other and then we came up with 'Mirror Mirror'. We wrote both of those songs in one afternoon.

'Handheld in Black and White' was the first one we made. Working at SARM East, I knocked it off in two or three days and had a lot of fun doing it. Bruce helped me by playing a great theremin solo on the middle eight. It was one of those instances you get where you don't know if it's good or it's bad, you just know it's different, and it was different because of the way I was working on the drums, trying out things I'd never done before. If you listen to 'Handheld in Black and White' it has a very specific drum sound that we achieved by recording all the drums separately and making the drummer play with one stick, to give it a certain feel. I played the bass on it, too, which was something I hadn't done for a long time.

It came out as a single and it did okay. It got to number nineteen, which was just good enough to persuade Warner Brothers that we should make another, so I began work on 'Mirror Mirror', which I recorded in my home studio, Despair Studios. It was just a bedroom that I'd repurposed as a four-track studio, and it was there that me and my brother-in-law, John, who is now a rabbi, spent nearly a week programming what turned out to be a very complicated backing track into a Roland TR-808 drum machine and a sequencer.

The TR-808 was still quite new at that point and was in the process of taking the place of the CR-78 in the affections of musicians. The CR-78 had enjoyed a great run, having first been heard combined with live drumming on 'Heart of Glass' by Blondie (1979) and appearing on hits as far and wide as 'Tainted Love' by Soft Cell, 'Vienna' by Ultravox and 'Mad World' by Tears for Fears. But the 808 had a punchier sound, and the way we used it on 'Mirror Mirror' made it leap out of the mix. There are no real drums on 'Mirror Mirror', it's all 808, which may well have been the first time I ever dispensed with a real drummer.

In one sense that was a cool step forward. In another, I feel bad, not only because it means a drummer loses out, but also because it's part of the reason why recording studios are going out of business. Whenever anybody asks me about this stuff, the analogy I use is that of a kitchen. If you have a kitchen where you're literally making everything from scratch then you need lots of pots and pans, you need to know what you're doing, and you need a great big cooker. But if what you're making comes from packets then you only need a hotplate and a saucepan and not much more. That's what it's like with music now. Nobody makes their own sauce any more. People buy programmes. They purchase instruments right out of the box. And it started with drums.

People these days are so used to those prefab drum sounds that they actually prefer them. I used real drums on a John Legend track a few years ago and I had to take them off. He said, 'Oh man, it sounds like church.' I always used to try to programme something in a drum machine that was a little bit like a drummer would play, but all of that's gone now.

Back in SARM, I was using both big and little speakers in order to make sure that Thereza would sound great whether you were hearing her on a big nightclub system or coming out of a builder's transistor radio. That reminds me of one of the tricks that Gary Langan and I used to use when we were mixing, which was that we'd put things extreme left and right stereo and then monitor the mix in mono to ensure that we could hear those things correctly in mono. That meant that when we switched back to stereo, the different elements of the track would jump out a bit; they'd be louder than you would have had them. I used that technique a lot over the years, particularly on 'Owner of a Lonely Heart'.

'Mirror Mirror' went to number forty-one but stalled. By then, I'd already started work on 'Give Me Back My Heart' and I got a visit from a guy called Tarquin Gotch, who was running WEA, who wanted to see if it was worth me continuing. I'd already spent about £10,000 (£40,000 in today's money) on 'Give Me Back My Heart', so we were chewing our lips for a while, until 'Mirror Mirror' suddenly took off, eventually going to number four.

For 'Handheld in Black and White', Bruce Woolley did most of the keys, while Simon Darlow played them on 'Mirror Mirror'. But, when it came to 'Give Me Back My Heart', even though the song was mainly written by Simon, I decided I wanted to use Anne Dudley. Our paths had crossed a few times over the years since that first meeting, but this was the first time that we worked together, and she was terrific. Her technique, her talent, her ability to read and write music . . . It just made her so complete and it made a huge difference to 'Give Me Back My Heart'.

Dollar themselves were great. True to their word, David and Thereza didn't get under my feet. Thereza was interested in the production process, but even so neither of them hung around much, and although it was obvious that there was history between them and maybe even, dare I say it, a bit of bad feeling, they always behaved with the utmost professionalism. I know that David has acquired a bit of a diva reputation in the intervening years, but he wasn't like that with me.

Really, though, Dollar was about a new bit of kit. It was all about the Fairlight.

———

When I listen to early 1980s records, I hear people dealing with technology in various ways. The young synth bands like Human League and the early incarnation of ABC were avant-garde indie types way before they became hit record popsters. People had grown tired of punk and the DIY culture that came with it, and most bands at one time or another decide that they'd rather eat than continue making challenging and abstract records. Some of them stick to their guns and remain underground. Others make the jump to the mainstream. That jump or lack of it is why most people have heard of, say, the Thompson Twins and Heaven 17 but not Clock DVA or Fad Gadget.

At the same time, these such bands were going to nightclubs and hearing stuff like Chic. They were deciding they wanted to make a dance record, the only trouble being that they didn't know how. They were only just coming to terms with the idea of synthesisers and drum machines. The nascent synth-poppers probably didn't know it yet, but they were waiting for a bit of kit called a Fairlight CMI, the first digital sampler. Not that they could have afforded one. In 1982, a Fairlight would set you back at least £18,000. It always makes me laugh when people say things like, 'Back when £18,000 was a lot of money.' It still is. Who's going to turn their nose up at £18,000? The thing is that in 1982, £18,000 was an *enormous* amount of money – it would buy you a house.

To those groups I'm talking about, a Fairlight was an unreachable ideal. But then they hadn't had a huge hit with 'Video Killed the Radio Star', and they didn't have the backing of a manager-wife with enormous vision.

'I've got to get this thing, it's going to change everything,' I told Jill, and she barely turned a hair. Geoff Downes, who was a complete keyboard nut, had bought one, so I'd seen what they could do, and what they could do was sample. *Digitally*.

Sampling was a revolution. Say you want to record the sound of yourself singing 'Ah-hah-ha,' in pre-Fairlight days you could record it. You could put it on half-inch tape or cut it to a record, or maybe play it backwards. If you were particularly committed, you might try making a loop by literally cutting the tape with scissors and pasting it together, which is how Pete Townshend and his producer Glyn Johns did the synthesiser part in 'Baba O'Riley'. But mainly you were tied by the restrictions of the analogue equipment. Actual tape instead of zeroes and ones.

With the Fairlight, the horizon didn't just broaden, it virtually disappeared. You could take that 'Ah-hah-ha' and put it anywhere you liked. Loop it, stretch it, overlay it, stretch it to sound like 'Ah-ah-ah-ah-ah-ah-ah-ah'. You could make it go to any pitch; you could play chords with it, up to five notes. And that was just what you could do with the voice. Imagine what it meant for sound effects: the world was your oyster. All you needed was an imagination. Drum machines were exciting. Mellotrons were exciting, but the Fairlight was on another level.

The trouble was that Geoff had gone, and he'd taken his Fairlight with him, so I no longer had access to one. So I had to get my own. I was perhaps the fifth or sixth musician in the UK to do so. There was Geoff, Kate Bush, Peter Gabriel, Pete Townshend and me.

It was an amazing-looking thing that came in a big flight case about the size of a small dog kennel, consisting of a white keyboard and a white screen. It also came with an airport-novel-thick manual that I flicked through and found a page that instructed me on how to load a sound. The first sound I heard was what was called an orchestra stab. Or, as it was known, an 'orch stab'. But I was clever and lucky at the same time, because I realised that I would never be able to read the manual and learn how to work the thing, because it was just too complicated.

Enter J. J. Jeczalik.

J. J. started life as roadie for Richard Burgess, the singer and drummer for Landscape, who you may remember from their hit, 'Einstein a Go-Go'. The fact that Richard had done some work on the second Buggles album, *Adventures in Modern Recording* (we exhausted him trying to get him to sound like a drum machine – successfully, I might add, he's an excellent drummer), had brought J.J. into Geoff's orbit, and when he clocked Geoff's brand-new Fairlight, it was love at first sight. J. J. wasn't a musician – he taught IT at Oxford High School and did so until 2013 – but he was a computer genius, and so he stayed on to help Geoff with the Fairlight.

For some reason, J. J. hadn't split for Asia in 1981 along with Geoff and so I nicked him. I did a deal whereby he'd work from a back room at SARM as my Fairlight enabler. I'd tell him what I wanted the Fairlight to do, and he would work out a way to do it – sometimes spending weeks working on it. And what that meant was that as the 1980s wore on, I was doing stuff with the Fairlight that nobody else had done, and nobody knew how I was doing it. Quite a few times in the early 1980s, I would find myself in a room with a record producer and I'd know what they were going to ask, and it would be this: 'How the hell are you doing what you're doing? There's something going on and I can't figure out what it is.' The answer was the Fairlight. You could rent one, but you'd only just scratch the surface of what could be done with it. You had to own it, you had to have the imagination to do crazy things with it, and, if you were lucky, get a J.J. to operate it for you. Having all those things meant that for a period of two or three years me and my Fairlight were the only game in town. I was the first idiot to get one, and I was the first who didn't treat it with kid gloves, who thought, *Let's have some fun with this thing.* Once I understood what it was capable of, I'd lie awake at night dreaming up shit for it to do. *We'll smash glass, just like I used to do when I was a kid. We'll smash glass and sample it and use it in a track, use it as percussion.* We'd sample the sound of a car engine (Gary's idea) and add echo.

Sampling soon became associated with taking old drum breaks from James Brown records, but back then, we were using existing recordings rather than taking something from someone else's record, mainly because we were nervous about copyright. Years later, of course, I'd be sampled this way myself. I'm credited as one of the writers on the Orb's 'A Huge Ever Growing Pulsating Brain That Rules from the Centre of the Ultraworld' for exactly this reason (it uses a sample from 'Slave to the Rhythm'). It got to the point where we had so many sample requests for 'Moments in Love' by Art of Noise that we started asking for 100 per cent of the composer royalties – and some people agreed.

Back to where we were, and although the Fairlight was used on the second Buggles album, it wasn't until I did the tracks with Dollar that I really got it to sing. Its most apparent use is on 'Give Me Back My Heart', where I did all of Thereza's backing vocals by playing samples of her voice on a keyboard. That breathy 'La la la la' you hear is a sample, and because it's gone through the Fairlight, it has a very specific sound distinct from what you might think of as a normal backing vocal. Why? There's an old saying about computers which goes, 'Shit in, shit out,' and with that in mind, I made sure when we put her voice into the computer that she sounded good. Each 'la la la la' was sixteen layered tracks of Thereza's voice and it came out really well. The first time we heard it, we were knocked out. It sounded . . . different. And different was exactly what we were hoping to achieve.

The songs were well received. The famous producer Arif Mardin was a fan of 'Give Me Back My Heart'. I bumped into Hans Zimmer at a party, and he was complimentary, too. Of them all, 'Mirror Mirror' was my favourite. A combination of Kraftwerk and MOR, a pop-techno single, it got to number four.

In all, I did four songs with Dollar – 'Mirror Mirror', 'Hand Held in Black and White', 'Give Me Back My Heart' and 'Videotheque' – all of which were released as singles ahead of the album. Two, I wrote with Bruce Woolley, two I wrote with Simon Darlow, who'd come on to help me finish the second Buggles album in place of Geoff Downes. All were top-twenty hits, but Dollar didn't use me for the rest of the album – time or money or some combination of the two prohibiting that.

Perhaps the most surprising thing about the whole project, though, was that it attracted some interest from an unusual quarter, the *NME*. One of their writers was Paul Morley. An early flag-waver for Joy Division, Paul was the main hit man for the *NME*. He's the guy that coined the phrase 'dinosaurs' for old rock bands after he reviewed a Foreigner concert and talked about how the band lurched about like dinosaurs in an ancient forest. But to my surprise, he began to write approvingly of the new Dollar material, particularly 'Handheld in Black and White', which had sent him into raptures.

I'd met him before this point. He'd interviewed me in the Buggles era and in the piece that followed had called me and Geoff 'dirty old men with modern mannerisms', which in a sense is exactly what we were. He didn't like the Buggles, but Dollar he championed. Perhaps in retrospect I shouldn't have been so surprised. I put a lot into those records, I had a whole picture in my head of Dollar and their world, wrote the songs accordingly, and I think he responded to that. I think he realised that there was something in there that you don't normally find in those situations.

The other thing that happened, of course, was that a band out of Sheffield had heard Dollar and liked it, too.

8

'Poison Arrow', ABC [1982]

In which I become a father and have a number-one album

In production terms, Dollar put me on the map. The fact that the records were hits and the *NME* liked me meant that I was combining commercial and artistic success.

One evening, Jill sat me down in front of *Top of the Pops*, during which the Sheffield band ABC appeared, singing 'Tears Are Not Enough' (or 'Tears of Noddy Nuff' as we later called it).

'This is who you should produce next, they're perfect for you,' she told me.

I didn't know what to make of 'Tears Are Not Enough'. This was the beginning of the 1980s and we were still looking over our shoulders at some of the great dance records made during the 1970s: the Bee Gees, Earth, Wind & Fire, and especially Chic. The combination of Nile Rodgers' production and Bernard Edwards' genius bass playing made for sublime dance records that went straight to the hips. Lyrics? Yes. We weren't yet in the days of house music. But usually very rudimentary ones. It was all about the groove.

'Tears Are Not Enough' was what you might call an English dance record, in that it had a very homegrown sensibility, an aspect that mainly came out in the lyrical content. I admired it. It didn't knock me out, but it had something. So Jill brokered a meeting with the members of ABC, who at that time were the singer, Martin Fry; guitarist Mark White; sax player Stephen Singleton; bass player Mark Lickley; and David Palmer, their excellent drummer, who these days plays with Rod Stewart.

It turned out that ABC admired 'Handheld in Black and White' which had come out a few months previously. I liked them. Not just because they were complimentary about my work but because they were intelligent and curious, and that's always a good start. They'd been to university in Sheffield, where they'd been inspired at local nightclubs Crazy Daisy and the Limit. Mark White and Stephen Singleton had formed a band called Vice Versa, very electronic, very avant-garde. But then Martin Fry came on board with dreams of commercial success and Vice Versa became ABC. After signing with Phonogram, 'Tears Are Not Enough' (1981), their first single, charted and gave them a taste for success. To follow it up, they had a song called 'Poison Arrow' that they played me, and I liked it. I liked the way that it was a dance song with brains, a literate floor-filler.

I didn't realise it at the time. Not then, nor when I subsequently went to the rehearsal room, but I was about the fourteenth producer that they'd met, and despite my enthusiasm over 'Poison Arrow', they were still a bit wary of me. What sealed the deal was the fact that the band and I shared a fascination for weird and wonderful magazines. Wrestling. Guns. Tattoos.

Any kind of weird sub-culture and I'd be reaching to the shelf in John Menzies. Fascinated, I'd buy a bunch of them and carry them around with me, flicking through them during breaks in the studio.

One of the guys in ABC had whipped out a magazine featuring a cool comic strip. In reply, I'd produced a wrestling magazine in which there was an article about the relative merits of a flame-throwing codpiece or a staple gun. And that was it. A rapport. They said to me, 'If you produce us, you'll be the most fashionable producer in the world, because we are the most fashionable band in the world,' and whether that was true or not I neither knew nor cared but I admired the self-belief.

Watching the rehearsal, it was clear that ABC were – with perhaps one exception – good musicians. They didn't have a dedicated keyboard player at the time, but that didn't concern me, thanks to my secret weapon in the form of Anne Dudley. They were creative, too. Talking about the middle eight in 'Poison Arrow', they came up with an idea for a couple saying goodbye to one another at a railway station, and right away, I thought, *Great. That's exactly the kind of thing I'd come up with. Exactly the kind of gag I like to do*.

We made a demo of 'Poison Arrow'. When I played it to certain key friends, they weren't very impressed, remaining unmoved when I tried to explain to them, 'This is like Bob Dylan but in a disco. It's dance music but *about* something. It has things to say about the human condition and the frailty of relationships.' I was met with empty stares and blank faces, but my faith in the song wasn't shaken. Instead, I decided it was simply a case of the old generation failing to understand what the new generation were doing.

The success of Dollar meant that I couldn't get into SARM, so I got ABC set up in RAK Studios near Regent's Park. RAK is a really good studio founded by the legendary producer Mickie Most, who was huge in the British Invasion of the mid-1960s. He produced the Animals, Herman's Hermits, Donovan, Lulu . . . you name it. Sadly, he died in 2003 of asbestosis, possibly contracted from the asbestos-impregnated fibres used in studio sound-proofing tiles.

ABC played 'Poison Arrow' at RAK. They ran through it a couple of times, during which time it never quite fired on all cylinders. There wasn't anything wrong, as such, but it sounded too much like an English indie band. I wanted Chic.

So I said to them, 'Is this what you had in mind, or do you want to get it better than this?' It's one of the primary functions of any producer: you must set the band a standard that they strive to meet. Okay isn't good enough. Even if they're bored or tired or can't stand the sight of each other, you must give them the belief that they can do better.

How to achieve it? That's the key.

'Well, yeah, but how do we do that, how do we make it better, what do we have to do?' they said.

I proposed programming the drum track into the TR-808, then programming the bass part and have the band play over the programmed bits. The idea was to do it the same way you might trace a picture. You lay your tracing paper on top of the picture, trace over it and then take the picture away. Whatever you end up with is going to be more accurate and focused than it would be if you did it freehand.

With ABC, it was a case of making them aware of the sound we were aiming for. It was a case of getting the foundation correct. That's the secret in a recording studio. Even if the over-all thing is complicated, you need to put it together from simple things done well, and the most difficult songs to get right are the ones that repeat the same thing but with very subtle differences. The Beatles were clever like that. Learning to play something like 'Get Back' is a good discipline. It shows you how much you can do with one simple idea. How if you do *this*, and then *that*, and then *this other thing*, it will all make sense. You can see it if you watch the *Get Back* documentary. McCartney finds one bit, then the next and then the next, and gradually the song is built into the classic we know today.

So anyway, the idea was that by programming everything, I'd focus the band; they'd know exactly what they were going to play, they'd play it and that's when the song would move forward. Look-ing back, it was quite a commitment. I started the programming early in the morning and worked until 7 p.m., at which point I had to go home for dinner. Jill was Jewish and Friday-night dinner was very much the custom. So I left them at RAK with Gary and the drummer, David Palmer, working on the drum track.

I was very lucky, looking back, because David was good. I said to him, 'Just play the same thing, but play it exactly with the drum machine. Literally sit right on top of it,' and he did. The thing is that dance records have got to be in time, or at least as close to in time as you can get them, because that's what people dance to, they dance to the repetitiveness and the certainty of that beat, while at the same time, a DJ needs something that's in time in order to match it with the next record. David got that; a lot of drummers don't.

Next, we did the bass part, the bass player playing exactly in time with the synth I had programmed, which really kicked the track into another gear. Mark White was an excellent guitar player and we did his parts quickly. After that I brought in Anne Dudley, who came in and did the keyboard overdubs in a day or two.

I told the band, 'It needs an intro. Somehow, we've got to have an intro.'

'Like what?'

I sat down at the piano and – I don't know what possessed me, it was one of the few times I've done this – played D A D, which became the intro to 'Poison Arrow'. According to Martin Fry, this intro entitles me to a place in the classic pop hall of fame.

Anne did a great job on the keyboards; we came up with a whole set of great countermelodies which livened up the song a lot. Writing a countermelody is one of Anne's strengths and she's all over the song.

Another thing I did on 'Poison Arrow' that I'd never tried before was at the end of the middle eight where we have the scene of them in the station, the bit where Martin says, 'I thought you loved me, but it seems like you don't care,' and she says, 'I care enough to know that I could never love you,' which is a pretty heavy thing to say to somebody. There was a drum fill after that when it goes back into the main song.

Mark White, the guitar player, kept on about that drum fill, how it wasn't big enough, and because he went on about it so much, I rented two Marshall 4 x 12 cabinets and a big Marshall amplifier, through which I ran a set of Simmons drum pads at deafening volume. When it came in, the drum fill practically knocked you off your chair: it was a real shock to the system.

'Is this drum fill enough for you?' I said.

Mark said it was.

In the 2008 documentary *The Wrecking Crew*, about that amazing bunch of LA session musicians who played on virtually every track that was produced in LA in the 1960s and 1970s, they talk about the secret ingredients that 'make the track pop'. As a producer it's my job to find those moments. It can be a gag that I add; it can be a case of teasing it out of the song, or adding little gags, or accentuating different aspects of the mix. But you're always on the lookout for those details – big or small – that add value, that people remember just as fondly as the melody and lyrics. We had a few of those moments with ABC. Those times that the track 'popped'. And that was one of them.

I remember Anne called me up when she heard the final mix of 'Poison Arrow' and said it was the best mix of anything that she'd ever played on because she could clearly hear everything that she'd done on the song. So that was encouraging. The band liked it. My team liked it. And . . . so did the rest of the world. 'Poison Arrow' went in at number fifty-two and three weeks later was in the top ten, eventually rising to number six, which meant of course that they got *Top of the Pops*, where something happened that surprised me. The presenter introduced ABC by saying, 'It's produced by Trevor Horn and it's great.' Which really blew my mind. Producers weren't regularly name-checked on *Top of the Pops*, if ever. Hearing it, I thought, *Wow, I'm going to be a famous producer.*

If I ever see him again, I must thank Mike Read for that.

'Poison Arrow' did well so I was signed up to produce the rest of the album. I tried to start work in SARM East, but I still couldn't get in, so now I had to go to Good Earth Studios, which was Tony Visconti's place. With me came Gary Langan, who up until then had been the in-house engineer at SARM East. My father-in-law was furious with me about that. They had two great engineers at SARM East, Gary and Julian Mendelsohn, and here I was, taking one of them. The thing was that I didn't want to use whoever was working in the studio at Good Earth. To a producer, an engineer is a bit like a director of photography is to a film director. The engineer's responsibility is to get everything down on tape and a lot happens between it being played and it going on to tape. You need someone you can rely on. Someone who gets your ideas. Someone you like. Recording engineers are some of the most conservative people in the world, but not Gary. He was funny and brave, and he'd do the stuff I needed him to do.

So I had a good team and the band were good. I was pleased with the drumming – Dave had bought himself a drum machine and learned how to programme it – I loved the sax, and I was happy with Martin Fry, the singer. I've never really given Martin his due when talking about the album in the years since, but although he was an inexperienced singer when we started, he has an unusual soul voice that really brought something to the project. He had a good way of bending his voice around unusual lyrics. This is partly because he sings in English, which not many people do. Neil Tennant of Pet Shop Boys sings in English, Dave Gilmour and Roger Waters both do, whereas Elton John, for example, sings in American.

Trouble was, I thought they needed a new bass player. Don't forget their ambition was to make a Chic-type dance record, and to make that work you need somebody who's really good at the fingerstyle, Bernard Edwards' style of playing. I said to them, 'If you want to make the record you want to make, you need a better bass player.' But the band needed convincing. 'Can you get a bass player so we can see what you mean?' So I found this guy, Brad Lang. He was the son of Don Lang, who'd been the trombonist in the Bob Miller Band and had sung the original theme for the *Six-Five Special* TV series. Brad was a brilliant finger-style player, so I got him to play a little bit of bass along with ABC, after which I think they understood what I meant, how much difference a bassist like Brad would make.

And Mark Lickley went.

It's not something I'm proud of. He got a credit on the album, but not as a band member, and he wouldn't work with ABC again. In terms of the album, it was worth it, because if you listen to the bass on *The Lexicon of Love*, it's great, but thinking back on it, I was a bit ruthless because I was young and thought too much about the work and not enough about other people's lives. But if it's any consolation, I've paid the price for it since, because, at one point, Chris Blackwell wanted me to work with U2 and, although I met them, they told him that they didn't want to work with me because they heard that I'd got the bass player the boot in ABC, and they were afraid that I might start something like that with them.

Oh well . . .

I'm pretty sure the first track we did on the album was 'The Look of Love'. As we were working on it, I had Anne Dudley with me in the control room. The band had worked it all out before we went into the studio, so we had a great backing track, but the end was still a bit speculative. I'd said to Martin, 'You're going to need to figure out something for the end because you need an end. I think, maybe, you should consider talking at the end of it,' and so he was thinking about that, and Anne and I were working on the keyboards when we received a note asking if David Bowie could come and hang out at the session.

I mean, I was a huge Bowie fan, of course I was, and so were ABC, so I said, 'Sure, yeah, if he wants to come in, he can come in.' That was the only occasion in all the time that I worked with Anne that I ever saw her rush off to the toilet and come back with make-up on.

Sure enough, fifteen minutes later, the door opened, and David Bowie slipped in. This was the first time I'd ever met him and although I knew upfront that his eyes were different colours, it struck me seeing him up close. He really did look a little like a visitor from another planet. He seemed very nice, and he sat there for a while, being Bowie, while we did some keyboards. As I say, there was one bit of the track that was speculative.

He said, 'I've got an idea for that if you're interested.'

'Sure, what's the idea?' I said.

He said, 'You could use a message from an answering machine.'

I said, 'Nah, I don't fancy that. I've got this idea where Martin's going to talk.'

He was fine with that, and it's not like I was rude or anything, but I've often wondered whether turning down his idea was the reason I never got to work with him.

We had a good gag in the middle of the song where the lyric talks about 'being left out on the pavement,' and a girl's voice says, 'Goodbye.' The girl we used for that is the actual girl who'd dumped Martin and caused him all the heartache that inspired the album. The words Martin came up with for the end of the song were 'And all my friends just might ask me. They say, "Martin, maybe one day you'll find true love,"' which I thought worked well, and we capped it off by a block of vocals at the end, during which you can hear me singing, 'Be lucky in love.'

All in all, a good song. I was impressed at how well they'd worked it out and I thought the things I added were good – making it longer, helping with the end – and that it came out well. It also made one of the best 12-inches that I ever did, where we combined all the different versions over two sides of the vinyl. The band liked that, too, although they drew the line at an idea J. J. had for using a tennis match in the mix. J. J. had sampled the sound effects of Wimbledon into the Fairlight, which I thought would be a great way to illustrate the perpetual back and forth of a love affair in freefall. You have the members of ABC to thank for the fact that that wasn't used on their 12-inch (although it did later show up on 'Beat Box' by Art of Noise).

Making that remix really marked the beginning of my love of the 12-inch. People had been telling me about versions of records they were doing in the States, where they would elongate the record for the dancefloor, like a special version of it. I especially liked the idea because it involved a foregrounding of the backing track and, as I always took such trouble over the backing tracks, I was more than happy for them to come to the front.

'Show Me' was an interesting one. Good Earth Studios is in a Soho basement and the room where we wanted to set up the guitar, bass and drums had a very dry sound. I noticed that there was a storeroom at the back, so what Gary did was place the drums near the door of the studio, open that door and put a microphone in the storage room, which was a few feet away, and that gave the drums a certain roomy sound.

I left the microphone with all the ambience on it open. I'd leave it open until the verse started and then I just touched a button and muted it. I did that every time the band played it. It makes me laugh, to think about doing something so manual and hands-on, but it's an effective trick. It means the drums are a little 'off', a little bit distant, and then I mute the ambience and the drums immediately come about 10 feet forward. It's the same on 'Owner of a Lonely Heart', where the intro is really big and powerful and then when the track comes in, it's bone-dry and in-your-face.

Remember the start of *Star Wars*, the first one? You get an interesting-looking spaceship, followed by a much, much bigger spaceship, and because of the scale of the first ship, you really get a sense of the sheer size of the second one, which has much more impact as an image. I was playing with the same sensation in my records.

Martin Fry once said that I see things in widescreen, which I probably do – and certainly did during that period. I tended to have a pictorial sense of the way things should be. If I was stuck with what to do with a track, I'd think, *Where is this happening? What's going on?* I'd think of it as a song in a musical or film; where it was happening and what was happening between the people.

Anne Dudley did all the keyboard overdubs for the album, and on 'Show Me', which was probably the second track of the session, she played the most beautiful Fender Rhodes part at the end. I liked it so much that I decided to add sixteen bars and make that little bit of playing a piano solo. These days I could add sixteen bars to a track in five minutes, if that, but back then the process involved a lot of messing about, which took five or six hours. As I was doing it, I had this thought, *Oh my God, this isn't my record, what if they don't like it?* After all, I'd had a couple of situations in the past where I'd edited somebody's track and they'd hit the roof. I remember thinking, *The band are away in Sheffield. God, if they don't like this, then they won't like anything I do, and that's really going to make this album a pain in the arse.* In a way, those sixteen bars became a test of whether ABC and I were a good fit for a whole album, or not. But they were bright boys, and when they came in on the Monday, they loved what I'd done with 'Show Me'. Hallelujah, this is going to be okay!

The Lexicon of Love also featured the first string session I had ever worked on as a successful producer. Unlike a film, where you've got maybe 120 players, an orchestra on a pop record will usually number around twenty to twenty-five. Even so, it's a big old machine and the musicians can tend to behave like they're working on a production line. Back in the late 1970s, I'd overseen a string session where the orchestra had literally stopped playing and started packing up in the middle of a take because the minute hand had swept through 1 p.m., which was their stop-time. I was so upset then that I threw their cheque on the floor, stamped on it and kicked it at the fixer. I said, 'That's the last time I ever use any string players on any of my records, ever.'

Perhaps there was fault on both sides. Certainly, what I've learned since is that if you listen properly and appreciate what an orchestra is doing, then they'll do it right and you'll all get on like a house on fire. But, if you're a tit and you don't treat them with enough respect, they'll just go into automatic mode, and a musician on automatic mode is not what you want: 'Tell me what to do and I'll do it.' That kind of thing. It's the least creative state anybody can be in.

So I got Anne to do the string arrangement. It was her first time with a big orchestra. We did it at Warner's De Lane Lea Studios in the West End, and although I was dreading it, it went so well that we did a second session, and that was even better. Mind you, I didn't go and talk to the orchestra or look at them. I just stayed in the control room and talked to Anne.

In the meantime, we were having problems with Martin's vocals. For some reason, we just couldn't 'get' them. I wasn't happy, Martin wasn't happy. Nowadays, I can move vocals all over the place. I can pitch them up and down, I can put them in tune. Back then all I could do was record lots of takes and keep the good bits but even that wasn't really working.

Jill chose that moment to give birth.

———

One Friday night, just before dinner, I spotted Jill in the vegetable garden. 'What are you up to? You're meant to be pregnant, you're not meant to be . . . What are you doing?'

'Gardening.'

Typical Jill – *I'll be okay, I'm fine.*

Our as-yet-unborn daughter Ally wasn't due for another six weeks, but that Sunday night I woke up and the bed was wet. Jill's waters had broken, so I had to get her to hospital at 4 a.m. The labour only lasted about an hour and she gave birth without any anaesthetic, which again was so very her. She was already breastfeeding Ally as she was being sewn up.

She stayed in hospital most of that week. Family legend has it that I went in two days after Ally was born, full of woe, sitting beside Jill's bed, moaning, 'Oh my God, I'm not getting anywhere with the vocals,' after which Jill decided enough was enough and checked herself out of hospital.

The next day we got great lead vocals on three songs in one morning. Martin was singing beautifully. One of the last tracks we did was 'Valentine's Day', which was a good tune but very much an album track, never quite a single. We did a second string session, again with Anne conducting. I had told her I wanted something like 'The Days of Pearly Spencer' by David McWilliams (which I ended up remaking with Marc Almond in 1992).

It was a triumph. Anne nailed the arrangement. The orchestra nailed the performance, and I was ecstatic. It was one of those ideas that just . . . worked. Like I say, you always remember the ones that work.

The album was getting better as we went along. There was a middle eight on 'Date Stamp' for which I suggested we get a female singer, and we used Tessa Niles, whose session marked the beginning of a beautiful friendship. She ended up singing on loads of things for me over the next two or three years, one of those singers where even the first take was almost useable. I'd go so far as saying that she's responsible for the fact that I refuse to auto-tune session singers. My philosophy is that if I'm shelling out for a session singer, they should be able to sing without needing enhancement. I'll auto-tune the lead vocalist because they're paying me but backing vocalists ought to be capable of singing in tune and in time.

I love session musicians, and session singers are a breed unto themselves. It's a bit of a calling to be a session singer, not many people can do it, but Tessa can. I think because it involves using the other side of your brain. For instance, if you're singing a harmony with someone you have to copy their phrasing exactly and some people find that difficult.

On the song 'All of My Heart', there's a moment where I took all the instruments out and made everybody stop so that Martin could sing, 'All of my heart,' and then, *bang*, it all comes back in again. That not only made quite a difference to the song but is also an example of where I'm primarily a songwriter, not a recording engineer. Sometimes people talk to me like they think I know all about frequencies and stuff like that, but I don't – I haven't got the brains for all of that; I'm a songwriter primarily.

ABC invited me along to where they were shooting the *The Look of Love* video somewhere in Wandsworth. They wanted me to be in it, but I'd had enough of such things. I didn't want to go on *Top of the Pops* again or anything like that. I was probably even a bit snooty about it, thinking it beneath me. Either way, I went along, and who should I bump into at the shoot but *NME* writer Paul Morley, and we had a long conversation about how English records weren't selling that well in America. At that point, I wasn't so keen on American music. I disliked that everything had to have a category – AOR, R&B, rock and pop – with hardly any crossover. Radio stations would concentrate on just one genre, whereas in the UK we had Radio 1, which while limited at least meant that everybody got to listen to a bit of everything.

Morley and I talked about that, how although we both respected the quality of American-made records, the scene lacked excitement. Paul was possibly a little drunk and at one point tried to kiss me. That week, there was a picture in the *NME* of me recoiling from Paul's attempted snog.

Heady stuff.

Around that time, I was approached by Spandau Ballet. They'd made their second album, *Diamond* (1982), two singles from which, 'Paint Me Down' and 'She Loved Like Diamond', had not done well. As competition, ABC hated Spandau, but I thought 'Muscle Bound' and 'To Cut a Long Story Short' were interesting and different. They'd said to me, 'Would you listen to the album and see if there's anything that you can do to make one of the tracks better?' I alighted on a track called 'Instinction'. Gary Langan and I listened to the multi-track, after which I had a meeting with the band.

'I want you to redo the vocal,' I said to their singer, Tony Hadley.

'Oh yeah? Why?'

'Because it sounds like you weren't happy when you were singing it.'

It all came flooding out. Turns out not only had somebody said something critical to him about his voice, but they'd made him lie on the floor and put a microphone on the ceiling. It was the dumbest thing I'd ever heard.

'It won't take you long,' I told him. 'I reckon you could sing the song again in twenty minutes.'

Although he was nervous, I was right. He did sing it again in twenty minutes, and it was great. Anne Dudley came in to overdub keyboards on it, we did a few other bits and bobs and it went to number ten, and while there was talk of me doing their next album, it never really came to anything. ABC weren't that happy about me working with Spandau, so I wound up Mark White by telling him that I'd put some of Gary Kemp's guitar on their album. I honestly thought we were going to have to scrape him off the ceiling.

'The Look of Love' was doing well so we knew that the album was going to be big. Gary Langan and I took two or three weeks mixing the album (missing every deadline) and then went into the Townhouse mastering room to put it onto vinyl. I took a reference copy home but decided I didn't like it and threw a spanner in the works by saying I needed more time. The label granted me another two weeks, during which time we pretty much remixed the whole album. The last track that we mixed was 'All of My Heart'.

Stephen Singleton was the one member of the band who would come in and listen to what we were doing, kind of riding shotgun on the mixing. He was a big help. The whole of the band seemed to like what we were doing. There was one bit on 'Valentine's Day', where I'd cross-faded one vocal with another right towards the end, that Martin didn't like, but, apart from that, the album was pretty much as we mixed it. This was unusual because it's been pretty much the opposite on every other record I've made, where I've sent people the mixes and they've generally not liked them or it's taken them a while to get used to them.

The last one up was 'All of My Heart'. It took us two days and the computer broke down twice. Stephen came in on a Saturday evening as the deadline approached. We had to get it done that night because Nik Kershaw had the studio booked for the following day, and we were finished – or we thought we were – when Stephen said, 'There's something wrong with the sax, it doesn't sound right.'

We tried hard to understand what he meant, and at first, I couldn't hear it, until something clicked: there was something wrong with the top end. On further investigation we discovered that the bearings had gone on the tape machine, which was a disaster, because we only had that one half-inch tape machine. This was in the days before you could just get the mix back on computer. If we broke the mix down without printing it, it would take us at least half a day to get it back and we'd never get it back the same anyway. So I spent about half an hour phoning around other studios at 2 a.m. – and nobody could (or would) help.

Luckily, we were in SARM East, so I called Jill, who was able to buy off the Nik Kershaw session while we got hold of a half-inch tape machine – which we eventually did on the Monday. The episode delayed the album even more, so Parlophone insisted that we approve the first pressings at the plant on Saturday morning.

The fact that I didn't know what they meant didn't stop me driving all the way over to Hayes in Middlesex on the North Circular, where I was met by a guy who wore a white coat and big wellies and was holding one of the first pressings of *The Lexicon of Love*. We went into a side room, and he played it back. Now, when you're working on an album, you're listening to it over and over again. By the time it comes to a playback of the whole thing you're sick of it, you just want shot of it. Listening to it, even just one more time, is literally painful.

'It sounds all right to me,' I said. 'How's it sound to you?'

He said, 'It hasn't got much bass on it.'

I was nervous because when I approved the test pressing they were going to press up 300,000 copies of *Lexicon* over that weekend.

'Well, can you play me something that has got bass on it?' I said.

He went off, came back with a test pressing of a Genesis live album, and sure enough, there was a huge bottom end compared to *The Lexicon of Love*, but in fact I felt myself breathing a sigh of relief because the Genesis album was all bass pedals and not at all the effect we were trying to achieve with *The Lexicon of Love*, which is very tight and designed to be played on a big system. I passed the album and days later, it was in the shops.

It did well. It went straight in at number one, spent fifty weeks on the chart and was the fourth best-selling album of 1982. All of which meant there was talk of me doing the follow-up, *Beauty Stab*. I'd heard some of the songs for *Beauty Stab* and I thought they were good, but the album I'd been working on, *90125* by Yes, had taken longer than expected, after which I had promised to do the debut single 'Relax' with Frankie Goes to Hollywood.

Frankie were signed to my own record label, so it wasn't like I could just walk away from that one. I asked ABC if they could wait and Mark White uttered the immortal line, 'He wants us to wait for three weeks. We wouldn't wait for God that long.'

Meanwhile, Gary Langan and I had gone our separate ways. He'd got worn out on the Yes album *90125* and wasn't too keen on Frankie, so he and I had an amicable parting. ABC knew Gary, and he knew them, so he seemed like the perfect choice to go and produce it for them.

I ended up listening to *Beauty Stab* a lot. Just after I finished Yes, and before the madness of Frankie really kicked in, my son Aaron was born. He had developed severe jaundice and had to stay in a hospital, so I have memories of driving around Watford at 4 a.m., listening to *Beauty Stab*. I liked it; I thought Gary did a good job. There were a few tricks he used that were favourites of mine, like altering the panning to make it jump. But although it was good, it clearly wasn't as strong as *The Lexicon of Love*. It's hard doing a second album when the first one's been so big. The fact that your debut album is successful means you've got to make sure that the second album is as good as it can be. Whether

I could have made it better is another matter. People like me are useful in certain ways and useless in others. Certainly, I got the better deal doing *The Lexicon of Love*. I had the material to work with. There are only eight songs on it but they're good songs. *Lexicon of Love* really put me on the map – I won Best British Producer at the BRITs for it.

I suppose it was a shame in a way that my relationship with ABC ground to a halt. I liked the band a lot. They'd come to see me when I was staying in America after I finished *The Lexicon of Love*. Jill had insisted we take a holiday, and since I'd always wanted to have a beach house in Malibu, because I'd read that that's where Richard Harris was living when Jimmy Webb wrote 'MacArthur Park' for him, off we went. There we had a visit from ABC, who were in the States promoting the record. I remember me, Martin and Mark doing that thing where you've got your shoes and socks on but you're running in and out of the sea and trying not to let it catch you. A great day, and one that capped what was a good working experience and a great album.

9

'Buffalo Gals', Malcolm McLaren & the World's Famous Supreme Team (1982)

In which I make the first British rap record with the Godfather of Punk

I'd just finished the ABC album and Jill was already looking for my next project. She narrowed the good stuff on offer down to two: one was a successful band who wanted something similar to ABC; the other was Malcolm McLaren, the infamous ex-manager of the Sex Pistols, who was making a solo album and needed a producer.

Jill thought we should meet him, but I was a little worried that her real motive was to tell him off for his role in making punk rock a driving force of the 1970s. She'd been a maths teacher at a rough north London school when punk had burst onto the scene, so her view of it was somewhat tarnished.

Malcolm once told an interviewer that the best piece of advice he'd been given was that it's 'better to be a flamboyant failure than any kind of benign success' and meeting him for lunch at SARM East, I could see that he lived by those words. What a fabulous sight he was: bright red hair, a weird, flattened cowboy hat, baggy trousers that hung low from his bottom to resemble a full baby's nappy, and the strangest pair of shoes I have ever seen. When we walked over the Mile End Road to Jill's production office, he ambled a few paces behind us, almost as though he was worried about being seen with two such strait-laced squares. Even so, the three of us must have talked for at least two hours before we remembered lunch, and although we had plenty of laughs, I had still had no clear idea what Malcolm wanted to do by the end of the meeting. All I knew was that whatever it was, it sounded great.

For our second meeting, Malcolm introduced me to South African township music. This was way before Paul Simon's *Graceland* popularised the kind of beats I heard that evening, so it was completely new to me, and as a bassman I was especially knocked out by the low end. But Malcolm wasn't finished blowing my mind. He played some weird voodoo-type Cuban folk music, followed by Peyote Pete's 1948 Folkways recording of 'Buffalo Gals' and then, most incredibly, a tape of a radio show where two guys called 'The World's Famous Supreme Team' scratched records. You must remember that back then the idea of someone 'scratching' a record seemed ridiculous. You spent your life trying *not* to scratch records. Deliberately doing so was one thing, doing so in order to create an entirely new sound was quite another.

According to Malcolm, the black kids in New York were into bands like Depeche Mode and Kraftwerk, and to prove his point he played 'Planet Rock' by Afrika Bambaataa, which used a sample from Kraftwerk's 'Numbers'.

I was so blown away by our round-the world musical journey, I almost forgot to ask Malcolm about his singing. He assured me there was nothing to worry about in that department because he'd sung 'You Need Hands' in *The Great Rock 'n' Roll Swindle* film, which was later released as a single. I don't remember whether I ever listened to 'You Need Hands', but I took him at his word. As I found out much later, I should have been more sceptical.

Meanwhile, I still wasn't sure what kind of an album he wanted to make, but he was so entertaining to be around and I loved the way he talked, so I signed on. Gary Langan? Not so keen. For some reason I couldn't sell the tapes the way Malcolm could.

Me, Malcolm and Gary flew to New York and took up residence at the Mayflower Hotel, an old establishment on 57th Street in Manhattan.

Back in 1982, New York was a crazy place. At that time, the club to go to was the Danceteria on 21st Street. Over four floors of wild bacchanalia, you could hear all manner of sounds, including hip hop, post-punk and disco, while DJ Mark Kamins was the main draw. It was a hangout for Madonna – so much so that it was later used for the nightclub scene in *Desperately Seeking Susan* – and of course it was a favourite place for Malcolm. I remember going to the bathroom there and seeing five guys all shovelling cocaine up their noses with tiny silver spoons. At the time, I was completely teetotal and, since Jill had threatened to divorce me if I ever started to do cocaine, much of this stuff passed me by, but there's no doubt it was a drug-charged atmosphere back then.

Malcolm dug up some Cuban players, and we arranged to meet them at a rehearsal room in midtown Manhattan. They turned out to be a rather motley collection led by a 6-foot redheaded Cuban queen called Eduardo, and when they started to play my heart sank. They sounded like Edmundo Ros, the

Latin-American bandleader – only not as professional. Totally unsuitable.

Malcolm turned to me and said, 'You're the producer, you go and tell Eduardo.'

Problem was that when I started to tell Eduardo that their music was not quite what we were looking for, he went off the deep end. I was bracing myself for the Cuban hairdryer treatment when luckily fate intervened and there was a phone call for him at that very moment. As he left the room, the conga player touched my sleeve, told me he knew what I was after and could get it for me, and he slipped me a card with his contact info on it.

That night, we drove out of Manhattan to the Bronx. We met the conga player at his apartment. He told us that he could find the people we were after, but it would cost us $5,000 as well as a steady supply of booze and illegal substances. We agreed. Driving back through Harlem in an armour-plated taxi, I knew we were finally getting somewhere with the project.

Three Cuban musicians showed up at the studio late afternoon of the following day. Suitably imbibed, they began to play a little number called '*E Lube Chango*', which I suppose would be a Cuban version of 'Sympathy for the Devil', '*Chango*' being the devil.

The assistants in the studio were utterly bemused. They kept asking us what kind of record we were trying to make, but at that time I still didn't have a clue.

When our little gang of voodoo priests finished playing '*Lube*', they indicated through their interpreter that they'd now like to sing over their wild drumming. After the three of them together had sung a rather incomprehensible tune, I asked if they would mind double-tracking themselves. I was curious to see if they really knew what they were doing, but in one take they double-tracked themselves more or less perfectly.

Those three priests were amazing. I've never heard drumming like it. As we listened, one of them looked at me and said, 'He got the spirit,' and, you know what? I had. Which proved to be a good thing.

After that session I became homesick and paranoid. I didn't know what to do to make these drummy bits into finished songs on a commercial album. Malcolm didn't appear to want to sing, and I couldn't figure out what to do next. Then Malcolm found a synthesizer player who understood the Cuban tunes, and the next day we recorded him playing the melodies our drummers had sung on an Oberheim synth. The sound of the synths and the real Cuban percussion was terrific, so I knew I'd be able to do something with these tracks even if we didn't have a song or a singer.

Next, Malcolm wanted to find some South American musicians so we could record a *merengue*, which is a fast salsa-ish beat, and some Andean folk music. He came up with Boris Khalaf and his Happy Dominicans. They ran into the audition room exactly two hours late, unpacked their instruments and then launched immediately into a lively salsa, which they played as effortlessly as you or I would brush our teeth. In a matter of minutes, they'd played the whole thing and then packed up and taken off to their next gig.

I booked the Power Station studio the following day to record the piece from 8 p.m. till midnight, but I told Boris the session started at six. Sure enough, the next evening at precisely 7.55 p.m., all ten of the Happy Dominicans – followed by a rather breathless Boris – rushed into the studio, apologising profusely.

The fact that Bruce Springsteen had been working in the same studio all day and had only just left, leaving bits of the E-Street Band's gear scattered around the place, must have given the session a surreal edge for the studio assistant. He kept looking at us, and then at Boris and his Happy Doms, trying to figure out what the hell was going on. I'd never imagined myself producing a South American wedding band but, as with the voodoo priests, the only way to do it was to set up the mics and roll the tape. Any musical input other than 'stop' or 'let's go' only caused major confusion.

It was around this time that Malcolm wheeled in the World's Famous Supreme Team. They arrived just as I was trying to get a handle on some uninspiring Andean folk tune we'd recorded the previous day. They were two tough-looking black guys who worked a con with cups and dice on Broadway during the day (I saw them in action later). When I told them I was a fan of their radio show they looked at me in disbelief, but I'd been listening to their cassette and I loved all the scratching and the druggy late-night New York voices.

Whenever I asked Malcolm about a possible single, he'd always say 'Buffalo Gals', which terrified me. How the hell were we going to make a corny old square dance into a hit single? But we soldiered on, mainly due to his blind determination, flying to Tennessee in order to record it. Malcolm had booked Tri State Studios just outside of Nashville and he'd hired a real hillbilly group called the Hilltoppers, who were famous for their appearances at folk festivals. The studio was a one-man show owned by the determinedly old school engineer, Randy, who also had a record pressing plant adjacent to the studio, where he pressed Gospel records.

The Hilltoppers were the *real thing*. They turned up in a purple VW minibus lined from top to bottom with pink carpeting, looking like characters from *Deliverance*. There was a boss-eyed girl who played the 'broom shank stuck in a biscuit box with string on it' bass and a man who must have been at least ninety, wearing a hat that said 'The oldest Hilltopper', but they were very friendly and said they were familiar with the song 'Buffalo Gals', so I had them run it through.

They were dreadful. Even Malcolm could barely control his face when we heard them.

'You're the producer,' he said, yet again. So I gave them $70 and they drove away perfectly happy in their purple hillbilly bus.

When I asked Randy if there were any session men around, he said, 'You must be talking about "utility pickers".' Within an hour or two we had a drummer, bass player, fiddle player and a few utility pickers who were very withdrawn but seemed to know what they were doing.

'Buffalo Gals' is a song used in square dancing. The lyrics describe the dance, so there are many very repetitive verses and without a lead vocal it's difficult to know where you are in the song. Malcolm was no help because, as I discovered, he couldn't sing in time or in tune. When I told him he should start singing after four bars, he asked what a bar was. I turned his microphone off in the monitors so he wouldn't put the utility pickers off. It can be difficult to maintain a performance when someone is singing the chorus where the verse ought to be. But at least if we didn't hear him, we could always see him in his funny cowboy hat, dancing and singing completely out of tune and out of time in the corner. Placed strategically behind a wall of acoustic screens so his voice wouldn't bleed into the recording of the band, he seemed to be enjoying himself.

The utility pickers were obviously veterans of a thriving local music scene and they responded to all our musical whims, if not with overt enthusiasm then at least with a certain grim dignity. We recorded a version of 'Buffalo Gals' which had the drummer playing the back of a chair with his sticks, and although that was the best thing to emerge from those sessions, it still didn't sound like a hit record to me.

Next, Malcolm flew out to South Africa to assemble a group of musicians who could play like the authentic township records we'd listened to. Gary and I followed on. This was the South Africa of apartheid, and I must say I was a little worried about the trip. Malcolm had been phoning me from Soweto with stories of recruiting street musicians the record labels wouldn't employ because of their militancy.

When we arrived, Malcolm told us we'd be working through the night for the next nineteen days in a studio run by a guy called Gallows. This guy not only owned the studio but also appeared to own most of the South African music business as well. Evidently, when Malcolm arrived they had tried to palm him off with their normal musicians, but he refused and, without any kind of official permission, took off into Soweto. At this point in time Soweto had no (or very little) electricity, and, there were on average twenty murders every weekend. Malcolm was wearing his funny hat and those baby nappy trousers that he made famous, and I can only imagine what the Sowetans must have thought of him. We were staying at the Carlton Hotel, which at that time was the only multi-racial hotel in Johannesburg, and Malcolm had some of the Zulu female singers staying with him in his suite. Consequently, his floor was patrolled by anxious-looking security guards carrying walkie-talkies.

Malcolm prepared the way for me by telling all the musicians I was a big producer from England, and they must obey me without question. He needn't have bothered as they turned out to be the nicest bunch of players I could have wished for. There were about fifteen of them – mostly Zulus: two guitarists, a bass player, a drummer and an assortment of singers – mainly Zulu women and one old man, a well-known local bass singer called Big Voice Jack. We spent the next nineteen nights together locked in the Gallows studios – we had to be locked in because, at the time, black people were not allowed in Jo'berg after dark.

The control room had a seat along the back wall where the musicians would sit between takes. On the first evening a white guy came in and introduced himself as David. He said if I needed anything, just to let him know. Without thinking, I said I'd like a cappuccino and turning to the assembled musicians on the seat, I asked if anyone else would like one. They all looked at me blankly. The man left to get me the coffee and one of the Zulu women told me that the white man was Mr Gallows. I told them that I was a paying customer in this studio and didn't care who he was.

The first night, I asked if anyone could get me some grass and the bass player volunteered. I gave him $15. The next evening, he arrived with a large carrier bag full to the brim with some pretty pungent herb. I was a little panicked as this kind of amount could land me in prison for life if the police caught me, so I gifted nearly all of it to my artists, who were very grateful. They rolled joints with wet newspaper, a technique I had never seen before.

In return, they were fascinated by the joints I rolled and so for the rest of our time there I would roll joints for them as a treat.

Malcolm was always a good judge of musicians and these guys could really play. The three female Zulu singers worked out all their own harmonies and no one seemed to mind Malcolm's crazy lyrics. We recorded about ten songs in these sessions, including two that turned into the singles 'Double Dutch' and 'Soweto', which was my favourite track on the whole *Duck Rock* album. Even now, I can barely listen to it without tears in my eyes.

I became quite friendly with the woman who had pointed out Mr Gallows to me on the first evening. One night she told me about a noise that Zulu women made as they killed someone. She shook her whole body and made this bloodcurdling shriek that sounded like a war cry. I recorded it immediately – it's the sound that starts 'Buffalo Gals'.

It's not easy working nineteen nights in a row and the hotel staff didn't help. I'd hang a 'Do Not Disturb' sign on my door, but as 4 p.m. approached, the cleaning staff would come around, banging and shouting until I finally had to let them in to clean the room.

One day Malcolm took us to Soweto. We left modern Johannesburg and headed out into the most beautiful countryside I'd ever seen. The first thing that came into my mind was that line from the hymn 'Jerusalem' about 'dark Satanic mills': there was no electricity, the coal smoke hung in a cloud above the whole place. As we drove into the township, it reminded me of Coalbank Terrace up in the Northeast, where I had lived for a time with my grandmother.

Malcolm wanted to work on another song called 'She's a Hobo'. The vocal harmony sounded brilliant, but the song itself was terrible, so I suggested we use the vocal harmonies with the World's Famous Supreme Team. I could have them cut onto vinyl and the WFS could scratch them. I only suggested this at the time because I was afraid of getting bogged down on what I thought was a crap song. Malcolm had another idea at this time that we'd do a rapping, scratching record called 'E.T. Come Home' as the film *E.T.* was big at the time. This idea horrified me, so without really thinking about it, I said, 'Why don't we do a rapping, scratching version of "Buffalo Gals"?' Malcolm loved the idea, which was a relief because to me at that point anything was better than some half-assed square dance as the first single.

When we finished our nineteen-day studio stint, we paid the musicians and singers £1,000 each. For them, it was an absolute fortune – they were used to recording a whole album in an afternoon and getting about £4.50 for it. They all talked about what they would do when they got the 'big cheque'. The guitar player told us that he was going to buy himself a wife.

'But don't you already have a girlfriend?' we asked him.

'Yes,' he said, 'but now I want a wife.'

We asked how much a wife would cost, and he told us about £500, a sum he never thought he'd see in his lifetime.

Later, we were at the hotel eating breakfast – which for us was supper – when reception rang to say there was someone for us at the front desk. At the check-in counter we discovered our inebriated guitarist carrying a crate of strong lager, accompanied by a smartly dressed young girl who looked little more than sixteen and seemed overawed by her surroundings. Our guitar-playing friend greeted us enthusiastically, the 'big cheque' sticking out of his top pocket, and told us he'd been trying to book a room.

Malcolm made sure he got one and paid for the honeymoon couple's room himself.

Malcolm was having such a good time in South Africa that he stayed on for a while. By then, he had about six or seven people staying with him in his room. Gary and I went back to England to begin work on the scratching version of 'Buffalo Gals'. The Supreme Team flew over from New York to work with us but came without any of their gear, which meant I had to find decks and mixers for them. These were quite specialised and could only be obtained in New York, so they had to wait in the Columbia Hotel for a few days. They hated England; they hated Radio 1 – 'Man, one minute they're playing one kind of music then some wack heavy-metal shit starts up,' they complained. I didn't know what 'wack' meant and it was also the first time I'd heard the word 'bad' used instead of 'good'. I found it quite confusing at first but, then again, I didn't find Radio 1 in the slightest bit confusing. It was what I liked about the music scene in the UK.

The Supreme Team also hated the fact that there were only three TV channels in the UK (they missed the launch of Channel 4 by a matter of months). While waiting for their decks to arrive, I had some acetates cut with various bits of the Zulu women's vocals – mainly pieces from 'She's a Hobo'. I tried cutting bits of the stuff we had done in New York, but it didn't seem as interesting as those female Zulu voices.

When we finally got down to work, I tried to explain the Fairlight to the Supreme Team. I was quite excited by the parallels between what they were doing by scratching the records and what we were doing with the digital mellotron. Much more excited than they turned out to be. I remember the look of absolute incomprehension on their faces as I explained digital sampling to them.

They were happier with the record decks and were quite fascinated by the acetates I'd cut for them.

I needed somewhere to start so I asked them what their favourite beat was. I think it took about eight hours for me to programme a drum and bass part into the Oberheim synthesizer and drum machine I had back then. They kept singing me the rhythm, but it took me a while to understand it. It was a pretty ordinary hip-hop beat by today's standards, but back then hip hop was just being invented, so I'd never heard it before. I looped the rhythm they showed me and got them to try some scratching with the acetates.

The results were amazing. I'd never heard anything like it before. The first jams we did with these acetates came out later as 'She's a Hobo Scratch' and they still sound as exciting today to me as they did then.

I showed them the lyrics to 'Buffalo Gals' and suggested they rap them over the beat they'd shown me. But they hated the idea: 'It's the fuckin' Klan! We can't rap that shit.'

I said Malcolm had paid for them to come over specifically for this purpose, but they were unmoved, so instead I offered to demonstrate how easy it would be to rap the lyrics. I went out into the studio, put some headphones on and rapped, 'First buffalo gal go round the outside. . .' When I finished, I couldn't see the Supreme Team in the control room and thought they'd left. Instead, I found them both on the floor, literally weeping with laughter. They put their arms around me and said, 'Man, we didn't know you could rap, Trevor,' and then fell back into paroxysms of laughter.

Malcolm came back from South Africa, and we started to try to make a record in the conventional sense with the World's Famous Supreme Team. It was tough. Anne Dudley was in one corner of the control room with a bank of keyboards, and J. J. with the Fairlight and assorted drum machines in another corner. The World's Famous had their decks and Malcolm would come up with these crazy scenarios that we'd try to make into a record. For example, 'Here I am flying over Tennessee with the World's Famous Supreme Team.' Cue scratching and music. I would shout 'music' to Anne and at first, she'd ask, 'What music?' But once she understood that I meant 'just play', she came out with some brilliant improvising. The Supreme Team loved her, particularly her piano playing. J. J. had sampled bits of the cassette of their radio show into the Fairlight and was doing things with the voices of the callers from the tape.

Two lines from that cassette intrigued me. Both came from a girl who was phoning the show late at night. They were, 'Hey, all that scratching's making me itch,' and the other one was when the DJ asked her how come she was up so late and she said, 'Too much snow white.'

Malcolm was a great guy to work with. If you saw him on a chat show on TV it didn't really do him justice. He was one of the few people who could entertain you for hours with stories and anecdotes and ideas. On the TV interviews I've seen they only give him a few minutes and he never really warmed up, but Gary and I loved to listen to him. He was so creative and, more importantly, very flexible. If his idea didn't work but something that we found along the way did, then he'd happily abandon the original idea. In every way but one he was wonderful to work with. His weakness? He had no sense of pitch or rhythm. This wouldn't have made too much difference in these days of direct-to-disc recording where it's possible to edit ice cream to concrete and fix anything, but back then it was a huge obstacle. Malcolm did his best but more often than not his performance would be – in the words of the World's Famous – a 'vibe killer'.

Two weeks of this kind of improvisation got us nowhere, and I was beginning to become desperate. We went back to SARM East and edited the best from the two weeks of experimentation. Although it was interesting, it still wasn't good enough for a first single.

I asked Malcolm if he'd leave me alone with the Supreme Team for a day or two so that I could put something together. I had an idea that if I constructed a backing track that followed most of the rules for a single – even if the content was abstract – I might be able to solve the problem, so we decamped to Good Earth Studios, where I used the Zulu ladies' war chant as an introduction and programmed a version of the Supreme Team's favourite drum groove into my DMX. I was working with Anne and whenever the track started to get too musical, we stripped it back down again, but by now I had a much better idea of what to do, and I seem to remember making the record in one day. Anne did a lovely bit of solo piano playing in the middle. I thought we all worked well that day. The Supreme Team scratched the old records I'd bought for them and Anne and Gary and myself made the record.

Lastly, it was obvious that Malcolm was going to have to do the lead vocal, and I still hadn't figured out how to get him in time. However, I got the Supreme Team to rap his 'Hobo' lyrics as a middle eight and I used the voices from the cassette of the

Supreme Team radio show as characters on the record. I put the line 'Too much of that Snow White' at the very end.

When Malcolm arrived at the studio to sing, he was thrilled by the track. 'How am I going to rap this?' he asked. 'I'm not exactly Dr Rhythm.' Then he came up with an idea – if I could beat my fist in time on his chest, he'd try to synchronise the words to my blows. This is what we did. By the time we had the vocal from him I was exhausted, punching him for take after take. If I flagged, he'd tell me off. Anyway, it worked and when we finally finished with the World's Famous scratching the original Folkways recording of 'Peyote Pete', Malcolm and I knew we had something.

Malcolm said, 'Well now I'd better play it to the record label,' which sobered us both up a bit, because even though I thought it was a brilliant track, I didn't know how the long-suffering Charisma Records would react to it. They were already 200 grand into the album and 'Buffalo Gals' wasn't your normal single.

Malcolm told me afterwards that when he played it to Charisma Records there was a silence after it was finished and everyone looked at each other. Then the mail boy stuck his head around the corner and said, 'What was that? It was fuckin' great.' So everyone decided to like it. Dave Lee Travis was an unlikely champion of the record when it came out and played it at least once and sometimes twice on his Radio 1 morning show. It wasn't particularly commercially successful, neither was the album *Duck Rock*, which was very ambitious but somewhat handicapped by the fact that Malcolm was not young and sexy, so although we broke new ground, we didn't make much money for ourselves or Charisma Records.

A year later, when I was in New York trying to produce Foreigner's new album – a project that ended up coming to nothing – I was taking a walk down Broadway and two black guys were breakdancing on the pavement in front of a huge crowd. As I pushed through the crowd, I realised they were dancing to 'She's a Hobo Scratch'. I thought they wouldn't believe me if I told them I'd produced the record they were dancing to, but it was a proud moment.

10

'Owner of a Lonely Heart', Yes (1983)

In which I have a pee on a barrel

By late 1982, I was a producer of some note, with hits under my belt, while the band Yes were in a state of hibernation. Chris Squire, having been introduced to guitarist Trevor Rabin, had joined with him and the original Yes keyboardist, Tony Kaye, to form a new band, Cinema. They asked if I wanted to come and see them. (Which I knew of course meant, did I want to work with them?)

I was interested, but Jill was much less keen. In 1985, Live Aid would make rock fashionable again, but at that time pop was very much in the ascendancy, and thanks to my work with Dollar and ABC, I was at least a tiny part of the reason for that. I was currently working with Malcolm McLaren on music that was an exciting, fascinating melange of hip hop, country and world music. What's more, Yes had ousted me from the band not two years previously.

Why would I want to go back?

The answer was that I didn't hold a grudge about being sacked. Jill would occasionally hold a grudge on my behalf, but that's love for you. As far as I was concerned, I hadn't been a good enough singer. If I'd been up to snuff, then I would have stayed in Yes and things would no doubt have been very different. And anyway, it wasn't strictly speaking Yes that I'd be working for, it was Cinema, and I was just going to see them. Nothing was set in stone. I could always say no.

I went along to see Cinema and they sounded fabulous in John Henry's old rehearsal room. Chris was playing bass and bass pedals together and I'm a sucker for that kind of thing, Trevor Rabin was obviously a virtuoso guitar player and Alan White was his usual brilliant self. Chris, with his usual persuasive charm, turned all the way up to eleven, wanted me to work with them. Trevor Rabin was songwriting now, he told me, and we made an arrangement to meet in a couple of weeks in LA, where Jill and I were going to rent a beach house in Malibu.

Trevor lived in Topanga Canyon so I drove over there one Tuesday afternoon to hear his songs. The rest of the band were there. The first songs Trevor played me seemed to me more suitable for Styx than Yes. As the tape reached its end, Trevor had excused himself to go to the toilet when something came on at the end of the tape, an extra song seemingly tacked on as an afterthought.

My ears pricked up. It had big guitar sound at the beginning followed by an amazing riff that kicked in like a jump-cut. I loved the way it leapt out at you, how it went from big to dry. Then the chorus: 'Owner of a lonely heart'. Amazing!

Trevor reappeared.

'What's this?' I asked him.

'Oh, that's nothing, that's not for Yes,' he told me.

'No,' I said. 'That's a number-one hit for Yes.'

'No, it's not for Yes,' he insisted.

It became the Trojan Horse for the rest of the album. I told them that if we did that song, I'd do the album. And so, despite the reservations of those around me, who thought I should be concentrating on either the sophisticated pop of *Lexicon of Love*, or continuing a process of branching out into more cutting-edge dance sounds as I was doing on the yet-to-be-released Malcolm McLaren album, I agreed.

SARM was currently the in-vogue studio and thus booked, so myself, engineer Gary Langan and the members of Cinema decamped to Studio One of the Townhouse in Shepherd's Bush to begin recording the album that would become *90125*.

For the first week I was like a rabbit caught in the headlights. I'd come from working with drum machines and sequencers. Suddenly I had to get used to dealing with people – people who talked back. They're starting. They're stopping. They're bitching and griping. They're not happy with the sound. They're swapping places. They're changing strings.

Chris refused to wear headphones. He said he needed to hear his bass coming out of the cabinet, he just had a monitor next to him so he could hear everyone else. At the conclusion of each take, where what we needed to do was discuss the quality of what had been recorded, the band would instead be complaining about the headphones: 'Can you turn me up? Can you turn him down? Can you do this? Can you do that?' Gary was going mad with it.

We solved the problem by giving each of them their own headphone mixer, so at last we could get down to business, but the episode was indicative of what was swiftly becoming a flight beset by turbulence. We had started with some of the other songs on the album – I thought it best to leave 'Owner of a Lonely Heart' until everybody was warmed up – but I was already beginning to teeter on the edge of regret. Perhaps Jill had been right.

As I got to know Trevor Rabin, I liked him more and more, but he thought that the drums should sound like Mutt Lange's drums. Lange, the legendary producer of AC/DC, Def Leppard and Foreigner, among others, was to Trevor the consummate producer. Uncompromising, very rocky, larger-than-life, all of that. But Yes weren't the same kind of band. The drummers in those bands, good as they were, were not in the same league as Alan White, who, aside from being one of the nicest men I'd ever met, was one of the best, most expressive drummers of his generation. In the end I said to Gary, 'Let's give Trevor a couple of hours,' and so Gary reluctantly relinquished his place at the board for Trevor to 'do a Mutt' on Alan's drums. Thank God that it didn't work and Trevor, to give him his due, accepted that fact and allowed Gary to regain his seat at the board.

It was a relief. I'm sure Gary was on the point of walking out, and given that he's without doubt one of the best engineers I've ever worked with, that would have been a huge blow. I had first met him when, along with Julian Mendelsohn – another superb engineer who went on to be an excellent producer – he worked as an assistant engineer at SARM. Gary had been involved with at least three Queen albums and had engineered for Jill's brother before working on the Buggles with me. Superb with sounds, he could do crazy things with echoes that would bowl me over and he was a complete trooper when it came to facilitating my ideas. Occasionally he'd admit defeat – 'I can't fit another thing on this track, Trevor' – and I'd know that I'd done enough, that I couldn't do any more, and I'd always listened to what he said.

Cut to a different scene. An office. A meeting or perhaps a phone call between two participants: Chris Blackwell of Island Records and Jill Sinclair.

The story goes that Chris Blackwell had fallen in love with *Duck Rock*, the album that I'd done with Malcolm McLaren, and wanted to meet me again. In a rare instance of grudge-holding, I resisted on the grounds that Island had dumped the Buggles, but Jill prevailed upon me and along we went. Chris did indeed wax lyrical about *Duck Rock* until, literally a propos of nothing, I said, 'What are you doing with Basing Street Studios?'

Basing Street was the Notting Hill studios built by Blackwell inside a deconsecrated church in 1969. Originally called Island Studios, it had at various times, thanks partly to the fact that it was one of the few studios to boast a sixteen-track recorder, played host to Led Zeppelin, Jethro Tull, Jeff Beck, Dire Straits and, of course, Bob Marley and the Wailers.

For me, Basing Street had a special allure. I make no apology for it, I am a huge studio fan. As far as I'm concerned, they're the best places on earth. Firstly, a studio is generally pretty comprehensively soundproofed, so you don't have ambient noise from outside; secondly, they're air-conditioned so the temperature's good; thirdly, you've got some of the best playback systems in the world, much, much better than any domestic hi-fi system; finally, you are, generally speaking, left alone, which means you can get completely lost in a tune, you can – and do – lose all sense of space and time. A lack of windows and clocks helps. Sometimes I'd enter the studio on Monday morning and still be going on Wednesday lunchtime, emerging into the daytime blinking, wondering what day it was.

I have favourite studios, of course, and least favourites. I never especially liked Abbey Road. Studio One is great for an orchestra, but it has a very specific sound, which, if it's not what you want, there's nothing you can do about it. Mind you, you must go to Abbey Road if you want to do strings for a film. You can get a 120-piece symphony orchestra in Abbey Road, a result of which is that their main business is film soundtracks. Me, I'm very rarely in the control room in charge of a 120-piece orchestra; that's Hans Zimmer's gig. For pop records, you get fifty musicians max. There's the expense for one thing: even the Beatles couldn't get EMI to cough up for a full orchestra when they made 'A Day in the Life'.

Real World in Bath is Peter Gabriel's studio and has one of the biggest control rooms I've ever seen but, because it's so big, you don't get any intimacy from the monitors. SARM East, where I did most of my work back in my early days, was tiny and had a great big set of monitors, but there was hardly any room in the control room, just enough space for me, Gary Langan and maybe a keyboard player and a guitar player, not many other people. Everybody else had to sit in reception and wait until I summoned them. I like it when a control room's small. You're more on top of the monitors. It took me a long time to get used to the idea of a great big control room. I didn't use one for probably fifteen or twenty years.

Putting my studio obsession to one side for a moment, there was also the fact that I was finding it difficult to get into SARM by then. I had to record parts of 'Poison Arrow' in RAK studios close to Regent's Park because I couldn't get into SARM. I finished off Dollar in the Townhouse, I did Spandau Ballet at Air. In short, I needed a studio to use as a base, and I wanted it to be mine. I'd asked Jill's father for shares in SARM, and he'd said, 'No, you don't give your best customers shares in the business,' which I thought was fair enough. So to think of having Basing Street . . .

Blackwell said, 'Well, I'm just about to sell it to Richard Branson.' Blackwell's lack of affection for Richard Branson was well known. 'Why do you ask? Are you interested in them?'

I was about to answer in the affirmative when Jill kicked me under the table as he continued, 'Because I tell you what, if you start a record label distributed through Island, you can take over the studios.'

'But we'll want to have an option to buy it,' said Jill, to which Blackwell agreed.

So initially we didn't buy it; instead, what we did was buy the studio business with all of the equipment for about £70,000 as well as taking up an option to buy the building. We decided to rename it SARM West, with the other SARM becoming SARM East, creating a small family. Meanwhile, work began on renovating the studio to my and Gary and Julian's spec. At the same time, Jill and I started to think about the label we were going to set up, and my thoughts went to an *NME* journalist I had previously met . . .

———

The year 1982 became the year 1983. In February came the BRIT Awards, where I beat fellow nominees Alan Winstanley and Clive Langer, George Martin and Martin Rushent to win

British Producer of the Year for my work on ABC's *The Lexicon of Love*. Meanwhile, in the studio we moved on to 'Owner of a Lonely Heart', where I overcame resistance from the band, who were worried that the whole thing was going 'too pop', and for the next six or seven days attempted to lay down a simple backing track for the song.

Operative word being 'simple'. Being brilliant musicians, these guys wanted to complicate it. Each take would involve extraneous and unwanted instrumental flourishes. They couldn't help themselves. On and on it went, with the group (still Cinema, by the way) pulling one way, me pulling another, until one day I arrived in the studio to find a deputation waiting for me: 'We think this song is wrong for the album, we don't want to do it.'

A red mist descended. 'Look, the reason I said I'd do this record is because I think we can get a hit single out of this song, and now you're telling me you don't want to do it?' This was quite an outburst for me. I was literally – I'm not joking, *literally* – down on my hands and knees, pulling at Chris's trousers. I was half-kidding, half-serious, half-losing-my-mind, half-being-manipulative. Either way, I was quite a sight. 'Do you want to ruin me?' I cried. 'I'm nearly the most famous producer in the world. Do you want to bring me down? Please let me programme it into a drum machine, please please please!'

Don't forget, I had once been a member of the band. Even so, my behaviour embarrassed them enough for them to agree to try the song again, at least starting it my way.

Work resumed on the track, and my thoughts turned to the drum sound. At this point I was listening to *Synchronicity* by the Police in my car. I loved it. Stewart Copeland's drums, perhaps the feature of the record I like the best, were pitched very high and I wanted to achieve something like that on 'Owner'.

The band and I decamped to the newly renovated SARM West for what would prove to be the studio's first-ever session in its modified form. It was there that I began work on my grand plan, which was to programme the drums and get Alan White to play over them. We used an Akai MPC60 for the programming, a great machine that found favour with the hip-hop community, mainly because it's just so instinctive to use, which is what I love about it. The band, meanwhile, spent their time complaining about the building dust that still hung in the air, coughing loudly at every available opportunity. They were mainly doing it to wind me up, insinuating that they shouldn't have to pay. The first thing that happens when you build a recording studio is that people will try to get in for free.

Over we went to SARM East to record the drums. I had never particularly liked the drum sound in SARM East. It just didn't have the right acoustics, but there you go, beggars can't be choosers, and at least the band weren't doing their coughing thing. More to the point, Alan played it, which was a big deal. Put it this way, Yes had never played with either a click track or a drum machine. Never, in all the time they'd been together.

I've mentioned how Yes/Cinema were always accompanied by loyal road crew, one of whom was a guy called Nu Nu Whiting, who as well as being a very hardcore guy, very naughty at times and a great bloke, was also Alan's drum tech. I remember I was leaving the control room of SARM East to go to the bathroom when I overheard Nu Nu telling someone, 'The drums sound like a pea on a fucking barrel. I've never heard Alan's drums sound like that. . .'

He caught sight of me. 'Oh, sorry, Trevor.'

'That's the way we want them to sound, Nu,' I told him, but the look on his face said it all, and although my treasured drum sound remained on the record, that doubt around the band and crew persisted all the way through the recording, the production, the mixing and release.

We started to do keyboard overdubs with Tony Kaye. He may well have been a founding member of Yes and thus commanded a certain amount of loyalty from all concerned, but he didn't really like 'Owner' or the drums we'd recorded so we only got a fender Rhodes playing an A-minor seventh chord on the chorus. I was worried. Next day, as I arrived at the studio, Trevor Rabin cornered me: 'I've got an idea for "Changes",' he said. 'Changes' being one of the songs we'd recorded. He sat down at Bösendorfer grand piano and played the most beautiful part.

'I didn't know you played piano,' I said.

'I was a child prodigy, I won lots of awards,' he told me.

'Well, fuck me.'

I immediately tried to get him to take over on keys.

'Oh no, I couldn't possibly do that. Tony is our keyboard player,' he insisted.

Later on that evening, Tony was playing a Hammond solo at the end of one of the tunes. Chris was sort of producing it because he could sense I wasn't happy with Tony. Take after take after take of a Hammond solo. In the end, something within me snapped: 'I'm just going to the toilet,' I told the band, and I put on my coat, left the building and went home.

An hour later, by now about 10 p.m., I got a call at home from Chris: 'What's up, Trev? What happened?'

'Well, I've come home, and I'm not going back until Tony Kaye leaves and you agree to Trevor Rabin playing all the keyboards on the record.'

'We can't do that. Tony's in the band, he's our keyboard player.'

'Those are my terms. I'm not coming back until Tony's off the session.'

I wasn't trying to get Tony fired from the band, you understand, just the session, but work on the album stopped for at least a week as various discussions were held. I stuck to my guns. *Either he goes or I do.* Eventually, they gave in and Tony Kaye went back to America.

'You really upset him,' said Chris.

I was sorry but I needed to do it for that record. Trevor Rabin was there at 1 p.m. every day in good shape to play and he had loads of ability. You can't ask for more. As a guitarist, he was the kind of guy to whom you could just say, 'How about a Hendrix kind of thing?' and he'd do it; he'd just pick up a guitar, hit a few pedals and bring Jimi Hendrix into the room. He was also turning out to be the most amazing keyboard player. Some of my best memories of *90125* are doing all the overdubs with Trevor.

On the original demo of 'Owner', all those big whizz-bangs that the song is famous for had been played on a Minimoog, but I said to Trevor, 'Why don't we do it with all the wrong sounds?'

'What do you mean?'

What I meant was using more abstract modern sounds. We started with Trevor playing guitar samples from a Synclavier then J. J. sampled some stuff from a cassette that Malcolm had given me. That's where the big band samples came from.

The reason that everybody remembers that first big stereo trick on 'Owner' is that it is set up so well. I know we loved it when we were working on the record. The rhythm track of

'Owner' is very simple and because of that simplicity, the effects we added really stood out and helped make the song the memorable experience I think it is.

———

It was that around this time I started to float the idea that maybe instead of being a Cinema album, it should be a Yes album – and that we should ask Jon Anderson to come back. Not only would Jon sing, went my reasoning, but he could also help with the lyrics. By then, there was an awful lot of heat under the album. Ahmet Ertegun, the legendary Atlantic owner, had visited the studio, heard the backing track of 'Owner' and loved it. Ertegun had signed Aretha Franklin, he wasn't a guy you impressed easily.

The idea to invite Jon back bobbled around as we booked ourselves into Air Studios at Oxford Circus, which for me was a trip, because it was then – and still is – the most illustrious studio in town.

Also, the most expensive.

'Be on time,' I told Chris. 'This place is £120 an hour.'

He was five hours late.

I'm ashamed to say that I attacked him. The crew prevented me from punching him in the face so instead I went after him with a pair of headphones that I pushed under his chin. In my defence, I'd like to say that was the only time I'd done anything like that. It's very out of character. I was just so . . . angry.

After that, to no one's great surprise, the session didn't go so well. I sat moodily in the back of the control room. Chris would play and say, 'What did you think of that?' trying to placate me.

'Bucks Fizz could have played it better. You should all join Chicory Tip,' I snapped.

It must have been a Friday because later the TV was playing and Frankie Goes to Hollywood came on *The Tube*. This was their first-ever TV appearance, and they were being trumpeted as a great new unsigned band. Chris happened to be sitting on the sofa next to me. 'Why don't you sign that band to your label?' he said, referring to the nascent label Jill and I were setting up. Because I was still cross with him, I didn't say anything, but the truth is that I was paying attention.

While in Air, we recorded a beautiful instrumental called 'Cinema'. It was nominated for a Grammy and is also the only track on *90125* which features my voice. We'd managed to get a really good drum sound for Alan in Air and alongside 'Cinema' we recorded a song called 'Red Light Green Light', but it didn't come out so well, so we dumped it.

Or did we? A couple of days later, working at SARM East on the then-new Fairlight CMI Series II, J. J. was fiddling with 'Page R', which was the in-built sequencer. He played me the loop he had subsequently made of Alan's drums from the discarded song. It was the first digital drum loop I'd ever heard and it ended up providing the basis for 'Beat Box' by Art of Noise.

Our time at Air ended. Everybody was happy but there remained this problem of the lead vocals. I was still pushing to invite Jon back and rename (or was it re-rename?) the group Yes. Alan White was adamant that he didn't want Jon back in the band, and Chris, who'd no doubt wanted to make a go of Cinema and had always had a bit of a turbulent relationship with Jon, was similarly resistant. The trouble was that we all knew the band would be better with Jon in it. What's more, they were a much more commercial proposition with him onboard.

We went into a studio in Willesden and had a great two weeks. Trev and Chris had a song called 'Leave It' for which I wrote lyrics. We had the best time doing that song, with Alan playing on top of a drum machine. Chris and Trevor's voices sounded wonderful together. We did this great a cappella opening into this rhythmic dum-doo vocal thing. Trev and Chris did stacked vocal harmonies on 'City of Love'.

We were nearly there.

We had all these great tracks, not least of them 'Owner', but were lacking lyrics and still needing to rewrite certain key parts of the songs to finish the album. Talk of inviting Jon back gained traction. Meetings were held.

Since there were at least two other bands laying claim to the name Cinema, renaming the band back to Yes proved to be a bit of a no-brainer. Getting Jon back would be a tougher sell, though, especially when it came to the man himself. I was therefore selected to go and meet him to ask him to rejoin the band – I knew it would have to be me because none of the others wanted to do it.

———

Jon Anderson was a musical hero of mine, but I'd never met him before, and given that I'd previously taken his place in the band I assumed he wouldn't be looking forward to seeing me and probably wouldn't be at his most charming.

I was right – he wasn't. It was understandable: the band had been his baby from the beginning. He'd led it to great success, only for sales to fall off, and for him to find himself ousted and crap old me there in his place. Still, I was prepared to put up with almost anything from him because I really wanted his voice on the record, and I wanted Yes to be Yes, so if he was rude to me, I would just ignore it.

When we eventually met, the first thing he told me was, 'They would have put a rubber monkey upfront just to do those dates, you know,' referring to the *Drama* tour, which had already been sold out on Jon's name when we started recording the album.

I wasn't expecting him to like me anyway, and to this day he probably still doesn't, but neither of us let it get in the way of what ended up being a productive meeting, in the sense that I got what I wanted. Once again, Jon was a member of Yes.

True to form, the sessions with Jon weren't fun. He rewrote plenty of lyrics, much to the distress of their original authors. I was impressed by a lot of his lyrics. He sang a great tune over 'City of Love'. His voice sounded terrific. He insisted on only ever singing from 2 to 5.30 p.m. and he wouldn't let me comp his voice, so we were always dropping in and out on the multi-track, which created all kinds of problems. Jon was constantly butting heads with Gary, the two of them having taken a dislike to each other.

And then we got to 'Owner of a Lonely Heart'. I'd never liked the verse on Trevor's demo of 'Owner'. It sounded terrible to me, even with Jon singing it. Nobody seemed able to come up with replacement lyrics, so I did something I never do – I got a little bit drunk.

This was very unusual for me because I almost never touch alcohol. I encouraged Trevor to do the same and the two of us stayed up, trying out all kinds of verse ideas on 'Owner', even one that made us sound like Chas & Dave. Until, with a flash of boozy inspiration, I decided to come at the lyrics from another direction. What would Jon sing? How would he sing it? I channelled Jon, and from that came the version we now know and love: 'Move yourself you always live your life. . .'

We laid down a demo vocal with this new tune and lyrics. To avoid antagonising Jon, Trevor sang it. The next day, we played it to the rest of the band, minus Jon. They didn't like it. That was a Friday and I went home exhausted and a little dejected because we had Jon back in on Monday. On Sunday, out of the blue, Chris phoned me and, in his usual way, said, 'Trev, I think you got that verse because that fucking tune has been going around my head all weekend.'

The day after, on the Monday, I played it to Jon.

'Why are you playing me this? I've already sung this song.'

'I've rewritten it.'

'You've rewritten it? As in you, Trevor Horn?'

'Yes.'

He looked at me. 'I know what's going on around here and I know why this album's taking so long, Trevor Horn. It's because you're jerking off, right? I wouldn't care if this song was "Send in the Clowns", right? A really good song, but it isn't, it's just a crap song.'

I only just managed to keep my cool. 'I know what I'm doing, Jon,' I said, 'and I'm not jerking off. I'm trying to finish the album and I'm trying to get you a hit record. That's why we rewrote it.'

During my drunken night I'd written a second verse, which I really liked but he changed it to, 'The eagle in the sky, how we danced one and only,' which I would never have written, and because we hated that lyric so much, Gary and I added in a gunshot after that bit, to symbolically shoot down the eagle. We were like, 'Let's shoot the fucking eagle.'

Truth be told, Gary was getting a bit loony by this point. Yes were driving him nuts, with Jon in particular really getting on his nerves. In the control room, we have a talkback button where if you press the button you can talk to the artist in the studio. Normally, I have that button set to come on automatically when the tape stops because there's nothing the artist hates more than watching the producer and engineer talk and not hearing what they're saying. The idea is to keep the communication between studio and control room really clear in order to avoid any misunderstandings.

Except that on this album, or at least the Jon Anderson portion of it, Gary turned off the automatic talkback. He used to do this thing where his fingers would hover over the talkback button and Jon would say something like, 'Spool to the middle eight,' and Gary would go, 'Okay, Jon, you twat,' but as he said, 'you twat,' his finger would have come off the button.

I didn't like it – 'Gary, you're going to mess that up one day.' But to his credit, he never did; his timing was impeccable.

Most of the band were absent when it came to mixing the record. Chris would join us in the late evening most days, but the others were in America, so it was mainly me and Gary in a darkened control room, mucking about with a glove puppet and a ventriloquist's dummy that I'd made from a pop shield, called Old Poppa Shield. Little tricks to stop us going mad from hearing the same songs repeatedly.

We were using two analogue multi-track tape machines, one sixteen-track with the backing tracks on it and one 24-track with the vocals and keyboards on it. We spent weeks but I thought we were getting really good results, so I sent the first four mixes to America for the others to hear.

There was just one more track to mix, 'Hold On'. During a break I realised there had been no feedback from America, so I called their manager, Tony Demetriades: 'I haven't heard anything back about the mixes.'

'The guys don't seem to like them.'

'What? They don't like all the great backward echoes we did on "It Can Happen"?'

'Well, yeah, well . . . There's a bit of a problem.'

'What problem?'

'They're not happy with the sound of it.'

'What sound?' I said, knowing exactly what he was going to say.

'The drum sound.'

I got angry. Again. I said, 'Do you know what? I'm fucking sick of you and I'm sick of your fucking band. So take your clapped-out old rock band and shove it up your arse, because I quit. I'm not doing any more.'

I downed tools and went over to SARM West, where a really good young engineer (Bob Kraushaar) and I edited together the first 12-inch for Art of Noise from hours of tapes, a thing that eventually came out as *Into Battle with the Art of Noise* and ended up being the first release on ZTT. I put all the anger into that edit.

There followed another stalemate, plenty of cross words with various people on the phone, but no work. Then I got a call from Chris's wife, Nikki, who I knew: 'Trevor, you've got to do something, man. Chris has just heard a mix of "Owner of a Lonely Heart" and he's in a right state. You need to hear what they've done with it.'

She sent me a cassette and God knows how they did it, but they'd replaced my high snare drum with a big fat Mutt Lange-type snare, while Jon had sung a load of new bits on top.

But. . .

(And it's a big but.)

Fan-of-the-song Ahmet Ertegun had heard this new mix and apparently had ripped the cassette out of his machine and flung it at the wall, demanding to know what had happened to the original.

In the end, hatchets were buried, Trevor flew over to England and we finished the final mixes together.

I was in America, working on what would ultimately be an aborted project with Foreigner, when I started to hear 'Owner of a Lonely Heart' on the radio. I'd done a 12-inch mix of it, the 'Red & Blue Mix', which was doing well in the dance charts. I went to see Genesis at Madison Square Gardens and bumped into Ahmet Ertegun, who greeted me by saying, 'How's my favourite record producer?'

He loved the remix, too.

Meantime I was hanging out with Lol Creme and Kevin God-ley, who were editing the video of 'Synchronicity' for the Police and staying at the Parker Meridian hotel, so when I wasn't work-ing with Foreigner, I was with them. We were in their hotel suite one Sunday afternoon pretty out of it on this weed they called Thunderfuck when the phone rang. Lol picked it up and said, 'It's for you, Trev.' It was Chris, who it turned out was with Yes doing a press junket two floors down from my room. How did he know I was there?

'Come down, say hello.'

'Is Tony Kaye there?'

'Yeah, but it'll be all right.'

So I did, and sure enough, they were all there, all of them looking slightly in shock, because they were back in business, and if they didn't exactly give me a hero's welcome there was at least a tacit acceptance of my part in their success. The single, while not doing so well in the UK, went to number one in the US. At the same time I was having huge success with Frankie Goes to Hollywood, which meant that I achieved something nobody's ever done before: a number one in the US and a number on in the UK with two different records.

They remain my favourite group, and I'm happy to say that even if I don't think that *90125* is the best Yes album – that honour would have to go to *Close to the Edge* or maybe *Relayer* – it is still the best-selling, and 'Owner of a Lonely Heart' is not quite their only hit single, but it's certainly their biggest. Every album has an 'Owner', a song that gobbles up all the time. Sometimes it's the best track on the album, sometimes it's the worst. With 'Owner', it was the best and, although it was the least Yes-sounding song probably of their entire career and surely the most problematic, I think that, in retrospect, it was worth it, whatever shit it put me through.

11

'Relax'/'Two Tribes', Frankie Goes to Hollywood (1983/1984)

In which Frankie say, Frankie do

Having to stand aside for ABC's *Beauty Stab* brought the idea of running my own label into sharp relief. I figured that even if I didn't produce an album, I could still have a hand in the musical direction of the band. Something else that had impressed me about ABC was the fact that they had drawn up a band manifesto. I don't think Yes had one. We certainly never had a manifesto in the Buggles, but the members of ABC had sat down and formed a cohesive, written vision for the group. I don't remember any of it now, but I do recall being impressed by it, even going so far as to conclude that maybe the Buggles wouldn't have got such a critical drubbing if only we, too, had created a manifesto of our own.

One of those drubbings had been courtesy of Paul Morley at the *NME*. He was famous for them, and I fully expected another one after our 'Look of Love' video-shoot encounter. My fears turned out to be groundless. The encounter itself had gone well, and Paul was very kind in the subsequent write-up. So gushing, in fact, that he even made an appearance in *Private Eye*'s Pseud's Corner on the strength of it. Most importantly, he had good ideas. He and I hit it off to such an extent that I began to think of him as someone who would be good to have on board for this label I was thinking about. The funding was already in place, of course, courtesy of the deal with Chris Blackwell. It was just a case of finding the right personnel, and maybe Paul was a good fit. I didn't know what I expected him to do, just that he could do *something*, and that something would be interesting.

Jill wasn't so keen on having him in the fold. When the three of us met to discuss the idea, he turned up wearing a blue mac and carrying a plastic briefcase, which for some reason only seemed to deepen her innate suspicion. Still, he duly came on board, forming a management triumvirate with me and Jill, and while the two of them would never enjoy a particularly warm relationship, they did at least tolerate one another. They had to. At the beginning it really was just the three of us sitting around a table, with Jill, who was in charge of overall management, doing her best to curb what she called the 'idealistic excesses' of Paul and me. I was in charge of production, of course. Paul took care of the marketing. He was designing the label, and you have to say that he succeeded admirably in that regard.

The first thing Paul did was to give the label its name, ZTT, or Zang Tumb Tuum, the name taken from a poem by Italian futurist Filippo Tommaso Marinetti – a 'sound poem' no less, with 'zang tumb tuum' supposed to approximate the sound of machine-gun fire. For the artwork we turned to Tom Watkins, who had designed improvements to SARM West (and who later went on to manage the Pet Shop Boys) and an interior designer, Gary Knibbs. Under Morley's direction they came up with the logo, as well as livery for the label, and before we knew it, we had a distinctive look, perhaps the strongest label identity of the 1980s. To this day, it retains a cult following.

I played Paul some material that Anne Dudley, J. J. Jeczalik, Gary Langan and I had been doing in between other sessions. Having been exposed to all that New York hip hop during our Malcolm McLaren sojourn, we'd started working with drum loops to make a track called 'Beat Box'. Paul came up with the name Art of Noise, wrote a manifesto, thought up with a set of titles, one of which was 'Moments in Love', and we began to make music to go with the titles. This was around the same time that I was struggling with the Yes album *90125*, when I would let off steam by working on material in my downtime. You may recall that during one particularly frustrating episode I ended up working on the EP that that was eventually titled *Into Battle with the Art of Noise*.

In September 1983, *Into Battle with the Art of Noise* became ZTT's debut release.

Chris Blackwell called: 'I just got that record, that Art of Noise record, and I love it. I don't know how many it'll sell, but I don't care. It's groundbreaking.' And, take it from me, you don't get that very often in the record business – that's why Island was such a good record label, because of Chris Blackwell.

Meanwhile, there was the business of ZTT's first 'proper' signing, Frankie Goes to Hollywood, who had come onto my radar, thanks to that performance on *The Tube*. I'd thought the drummer was interesting, and I loved the idea of the two chained-up dancers. Musically? There was something there, but

Left: My parents' wedding in 1945.

Below: At home with Marjorie, Janet and new-born Ken.

Right: Me, aged seven, my hair styled with Brylcreem, which I thought made me look incredibly handsome. Handsome people in films never got picked on, so I thought this would do the same for me – it didn't!

Below: With the youth orchestra – I'm bottom left, holding the double bass.

Left: At the Savoy Hotel in Blackpool with Johnny Wollaston and Arty the drummer. Note the Farfisa Compact Duo – the same keyboard that Richard Wright played in Pink Floyd.

Right: With the Tina Charles Band on our way to Thailand. It never occurred to me before I saw this picture that I was the shortest guy in the band.

Below: On stage with the Tina Charles band in Thailand.

In the studio with Yes. That's Chris Squire looking at me over the board.

An early picture of me at SARM West Coast.

With Seal at a house on Blue Jay Way, Los Angeles, while we were making his first album.

Left: Jill and I in the registry office before we got married.

Right: I carried Jill over the threshold on our wedding day before I went off to the studio.

Left: Me, Jill and a creative wedding photographer.

With Rod Thompson and Bruce and Tessa Woolley at our wedding party.

Jill and the kids in Los Angeles.

Anne Dudley, Lol Creme, Paul Morley and myself trying to look interesting with Art of Noise.

art of noise

Singing with Yes – not sure about the trousers – and playing my beautiful tambourine (before it broke).

After Geoff left the Buggles, I tried to replace him with shop-window dummies, but they were hopeless musicians.

it didn't really grab me at the time. Not until one night, when I was driving home from Morgan Studios and heard 'Relax' on David Jensen's Radio 1 show. Something clicked, and I went in the next day and announced, 'We've got to sign Frankie Goes to Hollywood.'

Paul Morley shook his head. 'Uh uh, Holly Johnson used to be in a group called Big in Japan. Not cool.'

'They've got a track. I think I can do something with it.'

I had fallen in love with 'Relax'. I loved Holly's voice. It had an excitement to it. Not only that, there was something about the band. A look and an attitude that I hadn't come across before. Because I liked them so much, I assumed that everybody else would be after them, too, but as it turned out, a ton of labels had already turned them down. Why? Search me. Maybe it was the promo picture of Holly and Paul, where Paul had a knife coming out of his trousers and Holly was pretending to give it a blow job. Exactly the kind of stuff guaranteed to scare your average deeply conservative record-label guy.

Jill asked around and we had dinner with Holly and Paul at a Japanese restaurant in the Kensington Hilton. They were both very charismatic and I liked them a lot. It didn't even bother me that Holly thought I'd produced Bucks Fizz, possibly confusing them with Dollar, which after all, is an easy mistake to make. Overall, that one hiccough aside, the meeting went well.

There were three other members of the band, who were collectively known as 'the lads': bassist Mark O'Toole, guitarist Brian Nash, or just 'Nash' or 'Nasher', and the drummer Peter 'Ped' Gill. Not long after our dinner with Holly and Paul, I met the lads downstairs at SARM West. They said to me, 'We want to be, like, a cross between Donna Summer and Kiss.' I didn't like Kiss, but I could see what they meant.

Right from the start, Frankie were an odd mix. Most bands, they're a gang. The Beatles, the Small Faces, Blur, the Strokes . . . They have a cohesive, singular identity. Frankie weren't like that; they had two distinct parts: Holly and Paul on one side, 'the lads' on the other. And yet they worked. Holly was a great lead singer and a brilliant presence. Quite difficult to reach but he had enormous charisma and the manner that made him a magnetic frontman; Paul was charming and very good-looking (he managed to seduce at least two of the ZTT crew that I know of), and never rude or short-tempered. People think of him as 'just' the Frankie dancer, but in fact he had a great voice and he proved an excellent foil for Holly.

As for the other three, Mark reminded me of a young John Wayne and was full of great ideas, coming up with the bass part for 'Two Tribes' and 'Welcome to the Pleasuredome' among others, neither of which were easy to play. Nasher was fun, very much the heart and soul of the band. Ped was great, too. Very solid. Good drummer.

What I also liked was that despite their outward appearance of having two distinct sides, they were a really close fivesome at first. You'd often see them all on a sofa with their arms draped around each other. Obviously, Holly and Paul were very gay and largely responsible for that aesthetic, and the lads were just about as opposite as you can imagine, but that was never the cause of any friction that I could see. Things fell apart for them later, which was sad to see and very much a result of the fact that Holly had brought a boyfriend, Wolfgang, into the circle. But at the beginning? They were as close as any band I've ever worked with. The lads were funny, witty and having a good time. And Holly and Paul were just . . . out there.

———————

I didn't have a clue what I was going to do with 'Relax', I just knew it wasn't going to be straightforward because it was more like a jingle than a proper song. But it was very catchy and there was something about the way Holly sang it, so I decided to get the band together in a studio to see what they were capable of, have them record another more polished version of the demo and then take a view on where to go next with it.

I took them into Manor Studios at Shipton-on-Cherwell in Oxfordshire. The Manor, as it's most commonly known, was a residential studio, the third of its kind in the UK (the first two being Ascot Sound Studios built by John Lennon in the grounds of his Tittenhurst Park mansion, in which he recorded *Imagine*, and Rockfield Studios in Monmouthshire).

So I booked them into the Manor and had them play, at which point, I found out that Nasher wasn't the guitarist on the demo that I'd been given. He'd only been playing guitar for a few months. In a three-piece band the guitar player must be really good for it to work. Just think of the great three-piece bands: Led Zeppelin, the Jimi Hendrix Experience, Cream, all had guitar players who had been playing for more than a few months. As time went by and the band became successful, Nasher's guitar playing improved immensely and he went on to make a valuable musical contribution to the band but the problem was that at that particular moment in time, he couldn't play. The guitar on the demo was played by Mark's brother, Jed. There wasn't much point in having them play the song, so instead I recorded them jumping into the swimming pool and made that into a sample that we did indeed use on the record (and, as it would turn out, the only appearance from the lads on the finished product of 'Relax').

So I was going to have to rethink. Don't forget I'd just come from working with Trevor Rabin, Alan White and Chris Squire. Brilliant, visionary musicians. They had all played thousands of gigs. The Frankies in their short career had played five. They had enthusiasm and latent talent, which are both fine qualities, but I needed a band. I needed people I could work with in order to mould the track.

To help me get a new angle on the song, I spent two days with Ian Dury's backing band, the Blockheads, who did a pretty good version of the song. It's a little bit like the final record, but still not right, and when Holly sang on it I realised it was too soft. Still, it was definitely a cut above the demo and there was one great idea in it which came from Norman Watt-Roy, the bass player.

I spent the next two weeks with the Frankies trying to record them playing something like the Blockheads' version, but it just didn't click. By now I was chewing my lip nervously, wondering how to get around this problem. If Frankie were just an act I had been contracted to produce I could have quit, but that wasn't an option because the band were signed to our record label and publishing company.

It was Paul Morley who suggested the band do a version of 'Ferry Cross the Mersey', so we gladly parked the growing headache of 'Relax' and went to work on that instead. Because Gary Langan was off producing ABC's new album I needed an engineer, so Jill found me Steve Lipson, a guy I had once worked with at Regent's Park Studios. Steve didn't say much and I got the distinct feeling – erroneously, as it turned out – that he didn't like me, but at that point I didn't care; I was used to recording engineers not liking me and I was probably missing Gary a bit.

Meanwhile, Julian Mendelsohn had turned me onto a keyboard player called Andy Richards, who had played on a session at SARM East. I called him up and he came down to London to work on 'Ferry'. The arrangement we did turned out well and I liked working with Andy. He was a good player and was very fluent with sequencers and sounds. I had this feeling that things in Liverpool weren't as optimistic as they had been when the song was written in 1965 so I had purposely inclined towards making the song sadder.

We went into SARM West and recorded it. Holly did a great lead vocal, Mark and Paul did some great backing vocals, J. J. surpassed himself with some great shipyard noises – huge clangs and bangs – but Nasher wasn't able to contribute anything. Despite being short of a guitar part, at this point everyone who heard 'Ferry' was much more excited by it than 'Relax'.

The band went back to Liverpool to sign on the dole and one Tuesday an old friend dropped by SARM West to see me unexpectedly with a gift. It was a Nepalese temple ball, the best kind of boutique pot. I had helped him out when he was passing through, on tour, and he was returning the favour.

'Now, Trevor, it's an evening smoke so be careful,' he warned me.

When he left, I was walking through the live room of Studio One when I heard 'Ferry' blasting out from the control room but someone was playing an excellent guitar part, kind of like the part we had been trying to get Nasher to play. I ran into the control room, thinking that Nasher had been practising, but to my surprise it was Steve Lipson playing the guitar.

'You never told me you could play guitar,' I said.

'I did, but you weren't listening.'

We finished off 'Ferry' and I was pleased with the results.

I thought it would be a good idea to smoke some of the temple ball as we looked at where we were up to with 'Relax'. Maybe I could figure out where we were going wrong? We put up the multi-track and listened. Despite my being fairly high at this point the third version of 'Relax' sounded awful and so I freaked out for a while, probably due to a combination of frustration and temple ball, saying things like, 'It's beaten me finally. Why didn't anybody tell me how bad it is? What are we going to do? Let's just wipe the tape and give up.'

Steve restrained me from erasing the tape, and after some more temple ball I decided that we should start again and maybe we could use that idea from the rehearsal room as a starting point. The idea was a piano playing eights on the note E, locked to a drum machine playing four on the floor. So we started work. There was me on Linn drum machine and guide vocal, Steve on guitar, J. J. on Fairlight and Andy Richards on keyboards. We didn't say much, we just got on with it –'Why don't we put some European chords behind it? Andy, try playing E-minor, see what it sounds like.'

Andy was too clever to play E-minor. Instead he played G6, which is a first cousin to E-minor. He started to play that and, boy, when you heard that over the sequenced piano locked to the drum machine, *that* was the sound. It was a sound I hadn't really heard before, so I had no frame of reference. But it was a great sound, and where before the song had been crap, now it just got better and better.

I had five drum patterns in the Linn and my favourite was pattern number 41. I soon found that by switching between pattern 40 (that was a straight four on the floor) to 41 as the verse started gave us a terrific gear shift. So I was switching between drum patterns on the fly while singing the song, Andy was coming up with some terrific keyboard sounds and Steve was engineering while interjecting cool guitar flashes. J. J. was banging out strange noises until finally, after five hours of playing, we said, 'Right, let's record it.'

We got it the first take.

If you listen to 'Relax', it's quite a complicated little arrangement, it's four minutes long and it's very specific. Holly calls the faithful to sex then the song starts with the beat and a pad that changes chords in unusual places – if you're not careful while listening to the intro you'll start the song in the wrong place. Because I only had a chorus and a middle eight to work with the intro goes straight into the chorus and it's the chorus run-out section that's important. We had some great flourishes for that section so we amped them up each time as the song progressed. The middle eight was easy but then we exploded into another verse with Steve playing a dynamic guitar solo. Then we played the chorus twice, changing the instrumentation a little, and on the run-out of the second-to-last chorus we start to wind it down as though the song were finishing, before we have the massive orgasm sound. That was pure Andy Richards and we all laughed our heads off when we heard it for the first time.

So that was it. For the next couple of hours, we went back through it, refining bits of it before we called Holly and Paul, who arrived at 10 p.m., a perfect time to make music, when there are no distractions, no phone, no postman, nothing. They arrived and I went running down to meet them.

'Before you come up, I've just got to tell you, it's changed a bit,' I told them.

'It's changed a bit. How much has it fucking changed?' This from Holly.

And I said, 'Well, quite a bit really.'

'I don't believe it. You haven't started again?' Which was understandable when you consider the different iterations of the song so far. This was version number four.

The pair of them ran up the stairs and I followed them into the control room, where I played them the song. They didn't like it, they loved it. They started dancing from the moment the bass drum began and, do you know, I hadn't even thought about that aspect of it. I hadn't even considered the fact that it was a dance track. Holly wanted to do the vocal right away, but I told him we needed an hour or so just to finesse the backing track. He in the meantime amused himself with an old alto sax of mine he'd found in an upstairs room. He'd been up on the roof blowing this sax when of a group of dreads from All Saints Road gathered below him, calling for him to play them a tune. He told us about this when he came in to do his vocal. Looking for an idea to start the record, I said, 'Why don't you play an E?' and so that sound you hear right at the start of 'Relax', that parping sound, is actually Holly on my sax. I had this idea of him like a high priest of sex on a minaret, calling to the faithful.

Holly was full of confidence and his voice sounded wonderful. He did the song in one take. Brilliant. At the end, I said, 'That was good but some bits of it may have been a bit out of tune.'

'Like, which bit?' he said.

I pointed out a bit.

'No, I meant to sing it like that,' he told me and I realised that this was an affectation, that he was doing it deliberately, and it worked, so I shut up.

After that, we were so pleased with ourselves that immediately afterwards on that same night we did a fourteen-minute version, 'The Sex Mix', which came out on the first 12-inch. When I went home that morning at 5 a.m. Jill was asleep, but she woke as I got into bed – 'I think we've got it, darling.'

'Thank God for that.'

Still, me liking it was no guarantee of success, and I was banking on a hit. At that point, I'd spent a year doing Yes, which wasn't out yet, and I'd done Malcolm McLaren which, while creatively satisfying (and advertised in the press as 'a Trevor Horn production') hadn't sold as well as ABC. Starting my own label was suddenly looking like it was easier said than done. We'd borrowed money and Jill was saying that I should take something with a guaranteed payday. 'Relax' had to be a hit; it had to be.

'It's a classic,' Steve Lipson told me. I hoped he was right.

————

Imagine a film of a studio session. The band is playing. They're not playing anything in particular, they're jamming. The jam is in E and is really loud and the band are into it. Good for them: nothing better than when a group of musicians hit their stride and begin operating as a unit. That's when the magic happens.

Now cut to the control room, where a producer sits with his head in his hands, listening to the jam through one small speaker, bored stiff. The producer? That would be me. The band? That would be Foreigner. Between making 'Relax' and its release, I'd flown to New York in order to produce them, leaving a heavily pregnant Jill to oversee huge building works at our house, but things weren't working out. On my arrival, Mick Jones from the band had presented me with a tape of twelve demos, which were supposed to be the album.

'Right,' I said to him, 'these nine songs are great, and this one's particularly good – "I Want to Know What Love Is". These three, if you'll excuse me, are crap, and you shouldn't even think of doing them.'

Mick said, 'I wrote the nine and the singer wrote those three, so you have to do them.' And that was that. I settled in for the Foreigner job – and spent a lot of time listening to them jam.

I think 'Relax' came out while I was there. Certainly I remember being sent a copy of the video, which had been directed by an up-and-coming director, Bernard Rose, and was a very near-the-knuckle orgiastic thing set at an S&M party, complete with an obese, dribbling Roman emperor. 'What's this?' Foreigner had said. *It's my new single.* 'Let's have a look, then.' *Sure.* Five minutes later, they were looking at me in disgust, like, what sort of depraved creature have we invited into our world?

Island's Chris Blackwell was in town. He took me to the Paradise Garage nightclub one Friday night. The Paradise Garage holds an important place in dance music history. It's where you could hear the legendary DJ Larry Levan mix the likes of the Clash and Sylvester. Where Grace Jones and Madonna would often perform, and where the future stars of British dance music such as Paul Oakenfold came to be inspired. Larry Levan and his Peach Boys were DJing the night we went and discovering we were in the club, invited Chris and I into the booth before playing half an hour of my records and remixes: 'Beat Box', 'The Look of Love', 'Owner of a Lonely Heart'. Not only did these tracks sound amazing on the Paradise Garage's world-famous sound system, but I got to see the effect they had on the dancers down below (another famous thing about the Paradise Garage was that it had a special 'sprung' dancefloor).

The next day, I called Jill. 'I'm going to do another mix of "Relax".'

'Good,' she said. 'We need one.'

There were two reasons for that decision: firstly, we'd been getting complaints that the fourteen-minute sex mix was disgusting, mainly because I'd made a load of suggestive noises on it using turnips, carrots and a bucket of water. Secondly, hearing the Paradise Garage PA – just being in that club – had inspired me.

Andy Richards was in New York. I'd brought him over to play keys on Foreigner – always good to have a friendly face on board. So on the Saturday, when Foreigner weren't working, Andy moved his rig and we set to work on the definitive 12-inch version of 'Relax'. We were working in a studio called the Hit Factory. More famous names than I care to mention have recorded there (the Stones, Billy Idol, U2, Bruce Springsteen, Robert Palmer. . .) but its reputation was built more on radio-friendly rock than the kind of material I was producing, and I could tell the engineer didn't like the track. Even so, I left him to it for three hours or so, which is what I'd always do if somebody's mixing a song: leave them with it to see what they come up with under their own steam. I knew that I was going to extend the song but he needed to know what was on the multi-track and get a good basic mix going.

When I came back, it sounded crap. I said to him, 'Look, this is just a drum machine. If you leave the faders where they are, it'll go through like a drum machine. You've got to push stuff, you've got to compress it, you've got to put echo on it, you've got to make it come to life.'

He tried to follow my instructions but it was like pushing a boulder up a hill. I started to do all of these edit pieces where Andy was playing the new stuff over the backing track, mixing them straight to half-inch tape. The mix we ended up doing was the New York mix, which is the UK's best-selling 12-inch.

What I liked about the whole 12-inch thing was that you weren't restricted by the fact that it was going to be played on the radio; you didn't have to worry about it coming out of a tinny speaker, you weren't concerned about getting the hook in by the first minute. With 12-inches, you could go crazy. Back then, a lot of 12-inches were just 'extended mixes' where somebody would simply mute some stuff and loop other stuff, but what I did was treat them like a Yes track. I'd add extra music, I'd use those ideas I nicked from dub reggae.

And as with so much of what I was doing back then, it was driven by the fact that recording technology had moved on. Nobody remixed anything in the 1960s because it was all on four-tracks. There was nothing you could do. By the end of the 1970s, you could lock two 24-track machines together for forty-eight tracks. And if that sounds like a lot, it's surprising how many tracks you can fill up. I starting out on eight, then sixteen, then twenty-four and forty-eight. At the height of all the insanity, I had two Sony 48-tracks locked together, and these days it's not unusual for a song to be across 120 tracks on the computer.

The reason that I left New York, and thus Foreigner, was that Jill gave birth two months prematurely. Her father, David, called me at about 5 a.m., New York time, and said, 'You'd better book yourself on a flight. It looks like Jill's going to give birth.'

I'd been in New York about three months by then so packing was no easy feat, but I got to work and booked myself on Concorde at the same time. The phone went again: 'Don't rush, Jill's just given birth. You've got a son.'

Our son was Aaron. When I arrived home at Letchmore Heath, it was to find that the house was a building site and Aaron had jaundice and was in hospital in Watford. Jill had said, 'Where am I sleeping?' to which the sister had replied, 'You can't stay here with him.' Jill said, 'If you think I'm handing my son over to you for the next four days, think again. I'm staying here, find me a bed.' Of course, they did, so she stayed there while I remained at home in the building site, calling on Tom Watkins to come help sort me out.

Also to greet me was the dispiriting news that 'Relax' had made a rather dismal showing in the charts. In with a bullet at number seventy-seven before rising to the giddy heights of fifty-four and then fifty-three, dropping down to fifty-five.

Now, ninety-nine times out of a hundred, to drop is a death knell. The radio stops playing it. People stop buying it. You're dead in the water. Jill was worried and rightly so. But then a couple of good things happened. Firstly, Dave Robinson took over running Island and decided that the only good thing they had on current release was 'Relax' and that it ought to be properly promoted. Secondly, Jill rang Malcolm Gerrie, who produced *The Tube*, to ask if he'd put the Frankies on the following week's edition, and he said yes. It's rare that people on TV are as good as their word, but he was and I've always been grateful to him for that: the Frankies were booked.

The elephant in the room was the fact that, of the band, only Holly, Paul and Mark were actually on the record (unless you counted the swimming pool). Not putting them on the record was, I freely admit, a mistake on my part. With a little bit more effort I could have figured out how to feature them, and not doing so was a lapse of bedside manner on my part. It's not like they were pissed off; they really dug the track, so it was fine, and they all went on to make significant contributions to the band. But I know it would have made a difference to them if I'd put them on 'Relax'. It also meant that when it came to a TV appearance like *The Tube* they would need a bit of coaching to convincingly play it, something that Steve Lipson and I did in the run-up to the crucial Friday night.

It worked. They played both 'Relax' and 'Ferry Cross the Mersey', and enough viewers liked it sufficiently to go out and buy the single on Saturday, pushing it up to number thirty-five in the first chart of January 1984.

Suddenly *Top of the Pops* were interested, but, they said, only as long as the Frankies behaved themselves. This was music to my ears. The Frankies had a reputation already. Of course, they'll behave themselves. Who wouldn't on *Top of the Pops*? And if you watch it on YouTube, you'll see they have a funny attitude, all wearing 'we're-behaving-ourselves' looks on their faces.

The morning after their appearance, Dave Robinson rang. 'I bet you won't guess how many we've done?' he said. 'We've done 54,000 units this morning. The phones have gone mad. Everybody's asking for it.'

If you consider that somebody coming out with 9,000 pre-sales now has a really good chance of going in at number one, you can imagine what 54,000 meant to us. Suddenly 'Relax' was going gangbusters and we were heading for the number-one spot.

And then Radio 1 DJ Mike Read 'banned' it. To be honest, I could see his point, because I was a bit shocked when I saw the artwork. I never get involved in the artwork for the bands I'm producing. Not then or now. But 'Relax' was one of those times that I wondered if it was the wisest policy. There was some text on the 12-inch about licking 'the shit off my shoes', which marked the exact point that Jill and I realised we'd have to keep a much closer eye on Paul. We loved him, but he tended to get a bit out of control. And it wasn't just Mike Read that he offended. Either way, offended by the sleeve and the lyrical content of the song, Read announced that he was refusing to play 'Relax' from then on. The song went to number six, then two, and then number one.

It's often said that the Mike Read ban – and then the subsequent BBC-wide ban (later reversed) – 'made' 'Relax', but it was the *Top of the Pops* performance that did that. It was people seeing the band and putting them together with the music. The ban certainly didn't do it any harm, it made sure of the song's notoriety, but if you ask me it wasn't the deciding factor.

Meanwhile, our thoughts went to a follow-up. Up for consideration was a demo of 'Welcome to the Pleasuredome', as well as 'Two Tribes' and 'Krisco Kisses', none of which was an obvious follow-up, so I started looking around for another song. Bruce Woolley had just written a song called 'Slave to the Rhythm' with Simon Darlow, which at that point was a title I liked more than the actual song, but we tried it with Holly singing anyway – a version that has since found its way onto YouTube – and it wasn't great. So the follow-up had to be 'Two Tribes'. No one was very optimistic.

The Frankie demo was quite different to the final version. It had a great bass part, not much song and it sped up and slowed down in a kind of tribal fashion. The intro was there on the demo played by the bass. Mark's bass part was the most interesting part of the song.

We got the band into a studio for the weekend and recorded their version of the song then started programming what they had played. Suddenly the song started to come to life. But the real turning point came when Steve Lipson ('Lippo') came up with that guitar part, which is sort of like the bass part but isn't and goes perfectly with the bass. I remember him playing it to me in Studio Two at SARM and being really impressed. The more I got to know Steve, the more I liked him and the more I was impressed by his judgement and musicianship. Along with J. J. and Andy Richards, he formed the core team for the Frankies.

'The song "Welcome to the Pleasuredome" was a groundbreaking moment for us,' says Lippo now. 'I figured out how to calculate offsets, which meant I could digitally lengthen the song from four minutes to sixteen minutes, repeating it four times. It was one of those moments when the future revealed itself, when we realised that the possibilities were now endless as we could move anything anywhere.'

Meanwhile, the band had to do all kinds of promo for 'Relax', so we went off to a place called Ridge Farm Studios in Surrey, another residential studio with a starry client list. Here's where we seriously started work on 'Two Tribes'. We also did a version of 'War', 'Two Tribes' having sparked the idea for that as a B-side. 'Relax' was still selling well and, at some point in January 1984, Dave Robinson rang me up – at 8 a.m. on Thursday – and said, 'If you can do me another 12-inch of "Relax", I can guarantee it'll be number one next week, again.'

So I gritted my teeth, did one more 12-inch and called it 'The Last Seven Inches', and he was right, it did push it to number one again, which was amazing because it had been out for a while at that point. I was over 'Relax' by then, though. I was really feeling the pressure of the next single, which I knew would either make or break us. If the next one was good, we'd have a career. But we got to a certain point with it when I said to Steve, 'I just don't think it's good enough, I want to start again.' Steve wasn't pleased because we had a pretty good version on the go where we'd used a 12-inch wooden ruler as the bass, but I wanted the next single to be bomb-proof.

I bought us a Synclavier, which was basically a synthesiser and sampler that represented a step on from the Fairlight. The Synclavier had something like sixty-eight seconds of memory, which was enormous compared to the Fairlight, and it sounded great, the best-sounding digital audio I have ever heard in my life, even to this day. It cost an arm and a leg, around $350,000. But I knew it would make all the difference to us, having that much sampling time, and thanks to decent sales of Yes and now Frankie, I had a bit of money behind me.

When the Synclavier arrived it stood in the corner for a while. J. J. showed no interest in it so Steve started learning how to work it. If the Fairlight was complicated, the Synclavier was *really* complicated, and at first we couldn't get it to do what we wanted. I'd used one before – a Synclavier is responsible for many of the whizz-bangs on 'Owner of a Lonely Heart' – but on that occasion I'd rented one with an operator. Getting it to work ourselves turned out to be a completely different matter, and we were constantly talking to Synclavier because their idea of what constituted rhythmic accuracy and ours were different. We'd call up and say, 'Look, we've programmed the kick drum playing four in the bar at 130 bpm, but it doesn't sound right to us. When we do it on a Linn drum machine, which is a fraction of the cost of this instrument, it sounds right, but it doesn't sound right on this Synclavier.'

They'd say, 'Well, that can't be, because the sequencer is accurate.'

'How accurate?'

'Accurate to within ten milliseconds.'

But that's not enough. I've worked with people who can hear one millisecond, so that's not good enough.

We started 'Two Tribes' again and we kept everything we liked from the original version, which was the drums and the guitar and the bass. Steve started doing great things with the Synclavier. The difference between the Fairlight and the Synclavier was that on a Fairlight, you could have a repeated sample, say, 'Ah, ah, ah, ah'. Whereas on 'Two Tribes', on the Synclavier, you could have that long 'Yeeeaaahhh' that you hear, that sounds like the mating call of some mammal. It's probably only ten seconds long, but the fact that we could hit a key and have that sound in perfect quality was a huge bonus for me.

Another thing that made a difference for the second itera-tion of 'Two Tribes' was that while the first version had been recorded to analogue tape, for the second one, we got a digi-tal multi-track. We had teething problems with our Sony digital recorder, though, and sorting out those problems took time. The Frankies were in Europe promoting 'Relax' and Dave Robinson kept saying, 'Where's the record? We need a follow-up. When are you going to be ready?'

Elvis Costello came to the studio, recorded and mixed an album, *Goodbye Cruel World*, then went away and came back a couple of weeks later to do some re-records for the BBC. I remember him saying to me, 'You're not still doing fucking "Two Tribes" are you? You're still on one single? I've done a whole album.' We were kept alive by the fact that 'Relax' continued to sell, so people were still interested in the Frankies.

The office of ZTT was in what later became Studio Four in SARM West, so I'd often bump into Paul Morley. One time he collared me and handed me a copy of a top-secret cassette that had been sent to radio stations for broadcast in the event of a nuclear attack. Somehow, and I never did find out how, Paul had managed to get hold of a copy – not the whole thing, just a chunk of it – but pretty alarming to listen to all the same, made even more so by the stentorian tones of the guy narrating it, the actor Patrick Allen.

I loved it. Knowing that the 12-inch mixes would be key to the success of 'Two Tribes' – certainly if 'Relax' was anything to go by – I was on the lookout for ideas for extended versions, and this was perfect. Maybe we could get Patrick Allen in to recreate his public service announcements for the 12-inch of 'Two Tribes'?

Paul had transcribed what was on this cassette as well as adding a few lines of his own. 'Mine is the last voice you will ever hear,' was one of his. Patrick Allen arrived and I handed him the script. He looked at it, and in a voice that seemed to shake the very foundations of the studio said, 'Oh yes, I well remember doing this.' His brow furrowed. 'But, you know, when I did this,

I had to sign the Official Secrets Act. How have you got a hold of it?'

I told him I had no idea.

'I could be in real trouble if I do this,' he said and then shrugged. 'Ah, fuck it. I'm going to do it anyway. What are they going to do about it?', which I thought was very brave of him really, considering he could have ended up in the Tower for his trouble.

So he began. A brilliant and seasoned voiceover artist, he was perfect . . . Until he stopped. 'You know, there was a bit in the original you haven't got down here. It went, "If your grandmother or any other member of the family should die whilst in the shelter, put them outside, but remember to tag them first for identification purposes".' When he said the last line, one that Paul had written for him, 'Mine is the last voice you will ever hear, do not be alarmed,' he let out an exclamation. I don't think he'd ever realised how heavy what he was saying was.

I couldn't believe our luck. *This is gold*, I was thinking.

Another idea Paul and I had was to use a *Spitting Image* voiceover artist, Chris Barrie, to play Ronald Reagan. Paul wrote a few lines for him, some of which I later discovered came from *Mein Kampf*. The great thing about the Synclavier was that we could put chunks of Chris on the Synclavier keyboard, which made them very easy to access. So what we had was the 12-inch beginning with an air-raid siren, and then the strings, and then Chris: 'Ladies and gentlemen, Frankie Goes to Hollywood – probably the greatest thing this side of the world.' Originally, we had a belch from Mark after that, but I decided it was too gross and instead we used Nasher saying, 'Oh, yeah, well 'ard.' I had Patrick's stuff on a quarter-inch tape machine, and during the mix

I started to play it back, except that I didn't just run it straight; what I did was start to play it and then stop it, rewind it and play it again and then did the same thing again. Steve did a brilliant job on that mix and it was a breakthrough for us because for the first time I felt confident that we had something to follow 'Relax'. This became the 'Annihilation Mix'. For some reason, after this 12-inch it became much easier to mix the single version and I think it still sounds good to this day.

I was proud of what I'd done with 'Relax', but I thought this was even better; I'd never heard anything quite like it. It was an anti-war song that sounded like war breaking out.

In the music business, people will be desperate for you to deliver them a song, but if the song's not right then they are either going to tell you it's not right or not tell you and put it out and have it fail. There's no toe in the water. The acid test is whether people buy it. I'd worried people might not go for 'Relax' but not this one: this one I knew was a hit.

———

When we finished 'Two Tribes', Jill and I were pretty tired, so we took a couple of weeks' holiday in Bournemouth. I think I probably left Steve Lipson with the band to start work on the album. By now, I really liked Steve. I have always been an optimist and Steve was generally a pessimist. I've always preferred people who tell me the truth and I envied the way he didn't seem to care whether people liked him or not. I could see how talented he was.

In Bournemouth we stayed at my in-laws' apartment in Sandbanks, and, when Thursday came around that week, I thought I'd better check the *NME* for its 'Two Tribes' review. In those days, singles tended to be released on a Thursday, too, so I decided that having read the glowing review I'd pop along to Our Price in Poole and buy a copy. I was superstitious like that, back then – I'd always go and buy a single copy of whatever I'd been working on when it came out.

The Poole branch of Our Price was in a shopping centre. Making my way there – not even in the shop yet – I could hear 'Two Tribes' blaring out. Entering the store, it was just ending. *What a shame*, I thought, *I'd like to have gauged the customers' reaction.* But then it started up again. It hit me that the shop was packed, and I swear to God, it was as though every customer had a copy of a Frankie record in their hand. Not just 'Two Tribes' – it was the 12-inch mix that was playing – but 'Relax', too. Everywhere I looked, there were people buying Frankie products.

I got in the queue with my copy of the record. Reaching the front, I handed over my credit card. The guy behind the counter looked at me, looked at the credit card, and said, 'Oh my God, are you . . .?' and I was, like, 'Yeah, yeah, but give me a break, right? Don't say anything.'

'It's amazing. Amazing, man,' said the cashier, keeping his voice down. 'All we have to do is play it to sell it.'

I'd known 'Two Tribes' was good. Even Yes bassist Chris Squire had called to compliment me on it: 'I've just heard this track on the radio. Is it one of yours? It's about putting your grandmother's body outside in a carrier bag.'

'Yeah,' I said proudly. 'That's mine.'

He said, 'I thought it was you. It was good. I liked the bass part.'

Did I ever tell Mark that? If not: there you go, Mark. Praise indeed.

'Two Tribes' was number one for nine weeks. Nine weeks is a long time, added to which at various points, 'Relax' nudged up to number two again, so we'd have number one *and* number two. Paul Morley meanwhile had come up with ideas for T-shirts. The 'Frankie Say' T-shirts were a big thing. We did start to get a bit alarmed by some of the slogans, like, 'Frankie say Arm the Unemployed', but there's no doubt that they sold, and the more shirts we sold, the more records we sold. Next job: an album.

The problem that we had with the album was the same one we'd had for the second single: a lack of material. The Frankies had come up with a couple of new songs, 'The Power of Love' and 'Black Night White Light', and of course we still had the song that would give the album its title, 'Welcome to the Pleasuredome'.

'Welcome to the Pleasuredome' was at first a threadbare affair. We had one verse, a bit of a chorus and a great bass riff, also courtesy of Mark. I remember coming into the studio one day and Steve saying, 'Listen to this.' He had the verse of 'Welcome to the Pleasuredome' on one machine and on the other, he had the chorus part of it. When he pressed play, I was hearing the verse and the chorus together – 'I've offset the two machines so that they're running perfectly in time but sixteen bars apart,' he explained. It made me realise that we could do this kind of thing called 'additive editing'. So we could copy the verse onto another machine, offset the machine and put another verse straight after that verse. It meant that we could put any overdub anywhere without losing the quality. So if you think that a song is made out of bars, the intro might be eight bars, verse sixteen bars, chorus sixteen bars. Before the advent of two digital multi-tracks, it was very hard to move anything around. When I was doing ABC and wanted to elongate the opening track, I had to go through all kinds of hoops. It would take hours, and if you didn't copy it carefully, it would lose quality because it was analogue.

Now, suddenly, I was in a position where I could move anything to another place. Like, for instance, you want all the backing vocals on one chorus. Before samplers, you'd have to sing and record each chorus separately. Nowadays, people can do complicated harmonies on one chorus and then immediately copy and paste them into the other choruses so that each chorus is exactly the same. Back in the day, you had to do it again. And if it took you four hours to do it on the first chorus, it'd take you four hours to do it on the second chorus, because although everybody knows it better by that point, the singing quality begins to degrade.

During those three months, I'd lie in bed thinking about what this really meant, and in those three months, we turned 'Welcome' into a completely different animal. A very good animal indeed. We loved it. The band loved it. I always knew that it wouldn't be good enough to stick 'Two Tribes', 'Relax' and five or six other duff songs on the album. I wanted something a bit more substantial and 'Welcome to the Pleasuredome' seemed like the song to do it. Having that one in the can took the pressure off.

In truth, Steve Lipson and I should have had writing credits on it – the whole middle section was ours – but as with 'Relax' and 'Two Tribes', I didn't ask for a credit. I never did in those days. For a start, we – as Perfect Songs – were the publishing company. But also because I was afraid that, if I started claiming publishing rights, artists wouldn't let me tamper with their song and I'd be forced to leave it the way it was.

Still, that section in the middle of 'Welcome to the Pleas-uredome', I always think of as being one of the best things we ever did. We were working on it the day after the Notting Hill Carnival, when they were clearing up. I said to Steve, 'Come on, let's poke a mic out of the window,' and you can hear it on the record, it's just people clearing up after the Notting Hill Carnival, but it's a great sound.

I brought in Steve Howe from Yes to play a slide guitar part, and Steve Lipson contributed a great guitar solo that he did on the spot: 'I hope you recorded that, because it was brilliant,' I told him. And that's the guitar solo you hear on the track. The same had happened with Yes on 'Owner of a Lonely Heart', when Trevor Rabin said, 'I've got this idea for a guitar solo,' one take to demonstrate the idea, Gary recorded it and that was what appeared on the record. It's true of many things but partic-ularly when it comes to guitar solos: the minute people become self-conscious is when you lose some of the magic. Sometimes when you don't care, you do the best work.

'Welcome' turned into an excellent epic, from three minutes to fifteen with great dynamic changes. Meanwhile the band were starting to assert themselves. They played the backing track for 'The Power of Love' and when Paul Morley came up with the idea of 'Born to Run' they worked hard on it and came up with a cracking version where Mark played the sax solo on the bass.

Now I felt that we had a good album on our hands, and so for some reason we came up with the idea of making it a double album. Part of the rationale was that most of the tracks we had – 'Two Tribes', 'War', 'Relax', 'Ferry Cross the Mersey' – had all been on so many singles, 12-inches and cassettes, we thought it would be a bit of a threadbare affair if it was all previously released material, and it would be much better if it was a double album. It did mean that we needed more material, though.

Paul Rutherford had been on the dole during the making of 'Relax' and he told me that the dole people had been unpleasant to him one day. I lent him a cassette recorder and told him to record whatever they said to him, and he came back with this recording, with him saying, 'I'm sorry I've left me card at home,' and the girl saying, 'You're late as well. That's three times on the run. If you're late again, we'll put you on early signing.' I loved this so I got an actress to re-record it and I put at the start of 'Born to Run'.

So that was encouraging. Another strong track. But then – God knows why – I decided that we should do 'Do You Know the Way to San Jose'. Maybe megalomania was starting to creep in. Perhaps I was a bit in love with a theme that was developing, of escaping, getting away from where you were. Maybe I was thinking that I couldn't put a foot wrong. We did it one afternoon with Luis Jardim playing everything on it and Holly delivering a great vocal, but, even so, I shouldn't have done it, and it probably shouldn't have been on the album.

I'd been into the local record shop one day and the owner there told me that he was really excited about the Frankie album, how he normally only ever ordered a few copies of an album but for Frankie, he was pushing the boat out. The next time I saw him, he was concerned: 'I just heard that there are two covers, like, "Do You Know the Way to San Jose" and "Born to Run" are both on the album?' Maybe the face he pulled should have been a warning to me. Perhaps I should have scooted back to the studio and put the brakes on the double-album idea.

The other thing was keeping an eye on Paul Morley. The artwork had gone to print but there had been a complaint from the printers, which was when we discovered that the 'Welcome to the Pleasuredome' sleeve had thirty-two depictions of animals involved in all kinds of sexual activity. Jill was horrified and the Island people were reading us the riot act: 'If you try to push this through, the women in the factory will walk out. You just can't do this, it's obscene.'

Paul was completely unashamed. He had tried to get it past us and failed but was still determined to get it out there. As a compromise, we ended up putting fig leaves over everything. If you look at the album cover, it's got fig leaves all over the place and each of those fig leaves covers a depiction of a sex act.

The album came out in October 1984. Shortly after, we decided to have 'Power of Love' as the third single, at which point we realised how hard it would be to maintain momentum, because Dave Robinson was immediately saying, 'Right, then, where's the 12-inch for "Power of Love"?'

You can't do a 12-inch of a ballad. Nobody wants to sit listening to a ballad drone on for fifteen minutes: it just doesn't work. We had to dream something up, which turned out to be a lengthy orchestral version, but I remember thinking it was all starting to feel little tired. Still, when 'The Power of Love' reached number one in December 1984, it meant that we'd had three number ones from our first three singles, which was the only time anybody had done that since Gerry and the Pacemakers in the 1960s.

Moving into 1985, and Dave decided that he needed another single. The obvious choice was 'Welcome to the Pleasuredome', which unfortunately meant cutting our fifteen-minute opus down to radio-friendly size. You might think that would be easy, but it wasn't. Rethinking it back to four minutes was so tough that it all proved too much for Andy Richards, who had to take a break. As it was, Steve and I did it and I think we did a good job. Only thing was that it didn't get to number one. We'd marketed it by saying that it was Frankie's 'fourth number one' but we paid for that hubris when it peaked at number two, kept off the top spot by 'Easy Lover', the Phil Collins/Phil Bailey duet. Hardly a disaster, but I guess, looking back, we'd already peaked and that number two marked the beginning of the end.

———————

If I had a time machine, I'd do two things differently regarding the Frankies. For one, I'd have put the band on 'Relax', for reasons I've already said. Secondly, I would have hired at least two people whose sole job it was to hang with the band and be 'my guys'. Because what started happening was that other people began circling. People who began dripping poison into the ears of the band. Sowing the seeds of doubt.

In the record industry, you often find yourself going into partnership with people who don't have a clue about business. When they need the money, they need you, they're obliging and amenable. But, when they get big, people start telling them that they don't need you, and they can't believe that they're constrained by mundane things like contracts. A good deal is one where everybody makes money, or so the old saying goes. But it's not like that with artists. 'Look how much money they're making off you,' is the kind of thing that gets said, and I was aware that the band were beginning to be exposed to that kind of thing. You could feel it in the air; it became apparent with the odd remark.

I first saw it when they were doing some shows in America. Because of a rule they have with TV shows, we had to re-record 'The Power of Love'. So I met up with the band in a big studio in San Francisco, where we had five hours to re-record 'Power of Love' (although we didn't in fact re-record it, I just remixed it). That night I saw them play live in San Francisco and they weren't very good. The band were all right, but Holly wasn't giving it everything. As well as the fact that he kept turning his back on the audience and saying things like 'Kiss my arse, America,' which is the kind of stuff that doesn't go down very well over there, he was holding back on the singing – 'Oh, Wolfgang's told me that if I sing too high, I'll get cancer of the throat,' he told me later. Wolfgang, Holly's new boyfriend, was another wedge – perhaps the biggest – that was slowly driving the band apart. I should point out that forty years later, Holly and Wolfgang are still an item, which at least seems to suggest that Wolfgang wasn't just there for the short term. But the problem was that the rest of the band didn't like Wolfgang, and the feeling was mutual.

It may have been on that trip that the band were doing a lot of radio promo and were on a show called *The Solid Gold Show* or something similar. They were meant to be on at 9 a.m. but showed up late and seriously hungover, only to get a bit of an on-air dressing down from the presenter. Having blotted their copybook, they made things worse by going on to the next interview and slagging off the first presenter, calling him a 'fucking solid gold plank' on-air.

Being rude to the hosts was one thing, but what really worried me was this issue with Holly's performance. Two things: if you're no good live then you'll struggle to have a career. Second, it was very early days for Holly to be at all jaded by the touring process.

Normally, people are still enthusiastic at this point. You can't blame anybody who's been on the road for a year for getting a bit tired of being on tour, but after just a few shows?

So this was all going on. But anyway I took a break from Frankiedom. That year – 1985 – I won Best Producer at the BRITs and the Frankies won Best Single for 'Relax' and Best Breakthrough Act. All amazing, but the whole thing was like being hit by a tornado. It had started off slowly and then suddenly caught fire like I couldn't believe. To be honest, I thought there were some parallels with the Beatles. Obviously not in terms of talent, I hasten to add, but in the way that the Frankies, for that one year, became really, really big – bigger than anybody else around – the difference being that the Fab Four were already an incredible well-drilled band. They were musically tight and having lived in each other's pockets in Hamburg, great mates as well. The Beatles had paid their dues, but the Frankies hadn't; they'd played a handful of gigs. To their credit, they were totally up for the idea of becoming a 'real' band, and we were getting there. If you look at the YouTube clip of 'Two Tribes' on *The Tube*, you'll see that there are nine of us on stage. That's all of the musicians who played on the single, including me. At the start of that week, the band couldn't play 'Two Tribes' the way that we made the record and I said, 'What are we going to do if you can't play it?' They said to me, 'The lads will be able to play "Two Tribes" by the end of this fucking week, we guarantee you that,' and, I have to say, they worked their butts off and they really could play it by the end of the week. But by this point, other labels were circling, hoping to nick the Frankies off us, while at the same time we were having financial problems with Island. For a while it looked as though the band might leave ZTT, but they didn't, and we sort of drifted along until it came time to make the second album.

Obviously, the band wanted to be much more involved this time around. They weren't the only ones who wanted to do things differently. Steve and I had spent a year in the control room doing that first album and the prospect of starting another one really didn't appeal, especially with the atmosphere in the band being what it was. There was something else, too. The Yes album, *90125*, had done well, better than any previous Yes album, and there was enormous pressure on me to do the follow-up, *Big Generator*, which certainly appealed to me more than working with the Frankies. I went off to do that (we all know how that turned out), while Steve knuckled down to the second Frankie album. This pissed off Holly, who felt that I should have been doing it. He had a point, but the real issue was that his relationship with the band was at an all-time low.

One of the ideas for a first single from the second album was a cover of 'Do Ya Think I'm Sexy?' by Rod Stewart. The band liked it and had done what I thought was a good version of it with Paul singing. I got a call from Holly, who wasn't one to bother with niceties at the best of times: 'I'm calling to tell you that I am the singer in Frankie Goes to Hollywood, not Paul Rutherford, and if you release this version of "Do Ya Think I'm Sexy?", I will immediately leave the band.'

Looking back, I should have called his bluff. Either way, I knew things were on a downward trajectory. They went to a residential studio in Amsterdam. I thought Steve was doing a good job but he was having to pull it out of them a little bit. It was the same old problem: the band were keen, Holly wasn't. The main track was a song called 'Rage Hard', which although a bit pompous was a good tune. Then there was another song called 'Warriors of the Wasteland'. Other than that, Lippo was having a really hard time of it. Songs weren't being written and people weren't talking to each other. One lot were doing the backing track and then Holly would come in and do something that they didn't like. Meantime, things went definitively south with me and Yes, so I joined Steve and put in maybe three months' worth of work on finishing the Frankie album

We thought that the finished album, *Liverpool*, was okay but not great. All the good vibes that had been in the band were gone. The lads and Paul were still friendly to us but things were bad between them and Holly. The songs weren't there, either. 'Warriors of the Wasteland' . . . What wasteland? What warriors? As a title, *Liverpool* was a lovely tribute to their hometown, but it still felt like a bit of a thud back down to earth after the eroticism and sensuality of *Welcome to the Pleasuredome*.

The moment that I knew the writing was on the wall, both for the album and the band, was when they had a spot on *The Tube*. Performing a tune called 'Lunar Bay', it was painfully obvious that they didn't know it very well, to the extent that Holly had to watch Mark for his cue. Earlier in the show, Simply Red had been on, and they'd been fantastic. Great song, great frontman. Next to them the Frankies looked pitiful, they really did.

Sure enough, the wheel became looser and looser. Next thing I knew, their new manager was ringing me: 'I don't understand this. They're fighting. Holly won't go on stage with Mark unless he has a bodyguard.' Apparently, Mark had got so fed up with Holly, he'd kicked him in the arse, so Holly was demanding protection.

I went to see them play Wembley Arena. It's possible that the kick I've just described happened at that show. However,

I took several things from that gig. Firstly, they were by now a good live act and could play the whole of *Welcome to the Pleasuredome*. It wasn't exactly the record, but it was pretty damn close. Secondly, you could tell there was obviously something going on with Holly. You could just feel it. Afterwards I stood talking to Holly and Wolfgang. No doubt I was being polite, because by that point we were all walking on eggshells, when who should come lurching over but Lemmy of Motorhead.

'Oi, Trevor, I've got to talk to you about this guy here,' rasped Lemmy. He was pointing right at Wolfgang. 'You've got to get rid of him. If you don't get rid of this guy, you're not going to have a band. He's ruining it, he's ruining everything.'

By this time the band had already insisted on having nothing to do with Paul Morley, who had apparently said something to upset them. That didn't surprise me, but, even so, it felt like another symptom of their slow implosion.

'I can't believe it,' their American manager was saying to me. 'I've never seen anything like this before. Do they know what they've got? What they're throwing away?'

The second album didn't flop totally, but if you consider that the first album sold 3 or 4 million and *Liverpool* sold a couple of hundred thousand then you get the picture. Nobody was popping the champagne corks over that one. The material was weaker, of course, but there was also a distinct lack of buzz around them. It was as though the public had picked up on the discord within the band. What normally happens is that a group makes the second album and the second album isn't as successful as the first, but it still does okay, and then you go on and make a third, fourth, fifth, sixth album and maybe have another big album along the way. Certainly, if you're Pink Floyd, you do. Or even Yes, who were up and down but still kept releasing albums and gigging. When you play live, you go around the world and cement your relationship with your fans, but even that wasn't going to happen with Frankie. Seeing them at Wembley Arena, I knew that was it for them. Sure enough, when they'd completed the tour, Holly left the band to pursue a solo career.

———

Holly leaving meant him challenging his contract with us. We were pretty upset about that. I felt like I'd gone out on a limb for him and his band. Without the team I put together, the Frankies might have had a minor hit, done a few gigs and broken up and that would have been the end of it. They would never have had that year of fantastic success; they would never have had the back catalogue that still, to this day, goes a long way to sustaining all of them.

Jill had a conversation with Holly and Wolfgang about renegotiating his contract and him doing a solo album, but that went nowhere. In the end one of the things that triggered the court case was Wolfgang saying, 'You can't afford him. You haven't got enough money. Sell your studio and then maybe you might have enough money to keep him,' which to us – and certainly to Jill – was proper fighting talk. As far as we were concerned, we had a contract and Holly was in breach of it.

Looking back, we should have taken Chris Blackwell's advice to let it go, but we were taking Island to court over unpaid royalties so weren't minded to heed his words of wisdom. We decided to take legal action against Holly.

It was a stupid decision – stupid because it was enormously costly and took two years to resolve, and stupid because history shows that, in nine out of ten cases, the artist wins, something that MCA, Holly's new label, must have appreciated because they funded his court case to the tune of £150,000. I think we wanted to make a point, though, because everyone was after our acts. We were hot shit and the sharks were circling. We didn't help ourselves sometimes: the triumvirate of me, Jill and Paul could be a bit good cop (me), bad cop (Jill) and crazy cop (Paul), but, even so, we wanted to keep those acts we'd nurtured. Just that some of those acts didn't want to stay.

Before we contested the Holly situation, we had to deal with the Island case, which turned out to be only one day in court, after which Island basically folded and paid everything that they owed us. The Frankie trial was a different kettle of fish altogether and went on for longer. It was interesting to see the methods their side used. How they came at us from three or four different angles. They implied that we'd spent ages in the studio wasting time. They said that Lippo and I spent our time in the studio taking drugs, which was true, but it was only pot, nothing else, although they tried to imply otherwise. 'I can see where this leading,' said the judge in a rare moment of things going our way, 'and I want to tell all of you, I am not interested in this line of questioning. This case has nothing to do with that [meaning drugs].'

I remember standing in the toilet once with Wolfgang and Holly, all of us taking a pee and nobody speaking, and I thought, *How fucking monumentally lame this is, that we're doing this.*

There was a band that we'd signed to ZTT called Das Psych-Oh! Rangers, who I had dropped in the middle of a label meeting they were at when I heard about something heinous they had done in SARM East while working on their record. This had happened just before the court case, and I knew they were still sore about it because they would turn up at court every day in order to jeer at me and Jill.

I walked past them one day: 'You guys should be making a record.'

'Yeah, but we want to see you get it.'

I said, 'Well, stick around, it's probably going to happen.'

At one point, the judge said to Holly, 'Mr Johnson, you've had huge success with these people and yet before you met them, you weren't successful. So why don't you want to continue with them?'

And Holly said, 'Well, Your Honour, because they've got no respect for me or my music.'

I whispered in Jill's ear, 'We're going to lose this, he's right.'

So the trial went on, and on, and on, and then, of course, it adjourned for a few weeks while the judge made up his mind, after which we all had to troop back for the verdict. I was in no doubt about the result. As the judge started to read his verdict, which was to mark the end of a very long two-year battle, I said to Jill, who was sitting next to me, 'We've lost this, but it doesn't matter, don't let it show on your face.'

The previous week I had turned down an offer from a perfume company of £100,000 to do a commercial for them. As the judge continued reading, Jill said, 'I'd better get back to them about that advert. I'll do it as soon as we get back.' I really loved Jill.

Sure enough, we lost. Holly didn't get the rights to his records back, but he got his freedom and he went off to pursue his solo career. After that, the other members of the Frankies left, too, although for one reason or another they were never able to get another Frankie project off the ground. History tells us that

Propaganda and even my own band, Art of Noise, followed suit, but that's another story. For the time being, the highs of the Frankie year had left me with a bad taste in my mouth. On the one hand, I think it's some of the best stuff I've ever done and some of the best mixing from Steve that anyone has ever done. On the other? Well, I was interviewed by TV after the case when I tried to be dignified about it all and wished Holly luck – and it's true that I've moved on and haven't really dwelt on it since – but occasionally I'd think, *What a waste.*

12

'Dr Mabuse', Propaganda (1984)

In which I help to launch Abba from Hell

Frankie were the only band I ever signed to ZTT. Jill used to get mad at me for not doing more A&R, but my problem was that I always thought most things were shit. I'd be in A&R meetings, never like anything, then fall asleep only to be publicly bollocked by Jill when I started snoring.

It was Paul Morley's idea to sign Propaganda. He had this idea that if jazz was an American art form, then techno was a German art form, and for that reason – and because Kraftwerk were already spoken for – we should sign a German electronic band: Propaganda were it.

There were three guys and two girls in Propaganda. No doubt Paul fancied one of the singers, Claudia Brücken (and did indeed end up marrying her), which may have added to the lustre, but he also had this grand plan for them, envisaging them as 'Abba from Hell'. Propaganda wasn't exactly replete with virtuoso musicians, and I was still a bit unsure about them until I heard a particular piece of music that I thought was promising, 'Dr Mabuse'. As is often the case, it was a track where I thought, *I can do something with this*. I particularly liked some of the lyrics, which although they were in English had a distinctly Germanic feel. The band had been formed by Ralf Dörper, who had also been a member of the industrial group Die Krupps, and who worked in a bank. He was responsible for the lyrics and, for instance, had written, 'He's a satanic gambler and you're just the pool.'

I said to him, 'What's the deal with this pool thing? "He's a satanic gambler and you're just the pool?" Are you sure it's not "fool"?'

'The pool of money,' he replied.

'Ah,' I said and left it. No English person would have said that – 'the pool' – but it's a good line.

I met them and liked them. Claudia had an unusual voice whereas Susanne Freytag had a beautiful speaking voice. So we signed them and I committed to producing the first single, 'Dr Mabuse'. It wasn't too long after 'Relax' and I had this idea that the equipment we'd used to synchronise a drum machine and Fairlight on 'Relax' could do 'Dr Mabuse'. At that point in time, I had a decent collection of drum machines and samplers, and the plan was to program the track into all of these boxes, hit a button and let the track play. We'd spent quite a few days sequencing the song into these various implements and had it almost working when a journalist showed up for an interview. I said to him, 'Ah, you're going to love this. We're just about to do Propaganda, but we're doing the backing track all in one go. Do you want to come and have a listen?'

It was in Studio Two at SARM. I got him down there, set it up, pressed the button and . . . it went for about two bars and then totally messed up. We never did get it working, but in any event the episode gave us a foothold on the song, because we got a lot of ideas from all that programming. We had to go back to a more conventional way of doing it, which was locking everything to tape and recording it one thing at a time.

At this point in my career, I had high hopes for whatever song I worked on. Anybody can make a flop. I was determined that everything I did was going to be a hit. I couldn't understand why people downplayed the importance of a single. As far as I was concerned, if you didn't have a single, the album would flop. Every album I've ever done that's done anything always had a hit single on it – even Belle and Sebastian – and all the albums that didn't have a hit single on them did nothing. So I wanted to do the same thing with Propaganda. There was a lovely instrumental line on 'Dr Mabuse' that I thought would be better off played by real strings so we had a thirty-piece orchestra play it. I said to the arranger, Wil Malone, 'When you've done the arrangement for "Dr Mabuse", can you do me a piece that's a little bit abstract, maybe one and a half, two minutes long, based on "Dr Mabuse" that'll just be the orchestra on its own.'

I was just looking for more content for the 12-inch, because at this point in time I felt that people expected quality from ZTT. The string session went down to the wire. It took them almost the entire three-hour session to play the single arrangement properly, which left us ten minutes at the end to do this other piece that Wil had written. They did it in one take. I remember the two violin players talking on the tape, one saying, 'Oh, I quite liked that. That wasn't bad.'

At that time I was interested in the German industrial band Einstürzende Neubauten and wanted to introduce an element of their sound into Propaganda. I had the Portuguese percussionist Luis Jardim booked for the day. Normally, when I booked him for the day, Luis would say to me, 'What should I bring?' and I'd give him a rundown: congas, bongos, typical Latin American stuff. But this time, with thoughts of Einstürzende Neubauten uppermost in my mind, I said to him, 'Anything metal you've got, bring. I'll think of something.'

On the day of the session I was having breakfast, looked out of the window and saw a large bathtub in the drive. It wasn't as though it had appeared by magic – we were having a bathroom replaced – but I looked at it and thought, *That's an idea.*

I got my roadie to pick it up and take it to SARM West. After breakfast I went to Woolworths, where I bought three or four complete sets of crockery. The assistant kept asking me, 'You want this? You want that? You want this set to go with that set?' and I didn't have the heart to tell him I planned to smash it all. Next, I bought a sledgehammer and a couple of other large and impressive-looking tools from a tool shop before carting it all back to Studio One in SARM, where we laid a large tarpaulin on the floor and put the bathtub, plates and loads of drinking glasses on it.

Luis was late; he was always late. If you wanted him for 4 p.m., you booked him for 1 p.m., knowing he'd show up about 4 p.m. He walked in and saw all my crockery.

'That's the percussion for this session,' I told him.

He was like, 'Great.'

And it was great. He stood on a set of stepladders with a bucket full of crockery, pouring it into the bathtub, which as you can imagine made a cacophonous – but lovely – noise. He belted the old metal bathtub with a sledgehammer on the backbeat of the song. After two takes the bathtub started to fall apart, but Luis was in fine form and by the end of the session we had a percussion track worthy of any industrial band you care to mention. We were having a such a great time making this stuff that everybody in the studio who wasn't engaged elsewhere had come in to watch what was going on in Studio One. It was general mayhem, Luis running around bashing the hell out of stuff while Steve recorded the band running up and down the stairs. The resulting chaos was the track '(The Ninth Life of. . .) Dr Mabuse: The Word', which appeared on the B-side of the 12-inch.

I suppose you might say that 'Dr Mabuse' is another instance where the band aren't really on the single, but that's because nobody in Propaganda played an instrument – or at least not to the standard that we needed on the track. They wrote the song and cobbled together a demo, but that was it. As with Frankie, what you hear is mainly programmed – and it was programmed by us in the studio. To be honest, I think it's one of the things that made the project more appealing as far as I was concerned, and it wasn't as though the band objected.

Paul hired the photographer and director Anton Corbijn to shoot the video, which turned out to be an homage to the old vampire film, *Nosferatu*. He also went on to do the photography for the album. Around the same time, the BBC made a short film about ZTT, which as far as I know is the only footage that exists of me, Jill and Paul together. We're arguing about the cost of the 'Dr Mabuse' video. Jill hated it because nobody would play it and it had cost around £20,000. I distinctly remember seeing the boom mic hover, then lower in order to better capture our disagreement. The point of the film was to shine a spotlight on our big three successes – the Frankies, Art of Noise and now Propaganda – but of course they loved the idea of us falling out, the pitting of Jill's pragmatism against the wilful creative impulses of me and Paul. Neil Tennant of Pet Shop Boys talks of bands as having an 'imperial period' – big hits, critical plaudits, huge success, a building of the fanbase – followed by a survival period. It's up to you to decide where your favourite band's imperial period begins and ends and where their survival period begins, but for ZTT that time of the big three was very much our imperial period, when we had somehow alchemised the music with the package, winning support from the press and record-buyers. Later – and with half of the label owned by Warners – ZTT would become a more regular record label, signing existing acts like 808 State and Lisa Stansfield rather than building our own, and Paul's more outlandish ideas would take a backseat, as indeed did he, as the music became less adventurous.

'Dr Mabuse' came out in March 1984, got to number twenty-seven and spent twelve weeks on the chart. Not a huge hit, but it certainly made an impression. The next song for them, 'Duel', was, if anything, even better. Paul came up with this idea of doing a punky version of it with Claudia shouting the lyrics, and although the idea didn't interest me, I had arrived in the studio one day to find Steve and Andy Richards doing some crazy, brilliant things with keyboard and guitar, almost fighting each other with sounds, which resulted in a finished product, 'Jewel', that was sonically a tour de force. However, it was around about this point that I started to back out of Propaganda in order to let Steve take over. If his treatment of 'Jewel' had proved anything, it was that he had a better handle on Propaganda than I did.

He got stuck into the Propaganda album, *A Secret Wish*, while I took more of an executive producer role. I have fond memories of the album – for instance, we got Steve Howe in to play a beautiful and very understated guitar solo on 'The Murder of Love' – but it was Steve's show. And in that respect, they were in good hands. Steve's a brilliant musician. Over the five years we worked together, he made me look good. I used to make a joke about it: I'd say to people, 'I'm Captain Pugwash and Steve's Tom the Cabin Boy.' Mind you, he could be eccentric. During the making of the album *A Secret Wish*, I was called in one day. Steve had started wearing a plastic sheep's head, which could be a little unnerving. That was bad enough but now he was refusing to speak to anybody except through a vocoder. Even with me.

'Steve, everyone's worried about you, man,' I said to him one day. 'They think you might be losing it.'

'Who's a pretty boy?' he replied, through the vocoder. 'Who's a pretty boy?'

He was talking like a parrot through the vocoder. It was funny but it was also weird and I could understand why people were concerned. Steve was, and is, a genius – I always considered myself lucky to have bumped into him. Sheep's head aside, he made a great job of the album. The only problem with it as far as I was concerned was that it didn't have another obvious hit single on it. 'Dr Mabuse' had done okay, but only okay. 'Duel' did slightly better, but never quite rose above 'okay' (number twenty-one). The next single, 'P. Machinery', which was excellent, only got to number fifty. Propaganda were good; they were critical darlings, and I'm pleased to say they've had a long tail-wind, but, crucially, they didn't sell much at the time.

The legendary producer Quincy Jones called me up. I must have talked to him for an hour and a half. What surprised him was that I knew all his old recordings. I told him that 'Smackwater Jack' was one of my favourite tracks on Carole King's *Tapestry* album (1971) and how I loved his version of 'What's Going On?' and all the stuff he did with Toots Thielemans. He was a bit taken aback. And then, of course, I had to say, 'What was it like working with Frank Sinatra?' because I love Sinatra. Quincy told me a story about arranger Nelson Riddle saying to Frank, 'I think you may have been slightly flat in the middle eight,' and Frank going, 'I wasn't flat, the orchestra was sharp.'

Quincy was producing Michael Jackson at the time and said he liked Propaganda so much, he wanted them on his label in the US. So I know that Quincy Jones was listening to Propaganda, and I'm positive you can hear its influence on 'Bad'.

———

There was of course discussion around a second Propaganda album, but we became aware that they were talking to Virgin. Same old problem: another label could offer double what we could afford. I was pretty upset at the time, I had a meeting with Michael Mertens of the band: 'Why are you going somewhere else? You haven't even talked to us about renegotiating your contract, and we could maybe get more money out of Island. Haven't we done well by you?'

He said to me, 'Well, you didn't get everything right.'

'What didn't we get right?'

His problem was that we'd put Claudia Brücken's name before his on the records. I thought, *God, talk about polishing the vase while the roof caves in.*

A couple of years later, by which point Propaganda had made another album, the terribly underwhelming and under-performing *1234*, I was eating lunch in the Townhouse when Michael Mertens came over to speak to me. I brushed him off, saying, 'I don't want to talk to you, Michael. You walked away from us after we did everything and you've screwed it up and pissed it down the drain.'

Anybody who had any sense would have seen that the combination of people was what made that record work. Andy Richards wasn't some jobbing keyboard player, he was brilliant. A brilliant keyboard player and brilliant with sounds. You could go out there and hire somebody, but you wouldn't get Andy Richards. Same with Steve Lipson. How Michael could not have seen that was beyond me.

You might wonder why the record companies who poached our talent didn't see it either. Some of the biggest people in the music business have got ears of tin. Someone like Chris Blackwell was the complete opposite: you could sway him with the quality of the music. He didn't like the Frankies, but he liked 'Relax' – he knew a good song when he heard one. But he's in the minority. Most of them couldn't hear a hit for toffee so they rely on statistics. Experience will tell them that if a band's last album has sold 3 or 4 million, then the next one will sell at least a million, regardless of quality. And that's it for them. They take the band off us, they get the act, and that's enough.

As for the band, they don't understand what they're leaving. I think of Berry Gordy, who founded Motown. He had a reputation for being controlling, but then half the people who left Motown ended up going back to him because what they found was that when you sign to a major and you take the big money, it's not the same: the people around you aren't the same people. They don't care about you. They won't tell you if you're out of line, they won't tell you if you're shit, they'll just drop you, and they'll do it with a smile on their faces or not tell you at all. I know three or four people who've been dropped and read about it in *Billboard*. And that's what happened with Michael Mertens and Propaganda. He went off with the name, got his money from Virgin, made his album (*1234*), which the label must have been so enthusiastic about while they were making it, talking about how much better it was than *A Secret Wish*, only for it to completely tank.

Claudia Brücken stayed with ZTT and formed Act with Thomas Leer, who I have to say I'm very fond of. 'Absolutely Immune' is a lovely song. They didn't do as well as we had hoped, though, perhaps because by the time of their emergence our whole ZTT schtick was getting a little tired. The Holly Johnson court case took place in 1988 when Act were releasing their first material and it's possible that the way Frankie fizzled out so publicly tainted the whole of ZTT in the minds of a lot of people. Also, we'd burned so brightly and there's always going to be a pushback against that. It's human life, you can't always be on top. By the time of the emergence of Act, ZTT was not necessarily past its peak but it was at least moving into another phase and that phase certainly involved a lot less of Paul Morley.

My father always used to say to me, 'If you're getting away with something, keep quiet about it,' and consciously or not, I heeded that maxim at ZTT, keeping a pretty low profile. After the Buggles and Yes, I'd had enough of the limelight anyway. Paul, on the other hand, was happy giving interviews. He was always interested in being controversial rather than diplomatic.

I didn't mind what he said. I knew why he was doing it, but the artists were more sensitive: the Frankies, Anne Pigalle and Art of Noise would all in the short term refuse to work with him, and in the long term develop a *We'll show you* attitude. *We'll do it without you.* Besides which, by around the time of 1987–88, I myself had reached the point where I needed to go and work with other people. I couldn't keep working with stuff that was on my own label, it was becoming far too incestuous for my tastes. I suppose you could say that our imperial period was at an end.

13

'Close (to the Edit)', Art of Noise (1984)

In which a plastic saxophone melts in the Coachella heat

Art of Noise was born out of a series of events. First there was
J. J. Jeczalik and the loop he'd made from the Yes session at Air
in 1983. Then it was me, J. J., Gary Langan and Anne Dudley,
messing around after hours, when we'd draw a line under whatever we were doing, unfurl a pirate flag that J. J. had made and
declare, 'Hoist the Jolly Roger, we're coming aboard,' and start
making music together.

The sound of Anne on the first Art of Noise album, *Who's
Afraid of the Art of Noise?*, saying, 'Oh no, no,' came from one of
those sessions. 'You're not recording me, are you?' she said,
because of course we were – we were recording everything. Just
doing stuff. Bouncing ideas off each other. Together we'd all
worked on ABC, Yes and Malcolm McLaren, so you could say
we were match fit and, having absorbed the same influences – in
particular, the New York hip hop we'd been exposed to making *Duck Rock* – we were all singing from the same songsheet

when it came to using the Fairlight in order to both replicate and advance those sounds. We had a great version of 'Beatbox' that featured Alan White's drums from 'Red Light Green Light', the failed song we did in Air Studios, as well as Chris Squire's voice, going, 'Dum, dum' from the song 'Leave It'. J. J. had also included the tennis match that ABC hadn't wanted on the 'Look of Love' remix.

The final piece of the jigsaw was me playing Paul Morley what we'd recorded. From that, Paul came up with the name Art of Noise, and drew up a set of titles, one of which was 'Moments in Love', which after 'Beat Box' became our next song. Paul was now in the band.

I had this idea that you could put 'Moments in Love' on while having sex, mainly because it had a nice slow tempo, a kind of romantic sound and it went on for a decent amount of time, but I needed something in the middle, some sort of a climax. In a folk record shop, a very earnest young fellow helped me find a selection of old blues records that he thought I was going to listen to, but I was just looking for a moment. This is where I got the 'noooow, noooow, noooow' sound from. When we started recording the song, it sounded a bit bland with just the Linn playing so we changed all the drum sounds to samples of orchestral drums. The *ah ah* voice was a nick from Laurie Anderson (not literally) and it created a great atmosphere. Anne did an amazing job with the keyboards; it's her song really. It is quite long and after we'd mixed 'Moments', I played it to Jill in the car.

'It's a bit boring, isn't it?' she said.

'It's meant to be,' I replied. 'Just stick with it for another minute and the guy comes.'

We were all surprised at how popular that song became.

Paul wrote a manifesto for Art of Noise: 'Sampling the Twentieth Century,' I think it started. We were all inspired by this and kept hard at it, sampling the twentieth century. By now we had lots of material, including jam sessions with weird samples, Anne playing beautiful grand piano over some mad shit J. J. had cooked up, and lots of weird bits of South American radio.

When I had the row with Yes over the *90125* album, I went to SARM and edited our first ZTT release from these tapes. Called *Into Battle with the Art of Noise*, the EP was released in September of that year. Not only was it the debut for Art of Noise, but it was the first release on ZTT.

We needed a single. 'Beat Box' and 'Moments in Love' were the standout moments from the EP, but I wanted something else, something even stronger. I was thinking of a long piece, seventeen minutes long, like 'Close to the Edge' by Yes, but Paul changed that to 'Close (to the Edit)'.

Gary Langan had brought in a sample of him starting his car and J. J. had put it into the Fairlight and turned it into a rhythmic loop – Gary contributed the amazing double-bass part, which, I can tell you from painful experience, is nearly impossible to play on a bass guitar. I came up with the bit of dialogue, 'To be in England in the summertime, close to the edge,' and we had Karen Clayton, who was a receptionist at SARM, speak it for us (Karen was also responsible for the spoken-word part in 'Poison Arrow'), while the 'hey' is the voice of Camilla Pilkington-Smythe of the Pilkington Glass family. Frank Ricotti played percussion.

'Close (to the Edit)' was an upgraded version of 'Beat Box', but it was a really interesting piece in its own right. One of the things that was so good about it was the dialogue between the different voices, the synths and the samples and the 'hey'.

The album took a while, but we were all happy with it at the time. In retrospect we were the first musos to have fun with samplers, and now we are being sampled, the 'hey' finding its way into the Prodigy's 'Firestarter' and loads of people sampling 'Moments'. When I hear it now, it seems so crude. Listening to 'In the Army Now', it's just me, a Linn drum machine and a sample, and I feel vaguely embarrassed by it. I really like 'Moments in Love', which was one of the best things we ever did, as well as 'Close (to the Edit)' and all the many different versions of 'Beat Box'. Even so, it all feels very primitive to me. Still, the fact that it's held in such high esteem is all very gratifying and of course I tend to see whatever advances we made as Art of Noise as part of a ZTT continuum: the cash registers we used on the ABC album, the way Gary used echo, the many, many things J. J. was doing with the Fairlight. I was watching the Super Bowl the other day and I could see so many echoes of Frankie in the music being played. Big stabs. Huge, doom-laden power chords. They and Art of Noise have filtered into the culture.

Taken from the album, the 'Close (to the Edit)' single did well, getting to number eight in the UK in 1984, which meant that all of a sudden, we'd gone from being a strictly studio project, where we were working out our mad creative impulses, free of any commercial imperative, to a band that had a hit. The trouble was that I didn't want to go on to *Top of the Pops*. I didn't want to do it because I'd done it before; I was more concerned with being a producer. And anyway, you end up miming with a keyboard, and it's the lamest thing in the world to mime with a keyboard unless you're Kraftwerk. Chris Lowe of Pet Shop Boys gets it right – he knows how to pretend to play a naff little keyboard.

My refusal to do *Top of the Pops* didn't help as far as the future for Art of Noise was concerned. What also didn't help was certain pronouncements made by Paul, when he told an interviewer, 'I am the Art of Noise,' which really wound up the rest of the band. They said to me, 'How do you feel about that?' and I said, 'I feel about the same as if he'd said, "I am Trevor Horn." He patently isn't.'

Gary, J. J. and Anne left. They didn't leave Art of Noise but they left me and they left Paul and they left ZTT. It all got a bit weird for a time. We had a ZTT show called *That's Entertainment* that we staged in a theatre, and because three of Art of Noise had left, it was just Paul in a stripy suit talking over the records. We owned the name Art of Noise, but much to Jill's disgust I let the other three have it. I thought it was more important for them than it was for me, I was more interested in being a producer.

Years passed. I watched from afar as things changed with Art of Noise. Gary left the group, meaning that it was just Anne and J. J. They'd had hits, one of which, 'Kiss', was with Tom Jones, but ongoing commercial success eluded them until, in 1990, they officially laid the name to rest. Then, in 1992, I produced a single for Marc Almond, 'Days of Pearly Spencer', which led to me producing the entire second half of his album, *Tenement Symphony* (1991), which, because I was obsessed with Debussy at the time, featured a Claude Debussy composition as an extended intro to 'The Days of Pearly Spencer'. This in turn got me into the idea of somehow modernising Debussy. Pet Shop Boys fans may think this sounds naggingly familiar, and indeed, I was producing 'Left to My Own Devices' for them when Neil Tennant asked me what I planned to do next. 'I'm going to try putting Debussy to a disco beat,' I told him, and he said, 'I'll use that line, if you don't mind.' I didn't mind. He gave me some publishing on the B-side for it.

Anyway, Anne and I talked about reforming Art of Noise and we roped Paul Morley and my old buddy Lol Creme into it as well. The result was *The Seduction of Claude Debussy* (1999), an album we called 'a soundtrack to a film that wasn't made about the life of Claude Debussy'. Paul Morley came back on board and we got the late John Hurt to add narration. He came over for breakfast, where I talked it over with him and got it all done in twenty minutes. We also had the rapper Rakim do a bit. I'd waited for him for three days in New York but he never showed, only to later turn up unexpectedly at our studio, Hook End Manor in Oxfordshire, which we'd bought from Langer and Winstanley in 1995.

Making the album was good, but the fun part was later. For this most recent incarnation of Art of Noise, we had hired Paul McGuinness as manager. Paul is a bit of a legend in the business, known chiefly for managing U2. At the same time, the album, despite being a very niche concern, mixing opera singers with drum 'n' bass, sold well on campuses in America. As a result, we landed a 6 p.m. spot at the first-ever Coachella Festival. I was wondering how we could possibly do it because of the drum 'n' bass element being so prevalent but then I went to see a DJ Shadow gig in Dublin, which was basically him playing and scratching records, and I thought, *If he can stand there playing records, then we can play on top of a computer and people will be entertained*, which is how we came up with a show.

We couldn't afford to haul a load of musicians around with us and so it was just the core members of Art of Noise, who at that time were Lol Creme, Anne Dudley, Paul Morley and me, as well as an opera singer and Tim Weidner, who had engineered the album and was going to work the computer and mix the sequencers and drums onstage with us. We were going to play certain parts of the record just us, and then on a signal the computer would kick in. It was a good trick. We started the show with Anne on her own playing 'Dr Gradus', a beautiful complex piano piece by Debussy. Hearing that lovely piano composition blasting out over the festival ground as we sound-checked Coachella was a real joy.

We used the Coachella booking as a springboard to build a small American tour around that one appearance, which marked the first time I had been on a stage in almost twenty years – since that experience in Yes, in fact – two decades in which I had gradually transformed into a Gollum-like creature of the studio, shunning the daylight, a near-stranger to normal human interaction.

We rehearsed and our first show was in a big bar in San Francisco. It held about a thousand people. When I first walked in my heart sank because the sound system looked underpowered, but then I saw that they had massive subwoofers at the sides. We soundchecked, and still Paul hadn't given us much of an idea what he was going to do during the show. Because Lol was used to having a roadie I had to look after him. This caused Paul to accuse us of being gay. To put his mind at rest on that first night in San Francisco, Lol and I ran onstage, hand in hand.

Paul arrived on the stage wearing a Gestapo-like trenchcoat and clutching a lump hammer. He proceeded to leap around and brandish the hammer in a dangerous way. We didn't know what he was going to say or do from one moment to the next so, in the bits where he talked, we just followed him with the music. I loved that first show in San Francisco.

On the plane to Coachella the next morning, Anne was listening to a tape of the show. She kept telling Lol not to play this or that and pointing out his mistakes. At the end of the tape she turned to me and said, 'You were okay.'

The heat at Coachella was unbearable. The plastic saxophone I intended to play for 'Dreaming in Colour' literally melted in the heat so we had to drop the song from the set. During 'Moments in Love', on which I was playing stand-up bass, I glanced up to see that Anne was looking at me aghast. It took me a moment to figure out what was wrong: the double-bass was way out of tune because of the heat. It was a beautiful evening and we were on between 6 and 7 p.m. so we got the sundown.

We completed the tour, which went well, but that, for the moment, is all as far as Art of Noise is concerned. Perhaps we might make another record, you never know.

14

'Do They Know It's Christmas?', Band Aid (1984)

In which I play a part in the biggest-selling single of all time (but not the part that many people think)

The first time I met Bob Geldof was in 1979 at the Houses of Parliament. I think Jill knew him somehow. Maybe the Boomtown Rats had recorded at SARM. The reason we were all at the Houses of Parliament was one of those 'everyone who had a number-one record this year' parties. Jill introduced me to Bob, who immediately told me he rated the Bruce Woolley version of 'Video Killed the Radio Star' to the Buggles' version and I thought, *What a twat*. Not because he preferred the Bruce version of the song – he's perfectly welcome to his preference – but because he had the pressing need to tell me on our first-ever meeting. Still, I liked the Boomtown Rats. I particularly liked 'I Don't Like Mondays', which had not long been at number one, and 'Rat Trap', which had got to number one the previous year, but other than that I didn't have much of an opinion on him. After filing him under 'rude fucker', I moved on.

Fast-forward in time to 1984 and Geldof, having been moved by reports made by the BBC's Michael Buerk on the famine in Ethiopia, proved that he was very much *not* a twat by hooking up with Ultravox's Midge Ure and coming up with the idea to make a charity record.

Bob and Midge weren't the only ones affected by Michael Buerk's report. It had seeped into the public consciousness in a way that I'd never really known before. When they contacted Jill asking if they could use SARM West for the record, we were happy to do our bit and let them have it for free.

The day it all happened, SARM West filled up with the huge stars of the day, the people who filled the pages of *Smash Hits* and *Number One* magazine every week: Boy George, Phil Collins, all of Bananarama, George Michael, Spandau Ballet and Duran Duran; members of U2, Status Quo, Heaven 17, Wham!, Paul Weller and Sting. I wasn't planning on showing up but Jill rang me from the studio, amid what was clearly a very high-spirited atmosphere: 'You should get your arse down here,' she called over the din.

'Why? They're only making a record, aren't they?'

'They're making a record, but they're not *only* making a record. It's incredible. Get down here.'

So I jumped in the car, went down and had that classic moment when I found myself facing a big guy standing at the door of SARM, who said, 'Where do you think you're going, mate?'

And for once in my life I got to say, 'Do you know who I am? I'm the guy that owns this building.'

In I went, and Jill was right: they were 'only' making a record, but there was a special atmosphere around it. All these big stars in one room, most of whom would pass each other in the corridors of *Top of the Pops*, refusing to give each other the time of day, but here they were, teaming up, working together, egos to one side and contributing to an atmosphere that was joyful and hopeful. Jill was right, it was incredible.

It was Bob who asked me to do the 12-inch mix. No, he didn't ask, he *told* me that I would be doing it. This is probably where the longstanding belief that I produced the 7-inch comes from.

My first thought was that the remix should feature something that wasn't on the 7-inch, so I tried to get the assembled throng to do something, a sort of in-the-round vocal bit. But it was too ambitious in the short time we had and I had to abandon that idea. Instead, we waited and got the multi-track from Midge at 6 a.m. and went straight into making the 12-inch. We already had one idea. Loads of people – including some who weren't on the single – had recorded messages for the B-side of the 7-inch. David Bowie had done one, as had Paul McCartney, and even Holly Johnson.

(Quick digression. Why weren't the Frankies involved with either Band Aid or the subsequent Live Aid? Well, if memory serves, they were in America at the time of the recording of the single – Band Aid would in fact knock 'The Power of Love' off number one – which is why they didn't appear on that. And as for Live Aid, they were asked but declined. According to Nash, they were worried about making a mess of it and committing career suicide.)

Anyway . . . We loaded all the messages into our trusty Synclavier so that we could play them on different keys and mess about with them. 'Hello, this is Paul Weller – a Weller-Weller-Weller.' Just silly things like that. We had a blast with it, probably finished it just after lunch. Not a bad job. But everybody still thinks I produced the 7-inch.

Then of course came the concert, which was a most fantastic event. I didn't go, but we watched it, of course, and what was great about it was that you saw a good cross-section of who was playing at that particular point in time but with minimal production. Status Quo were great. Sting was great. And it's a bit of a cliché now to say it, but of course Queen were even greater, too. Even though they were a big band, at the point they were no longer hip, but when you saw them on the day, almost singlehandedly making rock popular again, it all clicked. And, of course, the other big winner was U2, who were very well drilled. It was funny, because when I first arrived at SARM West that day, and was listening to all those famous singers doing their bit on the record, I said to Jill, 'Who's that kid in the hat? He's got a great voice.' Turned out it was Bono.

15

'Slave to the Rhythm', Grace Jones (1985)

In which I come to the end of an amazing run

'Slave to the Rhythm' is a record that shouldn't have happened. It had its seeds in 1984 when, in the wake of the success of 'Relax', we were hunting around for a follow-up. You may recall that Bruce Woolley had written a song called 'Slave to the Rhythm' with Simon Darlow, which we'd tried out with Frankie. It didn't turn out particularly well, so it was shelved.

Chris Blackwell, the owner of Island Records at the time, was putting together a greatest hits album for Grace Jones and suggested that we make a single of 'Slave' with her for the album. Bruce and I were long-time fans of Grace. Years before, Bruce had played me the original version of 'Warm Leatherette' produced by Daniel Miller as the Normal, and we'd both been impressed with Grace's sexy cover version. I also loved the records she'd made with Sly and Robbie and Chris Blackwell, like 'Love is the Drug' and 'Pull Up to the Bumper', so we were up for it.

Lippo and I put together some kind of backing track for 'Slave' and we met up with Grace at a studio just off Queensway in London. That studio is gone now; the whole area has been redeveloped, but I know for a fact that Sinatra recorded there in the 1950s.

Grace was smaller than I expected but somehow seemed to grow larger as I got to know her, purely through the force of her personality. She threw herself into the song with enormous gusto. Grace marched around the place, and we all had a good time, but I wasn't keen on the end result – it sounded a bit like one of those aerobic workout tapes that were popular at the time.

The thing was that I wanted to do a really good record with Grace, not just some throwaway song, and that's what the original of 'Slave to the Rhythm' sounded like. I listened to it next to Grace's greatest hits and it just didn't sound as good. In retrospect, I should have finished there and then, given Chris Blackwell the track, and saved loads of time, money and energy. Instead, I decided that we would rewrite the song and play it over a go-go beat.

Go-go was a movement that was happening mainly in Washington DC, courtesy of the city's large black population. The famous bands from the movement were Chuck Brown and the Soul Searchers and Experience Unlimited (EU to their fans), and although the beat itself was nothing new (people like Earth, Wind & Fire had used it, and I knew it as a kind of ninety-beats-per-minute funky feel), the ethos was different: go-go shows went on all through the night, the rhythm never stopping even when the bands switched over. The drummers would sort of hand over the beat to the next band on the bill and the beat would go on and on. My reasoning at the time was that if I was going to be a slave to any kind of rhythm, then it would have to be the one I found the most exciting, and at that time go-go felt fresh.

I told my idea to Chris Blackwell and asked him if he could hire a go-go rhythm section for me in New York. Somewhat baffled, since it wasn't an obvious direction for the song, he put a band together, an amalgam of Soul Searchers and EU guys, who we were to meet in the Power Station Studios in New York, scene of our Malcolm McLaren adventure.

Steve was with me when I went out to New York, as was Bruce Woolley. The first shock we had was when they told us that we could only have the studio from 9 a.m. to 6 p.m. because they had another booking. I'm not into 9 a.m. recording sessions. Still, we were there and we had the musicians there. But what we didn't have was Grace. The percussion player, a precocious young fellow by the name of Little Beats, kept asking when she was going to turn up. *Not here yet*, was the answer. *Grace keeps Gracetime, let's see what we can get in the meantime.*

The problem with go-go was that the band weren't used to playing to an arrangement. An 'arrangement' for them was start, play your heart out, and then stop. I spent the whole of the first day trying to get them to remember the simplest arrangement for 'Slave', mostly to no avail. However, I had a portable cassette player and when the band had been improvising at the start of the session I had recorded some of it. So when things were going badly and the whole thing seemed like it was pointless, I would play this one bit of the drummer Ju-Ju's playing from the set-up jam. Bruce picked up on it, and while the band were taking a break, used a Roland JX8P keyboard to play some chords over it – they're the chords you hear at the start of the record, and I immediately fell in love with them.

That evening at 6 p.m., we were kicked out of the studio and as the band headed out to their motel for a night of debauchery, me, Bruce and Lippo made our way back to the Parker Meridien hotel carrying drum machines, guitars, keyboards and loudspeakers. The staff eyed us with suspicion, but we managed to get everything into the lift and since I was staying in a suite we set it all up in my room.

That evening, Bruce wrote another version, aided by me and Lippo, and his beautiful chords helped us mould the song in a new way. Over the moon and overexcited, I phoned Chris Blackwell who was just around the corner in the Essex House on Central Park South. He came down, I played it to him, and he got the shock of his life that the song had gone from being this big bombastic, 120-bpm Frankie thing to something else, something funkier and more sinewy at 90 bpm.

Next day, we couldn't wait to get rid of the musicians. They had been up all night and were slightly hungover, so we let them go early. Despite everything we had tried, the only thing that worked was that little jam at the start of the first day.

Steve set about making a drum track using the two Sony digital multi-tracks. It was a laborious task because we had decided to make a drum track by copying two bars from that jam and repeating them, spread across seven or eight tracks, for four minutes. We also used the percussion that had gone with those drums. We recorded a sketch of the song over these drums then took drum fills from that original jam and edited them into the right places. I was particularly pleased with our middle eight, which consisted of some beautiful chords played over eight bars of wonderful go-go drumming, where instead of repeating two bars we used the original eight bars of Ju-Ju's drumming.

Bruce played some good keyboard parts, Steve played a rhythm guitar and a bass. Everything seemed to be going well and we were ready for Grace to sing.

I rang Grace to see what time she would arrive and found something was seriously wrong: 'Grace, we've got the tracks down, they're really cool, you should come down.'

She said, 'I've just set fire to the Dolph's clothes.'

This was the Swedish actor Dolph Lundgren, who was her boyfriend at the time.

'Well this'll get you out of it. You can come down and sing,' I said.

She was obviously pretty wound up and mentioned things like 'nervous breakdowns'. I painted pictures of exciting recording sessions, new versions. *Don't have a breakdown, come and make a record, the track is waiting for you and it sounds beautiful.* She finally agreed to come, three days late, on the Sunday. Better late than never.

A strange thing happened the night before she arrived. It was the weekend and the studio was now ours for as long as we wanted it, so of course we were working crazy hours. It was 2 a.m. on Sunday morning and the assistant on the session brought us a note from Jim Steinman, who was working in the next studio to us. Would we like to pay him a visit at 4 a.m. and hear the song he was working on? Of course we would. Jim Steinman is the guy who wrote 'Bat out of Hell', 'Total Eclipse of the Heart' and many other American working-class, trailer-trash anthems. I'd never met him, but what the hell.

At 4 a.m. we trooped into the next-door control room and there was Jim with a smart guy, about the same age as us, who introduced himself as Todd Rundgren. Lippo was impressed, turns out he was a big fan of Todd.

Our host Jim handed out lyric sheets with tea and then proceeded to play us his song, which was called 'Loving You's a Dirty Job (But Somebody's Gotta Do It)' by Bonnie Tyler, which was a true epic. Every time I thought the song was over and I was about to say something about it, it picked up again and went from plateau to plateau, up a mountain, then through a valley. Exhausted, we applauded at the end of the playback, and Jim asked us what we were working on. I told him and he came into our control room, where we played him the two different versions of 'Slave'. Jim was enthusiastic and suggested we join all the versions together and make it into an epic. He was obviously into epics, but it started me thinking.

Meanwhile, Grace showed up on the Sunday only three days late but fighting fit. We learned of Dolph's infidelity and the subsequent torching of his wardrobe. When we played her the track, she purred, 'I imagine it's a warm evening and I'm sitting on a bench on the deck of my house as the sun's going down.' With that, she took a seat in the studio and we got a mic in front of her and started rolling.

The mood was perfect. We had Bruce sitting beside her, giving her the next line, which was how we did the first few takes, just to get her warmed up. Now cut to the control room and what you see is me and Lippo dancing for joy, knowing that it was going to work. Her voice just fitted, it completely suited the song.

Grace stayed, writing songs with Bruce out in the studio, and when she left at about 5 a.m., Bruce and I helped her down the stairs. As we walked out into the crisp New York dawn a white limo started up and a chauffeur climbed out onto the snow-covered pavement and opened the back door of the car. Bruce and I gently lowered Grace into the back seat but she fell off it and lay on the floor of the limo on her back. I realised she was trying to tell me something, so I leaned in through the door.

'Make it great,' she said.

Okay, Grace.

Back in England, the new version of the song just seemed to get better but now there were four different songs called 'Slave to the Rhythm'. Thinking back to Jim Steinman's advice, I had started mulling over the idea of a true epic. An album featuring different versions of the same song.

When we told our idea to Chris Blackwell, he went into shock. After all, he'd only wanted one song. Still, we were doing it anyway, especially when we got in touch with Grace, who was totally up for the idea. Back at SARM West, I got Paul Morley to interview her, and her ex-boyfriend Jean-Paul Goude to talk about her. Steve took the rhythm that we'd done in the Power Station and translated it into the Synclavier along with the beat, and that became a track called 'The Fashion Show', which Pink Floyd's Dave Gilmour played on. Bruce had a lovely thing that we called 'The Crossing (Ooh the Action)', and there was a song called 'Operattack', which is unlistenable so the less said about that the better. Then we had 'Don't Cry It's Only the Rhythm', which is one of my favourites. It started out as a loop in the Synclavier that Steve was messing with. I loved it and said let's record it so we started to turn it into a track for the album.

Luis Jardim came in. I wanted him to play some percussion, but he said, 'Rather than playing a shaker, why don't I just do it with my voice?' which he did, and it's a really cool sound.

One night, I was out at Giles Fish & Chip Shop when I happened to look across the room and saw the actor Ian McShane.

He had been a Yes fan, and in return I loved his work, so I went straight over and said, 'What are you doing? I need a voiceover on this record I'm making.'

He remembers it slightly differently, saying that I opened proceedings by saying, 'Ian, Orson Welles is dead, so only you will do,' but either way, he came down and he did it in one take, all of it, 'Ladies and gentlemen, Miss Grace Jones, Slave to the Rhythm,' and off he went again.

I told him, 'I'll send you a crate of champagne,' but I never did although I think he'd stopped drinking by then anyway.

All in all, we worked on the album for about six weeks in London, during which time Grace came into the studio a few times. I loved working with her. There was one point where I was a bit rattled because she came in with an entourage who wouldn't stop talking and I got a bit cross. I could see I wasn't the first person to get cross with Grace – she was well used to people being cross with her and knew how to deal with it by being warm and funny. Back in New York, there had been one night when we went to see Jackie Chan's film, *Police Story*, me, Grace and Chris Blackwell. When we came out, me, Grace and Jackie Chan all piled into a friend's car that was in fact a van with no seats in the back, just some duvet thing: me and Grace lying in the back, Jackie Chan in the front. We drove to Grace's restaurant downtown and all sat at a big table surrounded by pictures of her and had a fabulous dinner. That was a great memory.

By now our epic needed a climax. The song didn't have one written in it, so we had to come up with something. I saw Grace on *The Tonight Show Starring Johnny Carson* promoting some movie she was in and thought, *Why not use the opening line from his show?* Hence, 'Here's Grace!'

Grace loved the idea and did it in one take. When Richard Niles created the horn arrangement for the song, we got him to do a kind of swing talk-show thing on the 'Here's Grace' bit and Richard got it spot-on. Steve and I laughed out of pure joy when we first heard it.

Slave to the the Rhythm, the 1985 album, proved to be expensive, though, partly because I flew to New York on Concorde to master it, partly because we had a horn section and string section – arranged by Richard Niles – on it. I think it's fair to say that I got carried away.

The funny thing about the single of 'Slave to the Rhythm' is that although everybody remembers it now, it wasn't a huge hit at the time. The video by Jean-Paul Goude was brilliant. He used it as an opportunity to showcase some of the wonderful commercials he had done featuring Grace. Grace performed it on *Wogan* in a full-face covering. I know now that she was years ahead of her time. It probably wasn't great for the song's commercial prospects. Chris Blackwell said the single was just about the best-sounding record he had ever heard. Steve was amazing all the way through the project and his mixing of the song was inspired.

Looking back, I think people were shocked that the song 'only' got to number twelve because up until then just about everything I'd done was such a big hit and it felt like the ultimate Trevor Horn remix project. For maybe that reason it was after 'Slave' that I stopped doing 12-inches. I was tired of them. So that was where that period ended. The end of an era, you might say. Still, even if I'd had enough of remixes, I was still in love with orchestras.

16

'Left to My Own Devices', Pet Shop Boys (1988)

In which I make an epic

I knew of the Pet Shop Boys because they were managed by Tom Watkins, who as well as doing some interior decoration for Jill and me had designed the ZTT logo. He was always trying to get me to hear his new band, Pet Shop Boys, but at that point – and still today, in fact – people were always trying to get me to listen to things, so I dare say I demurred. But then, on the radio, I heard this record, 'West End Girls'. I really liked it and was surprised to hear that it was the very same Pet Shop Boys. I was like, 'Fuck me, Tom, is that your band? God, it's a gift, that record; it's going to be a huge hit.'

I was immediately a fan. The Buggles had been a two-man thing, but we didn't have the presence of PSB. Neil Tennant and Chris Lowe just looked the part, plus I really liked Neil's voice. I used to call him the 'Iron Choirboy'. He was another one, like Martin Fry, who sang with an English accent. So anyway, they had a few hits, and suddenly Jill was saying, 'Tom's talking about you producing the Pet Shop Boys,' an idea that I liked very much.

I met them. My thoughts went back to Richard Niles, who had done such great string work on 'Slave to the Rhythm' – 'How would you feel about having an orchestra on the record?' It turned out that Neil and Chris had never used an orchestra, but I thought that the song they played us, 'Left to My Own Devices', was perfect for an orchestral arrangement. It was to be the second single from their third album, *Introspective* (1988), and was Neil describing a day in someone's (probably his) life. The other great thing about the song – and possibly the reason they had come to me with it – was that they were keen for it to be a bit of an epic. For their first two albums they'd been making standard-length pop songs. Now, however, they were ready to stretch the format.

Steve Lipson and I got to work. We made a backing track and Steve did the drums with the Synclavier. He used some great sounds, but to me they sounded more like Steely Dan than the Pet Shop Boys. I had a crude music workstation, the Akai MPC60, which I took home at the weekend and used for programming some basic, simple garage beats.

Come the Monday and Steve didn't like my new drums much. He grumped a bit then replicated my laborious programming in a few seconds on his rig. He came up with this amazing synth bass part which really worked beautifully with the new drums. At this point the track began to coalesce, growing as we worked on it. Around this time, I was listening to a lot of Debussy, which began to creep into the track like King Charles into Mr Dick's head in *David Copperfield*. A soft section in the middle, where Neil talked about his childhood, had a little bit of 'Clair de lune' about it. We extended the song at the end because Neil had this idea that he was asleep and dreaming about what he'd been saying in the song.

I loved the sound of the female singers on the Debussy records I was listening to. I asked around and was directed to a singer, Sally Bradshaw, who sang Debussy well. We brought her in and the first thing I got her do was to sing the word 'house'. House music was very much in vogue at the time and I was being silly. Then she sang the chorus at the end.

The great thing about working with Neil and Chris is that you know where you stand – they're very decisive. We had tried an electric piano on the song. They didn't like it, too Bruce Hornsby. We played something else, they liked it. There was nothing in-between with them and in-between is usually where there's a problem.

The string session loomed. We were doing it in Studio One at Abbey Road with fifty players (those were the days). A couple of days beforehand, I went over to go through what Richard Niles had written in the arrangement. It all seemed good until we got to the end. The whole end part seemed very complicated. Richard assured me that it would sound fine when it was played by the orchestra, but I wasn't so sure.

When we were in Abbey Road two days later recording the strings, I was sitting with Neil and Chris in the control room, everything was going swimmingly, the strings in the middle section sounded beautiful and in the third verse they were even better. Then we got to the end. The strings suddenly sounded like *Oklahoma!* on glue. Chris, who up to this point had been liking what he was hearing, jumped up and started to shout, 'I hate it, I hate it, it's awful.' As I've said, we had fifty string players out there. I had to calm everybody down, telling Chris, 'Right, okay, don't say you hate it. Just let them play it and I'll deal with it.'

He was right, the strings at the end were way too ambitious so I got Richard into the control room and with a red pen we went through the score. I thought that since it was a revolving chord sequence he could write chords in footballs (semibreves) for the strings, starting low and gradually getting higher. To his credit he did an amazing job of the re-orchestration. It took him forty-five minutes – forty-five minutes while a fifty-piece orchestra chilled. We recorded this new arrangement and here and there, we dropped in bits that we liked from the *Oklahoma!* arrangement; everything came out well. Richard's arrangement ended up sounding absolutely inspired. The extra things like the harp and Sally's singing really added to the whole thing. I loved the lead vocal and the way Neil delivered it. I sang harmonies on the song along with Bruce Woolley; I used the strings on their own for an intro to the song.

I really enjoyed working with Neil and Chris, they always know how to treat an old producer. We've stayed friends ever since, and much later – in 2006 – I ended up producing their album, *Fundamental*. Just spending every day with them in a control room was something I looked forward to. When I started, Chris had already programmed nearly all the music and Neil had already done his vocals, so all I did was to replace the plug-in synths with real synths, re-did the drums and then did a lot of working-out for Neil's vocal harmonies on tracks like 'Luna Park' and 'The Sodom & Gomorrah Show'. I also produced their live album, *Concrete* (2006).

I've always loved the Pet Shop Boys. 'Being Boring' is probably the song I would like to have played at my funeral. When I was in LA and missing England, I would play Pet Shop Boys albums. In the car, my son would say, 'Can we listen to the Ketchup Boys?', which was a very good choice on his part because they were – and are – a very special band.

17

'Rough Ride', Paul McCartney (1989)

In which I get a proper telling-off from the man himself

Like a lot of Beatles fans back in the day, I was more of a John Lennon than a Paul McCartney fan. I suppose it's that old thing of liking the person who obviously doesn't care whether you like them or not. Things changed post-split, when I found myself preferring McCartney's stuff, 'Band on the Run' and 'Ram' especially. John had become a bit self-indulgent for my tastes. Obviously 'Imagine' was good, but on that same album was 'How Do You Sleep?', his childish dig at McCartney, and overall his material lacked what I liked about McCartney's, which was leaning towards straight-up pop, tuneful but with a twist – more up my street.

I'd met Paul a few times over the years. The first time was when I was in Air doing *90125*. I was on the Space Invaders machine when he appeared behind me and showed me how to rig the machine so I had the highest score. It's a unique feeling to have one of your childhood heroes not only recognise you but speak your name *and* show you how to cheat at arcade games. We bumped into each other a few times after the Space Invaders' encounter. One time I was at an awards do when he brought Michael Jackson over to meet me, and then, for some reason, wandered off, leaving me alone with him. I remember noticing that Jacko had painted part of his head black – I think it was where he'd lost some hair in an accident and put some sort of boot polish on there. I had very brief conversation with him.

'I saw you on *The Andy Williams Show* many, many years go, and you were great,' I said.

And he said, 'Mmph, mmph, mmph.'

And I said, 'What?'

And he said, 'Mmph, mmph, mmph.'

And I said, 'I'm sorry, I don't know what you're saying,' before the penny dropped and I realised he was saying, 'With my brothers.'

'Ah, yes, you were with your brothers.'

And that was pretty much that.

In the '80s, Paul McCartney hired a manager, Richard Ogden, who used to manage the American rock band Camper Van Beethoven. If you know Camper Van Beethoven, whose big indie hit was 'Take the Skinheads Bowling', then you'll know how surprising it is that their manager should go on to manage Paul McCartney. Richard said to me, 'How would you like to come down and write with Paul?' Up to that point I'd only written with Bruce Woolley or Geoff Downes in my life, and mainly to order, so I didn't really fancy the idea of writing with Paul.

At the same time, he told me that Paul was auditioning for a band – he needed a bass player, drummer and piano player. I thought it would be interesting to try out for that on bass to get to know him, so I offered to go along and audition. I found myself setting off for a rehearsal room with my Wal five-string bass and, having miscalculated the London traffic, realised I was going to be late.

The guy organising the audition rang me: 'Where the fuck are you?'

'I'm sorry, I'm just going down Park Lane.'

'Oh, my God, you won't be here for nearly an hour.'

'Yeah, sorry.'

'Mr McCartney wants everyone set up and ready to go a half-hour before he arrives.'

'Well, I won't be, sorry.'

In the end I got there just ahead of Paul. I plugged in, put my bass on a stand and then lit a cigarette I had prepared earlier. The crew weren't totally happy, but I had decided I was going to enjoy myself. Paul swept in with Linda, sniffing at the air. I was always a Linda fan, as it happens. Steve and I agreed on this. We always believed that she'd had a bit of a bum rap from Beatles fans and the media, and I like to think that time has proven us correct on that one.

Auditioning at the same time as me was a drummer and a guy called Nicky Hopkins, a brilliant piano player, very famous, who had played with the Stones, the Kinks and the Who. Paul was really intrigued by the bass I was using. He loved that it had a fifth string because it could go down to a low B. You've got to be careful with that B string, but I still play a five-string bass to this day, and that low string's really useful.

All told, I had a good time at the audition, and particularly liked talking about music with Paul. I spoke to Richard Ogden afterwards. I told him that I still didn't want to write with Paul, but I'd had an idea. How about I listen to whatever songs he's currently working on, choose one and then produce it in two days straight?

After some initial hesitations from Paul, Steve and I were summoned to his beautiful studio in Rye, which was full of amazing memorabilia: his old Beatles bass, with a setlist from the last Beatles show in Candlestick Park, San Francisco, still glued to it; the bass that Elvis Presley's double-bass player had used on 'Heartbreak Hotel'; and the most incredible Mellotron I've ever seen, one that Paul had used on 'Live and Let Die' when he played it live, which to me is the best Bond theme ever.

Even though it was a beautiful studio the first thing I did was close all the blinds. I didn't want doors open; I didn't want to see the sun. I wanted to pretend that we were in a studio in Denmark Street. Sunlight's fabulous but it can be overrated when you're working on a record. It's quite good to be . . . incarcerated.

Steve Lipson began setting up our gear while I went off with Paul, who played me five songs, one of which I really liked, which was 'Rough Ride'. I thought it was slightly autobiographical, and I also had an idea that it might fit the Experience Unlimited beat that Steve and I had cooked up in New York. From that, we got stuck in.

Paul was approachable. For instance, he had certain chords in the middle eight of 'Rough Ride', but I'd changed them.

He said, 'Trevor, those aren't the right chords for the middle eight.'

'They are now,' I insisted.

There was a pause and I wondered if I might have overstepped the mark, but he didn't argue, and we went on to put down a very basic track.

I forgot that he was a vegetarian. It was a little later, while working with Simple Minds in Scotland, that I gave up meat, but at that time, I still ate it. During the afternoon, one of the crew offered to get pizza and I ordered salami. It never arrived; I got a margherita instead. Pointing out the error, I was met with resounding silence, so I figured that that's just the way it was – there was going to be no meat coming into that studio.

That first night, he and I were having coffee in the kitchen of the studio at about 2 a.m. The TV was on and happened to be playing an old American Beatles cartoon. The Beatles' voices had been done by American actors, but the music was Beatles. I remember thinking how potent the music still sounded.

'That must be strange, to see yourself animated like that,' I said.

'Oh, not any more, I've given up finding anything like that strange,' Paul said. And then he told me a story about getting busted for pot in Japan in 1980. It wasn't his pot, or at least it wasn't his suitcase, but he thought that if he owned up then he'd get off, being Paul McCartney. But the Japanese weren't about to show leniency and they banged him up anyway.

Paul was nervous, but shortly after he arrived in prison, one of the guards said, 'You've got to come and meet the guy who runs the prison,' to which McCartney said, 'Well, I've met the guy who runs the prison. He said hello when I came in.'

The guy said, 'No, this is the guy who *really* runs the prison. You're going to meet him.'

Paul was led to a room and asked to wait until a wizened old bloke was brought in, complete with interpreter. Everyone sat on the floor. The old guy asked him what he was doing in the prison, Paul told him and was taken aback when the guy just laughed.

'You've had some really bad luck,' he told him.

And Paul McCartney, who thanks to a chance meeting met John Lennon and formed the greatest songwriting partnership the world has ever seen, said, 'Yeah, I've had some bad luck.'

The old guy said, 'Don't worry. Nothing's going to happen to you in here, you'll be fine. You'll be out in a few days. Stay sane and just don't worry, nothing will happen to you.'

And it was fine; everyone was nice to him after that, and he was indeed released after a few days.

What I learned from that encounter is that Paul is a fundamentally cool guy even though he knows that he's Paul McCartney. His ego is there, but he doesn't wield it like a weapon. The way he dealt with Steve, for example. Steve and I are very different in our approach. I would always be much more obliging and try to be charming, whereas Steve didn't give a fuck. There was one time when Paul came into the control room after singing a few takes and I said, 'That was great, the third take in particular,' but Steve said, 'Yeah, the first two were rubbish, but the other one was good.'

Paul might have flinched a little at that, but it wasn't as though he kicked off or anything. Instead he just got on with it, finished the track and everybody liked it – including Linda, who did a very good synth overdub on it. Overall, Steve and I felt good about the session as we drove home.

Hoping for lightning-in-a-bottle twice, we attempted another track a couple of weeks later, 'Figure of Eight', but this one was less successful. We were trying to stick to the same two-day routine, with it having worked so well on 'Rough Ride'; the trouble was that 'Figure of Eight' was a rock 'n' roll throwback thing and I never much liked rock 'n' roll. We changed the chords, so it ended up sounding more like U2 than Chuck Berry, but Paul wasn't sure about that. We left at the end of the session, and I think that one may have been subject to bit more tinkering from somebody other than us but, still, Paul must have enjoyed the experience overall, because he invited us to work on the forthcoming album, *Flowers in the Dirt* (1989). The trouble was that we were working with Simple Minds, who suddenly wanted to get their record finished. We couldn't make Paul McCartney until the middle of October.

I told Richard, Paul's manager, about the change of schedule and he said, 'Expect a call from his fabness.'

Paul got on the phone from the States and really started yelling at me: 'Who do you think you are? You think I need you? You're meant to be starting with me in August. You're telling me you can't start until mid-October?'

He was really going for it. So much so that I had to hold the phone away from my ear. I let the fire burn out and then said, 'Does this mean you don't want me to come in October?'

And with that, he banged down the phone.

I could see why Paul was cross, but in my defence, I had only ever signed up for doing things piecemeal, two days here, two days there. It wasn't as though I'd given him any assurances, I never committed to making an album.

Things calmed down and in October I went over to see him in his Cavendish Avenue home. As we sat chatting, I found myself marvelling at him. He was genuinely interested in me and what I was doing – a real rarity with famous people – and I saw, too, that he was very bright indeed. Years later, I read an interview with Gerry Marsden, who was a sweet guy. (I know he was a sweet guy because he called to thank me for doing 'Ferry Cross the Mersey' with the Frankies. 'Trevor, I've got a cheque here for £150 fucking grand and it's all because of you!' he'd said.) During this interview, Gerry had said, 'The difference between us and the Beatles was that the Beatles were intelligent; they'd been to art school,' and I saw that so clearly during that afternoon with McCartney. I saw the art student in him. He hides that a bit, I think, but it's there.

When Simple Minds wrapped, Steve and I returned to Rye and made a couple more songs with him. He took us out on his boat one afternoon, generous to a fault. And so while they say you should never meet your heroes, let alone produce for them (they don't say that second bit, but you know what I mean), my experience with Paul McCartney was on balance a good one.

McCartney is probably the biggest artist I've ever worked with (they really don't get bigger, do they?), but over the years I've been fortunate enough to work with a lot of people you might say are legends – Tom Jones, Tina Turner, Rod Stewart, Bryan Ferry. On the other hand, I've produced plenty of first-time artists – Kid Harpoon, Lee Griffiths, Mint Julep. There's good and bad with both. The downside of working with new artists is that sometimes their inexperience can get in the way, they don't quite understand what you're doing.

When Seal was starting out, 'we haven't got the record yet' was my common refrain and it took him a couple of albums to work out what I meant, which is that it's one thing having a song, but you have to turn that song into something you can play on the radio, and that's never truer than when you're making an album. To find one or two songs you like isn't easy, to find twelve is hard. But that's the job. I'm paid to take a song that somebody's written and improve upon it. Here's the thing: I know for certain that the first thing to happen when I try to make a song better is that it'll get worse. Because the way you get something better is to launch yourself at it. You think, *I'll do this, I'll do that, I'll do this, I'll do that*, and you do all those things, you try out all your ideas, you storm the beaches, and then you stand away from it for maybe a day or so, listen to it and realise that you've spoilt it. It's worse than it was before. Inexperienced bands reach for the razors at that point but I know that hidden in that storming-the-beaches version will be a good idea. And so I start another version where I incorporate that idea and work from that base until however much time was spent writing the song, at least ten times as much is spent rewriting it.

People who've been in the studio a lot understand. When I worked with Robbie Williams in 2009, I said to him, 'What hours do you like to work?' And he said, 'Friday,' which suited me fine. I'd work the other four days and then he came in on the Friday and because Robbie's experienced, he could say, 'I really like that and that, but I don't like that,' and we'd change it. We didn't have an argument over which way was the best. We both understood that it's a matter of taste. With the Pet Shop Boys we used to say, 'It's a strictly no-feel zone', meaning that everything had to be bang on. No rock-'n'-roll sloppiness. Yet if you did that for somebody else, they'd hate it. Some people love the edge and frisson of rock, some people don't. It's up to me to walk that line between the demands of the song and the demands of the artist. Integrity is relative.

It's also different making a single as opposed to an album. To produce an album for somebody, you have to really like them because you're going to be spending a shit-load of time together. Seal and I always got along well to a large degree because we both have the same love of innuendo and English humour and as I've said, the Pet Shop Boys were excellent companions, too.

Once Robbie had learned that my sessions weren't like normal boring sessions, and that actually it's a very open, creative atmosphere, he started to come in on days other than Friday, just for the crack. He liked the vibe in the studio, which I take as a compliment, because I always try to keep it nice, make sure everyone's being looked after and having a good time and being fed well. I tried being tough and assertive when I first started out, but it doesn't work for me. It might work for some, but the minute you start to make people afraid of telling you the truth, then you're fucked.

Which I guess brings us back to Paul McCartney, who over his many years in the business seemed to have intuitively absorbed all those lessons. It's why the only time he really lost his rag was over the Simple Minds thing, never once over a difference of musical opinion. I saw him again in 2010, when I was getting my honorary doctorate at the Liverpool Institute for Performing Arts, a couple of years after Jill's accident. He made a point of coming over and asking how she was. Like I say, a fundamentally lovely man.

18

'Belfast Child', Simple Minds (1989)

In which I go into loch down

As was so often the case back then, it was Jill who suggested I work with Simple Minds. From afar I had watched their progress, starting life as a post-punk band, gradually becoming more anthemic. What once was an urban soundscape was now more redolent of windswept clifftops, and by the late 1980s, they were a fully fledged stadium rock band. Mind you, I liked what I'd heard of that period. I loved 'Promise You a Miracle' and 'Waterfront'. I thought 'Don't You (Forget About Me)' was good, and I liked 'Alive and Kicking'. They all had a universal quality that I enjoyed, and in this regard were clearly giving U2 a run for their money – at home at least. Across the pond? Not so much. But I thought they had the raw materials to really break the US.

So we had a meeting, by which I mean that I spoke to their frontman, Jim Kerr, who along with guitarist Charlie Burchill was very much the heart and soul of Simple Minds. At that stage they also had the keyboard player Mick MacNeil with them – a third surviving member from the old days of the band – although Mick left in 1990. Anyway, we had this talk, during which I said, 'Have you guys ever thought of doing a folk song? Like, rearranging a folk song?' And Jim being Jim, very direct, very Glaswegian, growled, 'Like what? Which folk song?'

The reason I'd mentioned it was that I'd been listening to a lot of Irish folk at the time. It's always the way with me. I'm playing stuff looking for ideas, and more often than not I'll put those ideas into practice on whatever project blips on my radar. Debussy was like that. But since then I'd moved on to Irish folk and there was a particular song I liked called 'She Moves Through the Fair' a traditional Irish folk song that I suggested Jim should hear.

Things went quiet. I assumed that Simple Minds had found another producer. At the same time exploratory talks were being held with Paul McCartney, and Rod Stewart was on the horizon, too. A new, more 'heritage-focused' aspect of my career was about to start. So long, 12-inch mixes. But then I got a call from Jim. He said, 'That song that you told me to check out. It's working, we've come up with something. Why don't you come over and listen?'

Off I went to their rehearsal room, where they played me a song that was indeed inspired by 'She Moves Through the Fair'. A powerful, epic song about the Troubles in Northern Ireland, it was called 'Belfast Child'. It was good. From there we talked about making an album, their eighth. The band had bought a house by Loch Earn, a place called Lochearnhead, and started building a studio there. This was where they wanted to record the album, but because the studio wasn't quite ready, they'd booked another house beside another loch, Glenstriven.

First, though, we recorded the song, 'Mandela Day'. They were going to play it at the Nelson Mandela 70th Birthday Tribute concert at Wembley. We recorded it in one day in Studio One at SARM, where I persuaded the drummer, Mel Gaynor, to play with brushes, which gave it a slightly lighter touch. With that one in the bag, we then moved to Glenstriven.

To get to Glenstriven, you had to catch a plane to Glasgow, take a rented car to Dunoon, board the ferry and then drive 10 miles to your destination, but it was worth it. It was a beautiful house and had loads of rooms, including a snooker room, which always comes in handy when you're making an album.

We set up. Not unreasonably, I had expected Simple Minds to want to record much like a traditional rock band, all playing on real-life three-dimensional instruments. But no. It turned out that they were fine with programming stuff, nor were they bothered about having a drummer around. This to me felt like a problem: I thought the band needed to be playing together.

After a while, it became clear that they didn't want to play together for whatever reason, so I said to them, 'If you could pick any drummer to play with, who would you pick?' Stewart Copeland of the Police was the answer, a good answer, not least because I knew him and could call him: 'Stewart, do you fancy coming up to Scotland?'

Literally the next day, Stewart got on a plane for Scotland. I picked him up from the airport and then sat in as he chatted with Jim, Charlie and Mick for a day. Stuart was much too clever to actually play anything but suggested that they use a guy called Manu Katché who played with Peter Gabriel. In short order we hired Manu and he ended up playing on most of the album.

Hiccoughs aside, I enjoyed the process, and I especially liked Scotland. I'd return to London every weekend to see Jill, Ally and Aaron and then on Monday morning be on the plane back to Dunoon.

Workwise, we got a lot done. It turned out that the gatekeeper's wife at Glenstriven was a member of a little folk band and it's their flute and ocarina you hear at the beginning of 'Belfast Child'. We also recorded 'Street Fighting Years', for which Jim hadn't written any lyrics. Instead he was trying to improvise it, taking a sort of jive-singing approach. We got nowhere with that so I transcribed all eight of the jive vocal takes and edited together a lyric that he would sing – 'You've already written it. I've just put it in order for you,' I told him. It ended up working well. Sometimes you must do that as a producer. You hack a path through the forest. As I've already said, a producer's job is to make a record. You want to make a good record, but primarily it's just to make a record, and your job is to find a way of doing that.

From Glenstriven we moved to Lochearnhead. The studio was supposed to be ready but wasn't. The band stayed in a house next door while Steve Lipson and I were five minutes down the road in a log cabin. I didn't mind the log cabin. It was a bit basic, but once I worked out that you could warm the bed with a hair-dryer, I was fine.

The band spent a long time on guitar tracks with Charlie, which meant that for long periods there wasn't much for me to do apart from just 'be around'. Instead, I began to study the local railway system, which was now no longer in existence but had once been quite a transport hub. At one point, to much hilarity, I insisted that we all hike into the forest so I could show them an abandoned railway station. Nobody believed it would be there, but all came anyway and sure enough, I found the station in the middle of the woods. There it was, and it was amazing.

Lou Reed appears on the album on a song called 'This Is Your Land'. I didn't go and meet Lou. The band, who were all fans, went to Amsterdam to record him. Listening to the results, my first comment was, 'He's a bit out of tune,' which made them a little bit cross with me, so I just accepted that that was part of Lou's thing.

Work continued on the album, but I thought they were lacking a really big song. I knew 'Belfast Child' was good, don't get me wrong – it's often cited as Simple Minds' very best song, in fact – but I also thought it was too slow to put them in the U2 category, which after all was our aim. Personally, I thought that the band should have bided their time and recorded at least one more song, a bigger song. As I knew only too well, a big hit single can make a huge difference as to how well an album performs.

The trouble was that Steve didn't agree with me. Perhaps more importantly, the band disagreed with me as well. This was one of those moments that led to a parting of the ways where Steve and I decided that it might be better if he were to go off and pursue his own projects.

The thing was that Simple Minds were – and still are – a great bunch of people. Jim Kerr was so much fun to talk to and I thought he was a much better singer than he gave himself credit for. They were the first band I ever met who went out of their way to be kind and considerate to everyone around them, from the locals in Scotland – you should have seen the party they threw for them – to their record label, who loved them for it. They were not the sort of group I wanted to butt heads with. Same with Lippo, I didn't want to fall out with my right-hand man. So I began to back off. At the same time, Charlie Burchill was starting to get a bit feisty, convinced that I'd 'done something' to one of the tracks – 'I haven't touched it, Charlie, I'm not guilty, I haven't done anything on that track.' And with tensions running a little higher than I was comfortable with, I decided to let Steve finish the album. Jim got a bit cross with me about that, insisting I stay to mix 'Belfast Child', which I did, and when that was done, I sort of semi-bailed on it.

People have wondered if taking on Simple Minds was a deliberate move on my part to move away from the synthy sound with which I was identified, but nothing was deliberate back then and still isn't. There's no plan. Besides, unless you're the writer of the material as a producer, you don't really decide how the song's going to be done. The material decides itself. You must play to the strength of the song and the band. The one thing I'd say was deliberate was that when I'd finished one record, I was trying to do something different for the next one, if I could. Back then, I didn't want to be tied to ZTT. The trouble with owning a record label is that not everything sells. So for all kinds of reasons, some of them financial, I was actively seeking work outside of the label. One of those projects had been Paul McCartney, another was Simple Minds. And another . . .?

19

'Downtown Train', Rod Stewart (1989)

In which I discover that Tom Waits for no man

As the 1980s ended, I was restless. Steve Lipson and I had indeed had a parting of the ways and he'd gone off to be his own boss, leaving me to put together a new team. It wasn't easy, but Jill found an excellent keyboard player and programmer called George De Angelis from Greece and a new engineer for me to work with.

Rob Dickins, the head of Warner Brothers UK at the time, asked me to do a track with Rod Stewart for a greatest-hits package that Warner in the US was releasing. Rob, who has a great ear for songs, had come up with the idea of Rod covering 'Downtown Train', a song written by the cult singer-songwriter Tom Waits, which was a great idea that came with one major problem: we had very little time to do the single – about ten days.

I'd never met Tom Waits, but I knew that he was a gravel-voiced guy who looked like an intellectual vagrant. Resolutely uncommercial, his material was underproduced in a rather perverse way and the song 'Downtown Train' was tucked away in the middle of an album, *Rain Dogs* (1985), that I found difficult to listen to. Despite all that he has a huge and enthusiastic following, no doubt because he's one hell of a poet.

The song is about a man's love for a girl he sees on the train every morning and consists of two verses, two bridges, two choruses, a bit of aimless bashing around, and then a final chorus. After listening to it a couple of times I knew it could work for Rod; however, I felt like it needed a middle eight.

Tom Waits is one of those guys regarded as godlike by his people and the public at large, so there was an air of disbelief hanging around all concerned when I asked to talk to him about the structure of the song with a view to changing it. Finally, I was given the number of a hotel somewhere in Germany and told that he would take my call at 11 p.m. that evening. Our conversation was brief – Tom was no Buggles fan – he was a little startled that I was going to record his song with Rod the Mod and when I mentioned the middle eight, he gave a non-committal grunt. I wonder if he'd have been more friendly if he'd known he was going to earn over $1 million from Rod's version of his song. I found that out later because Tom was fighting a court case where he had to disclose his earnings. Either way, I never got a definitive answer about the middle eight.

This was 1989 and I had a small Compaq computer and a sound module, so I programmed a crappy version of the song into my computer with midi so I could change the key at will and met Rod on a Friday evening in Studio One at SARM. I'd been curious prior to that encounter, having grown up with his music in the Faces and as a solo artist, and he surprised me, because for some reason I'd always imagined him being a little fey and otherworldly. In fact, he was actually very fit and much stronger-looking in the flesh. As is so often the case with a bona-fide legend, he also turned out to be extremely charming.

We tried the song with Rod in a few different keys and in the end decided on G major, which is a great key for guitars. Rod said that, when his voice was in shape, he could sing higher and would prefer a higher key but, like an idiot, I didn't listen to him. His voice sounded pretty shagged and G seemed like it would be the best key for him. It was a decision that would come back to haunt me.

I asked Rod if he'd stay on and sing the song again in a few days' time, after we'd done a better backing track. At first he seemed keen on the idea, then later he said his current girl-friend would not allow him to be alone in England for one more day, so we made a plan to meet in a week in Los Angeles, the plan being that I would finish the backing track and bring it with me.

I booked us into Nomis Studios in Olympia to record the backing track. George De Angelis suggested a guitar player called Bill Lisengang from a band called Gas Attack. Synclavier lent me their new direct-to-disc system so we could play Rod's guide vocal back while we recorded the basic backing track.

We began on Monday and in the afternoon was when the calls from America started: an anxious Warner US constantly checking to see how the record was going. When you record a backing track, it's like a battle to find a way to do the usual musical clichés in a fresh way. It was taking me a while to get a handle on how to make the record and the calls weren't helping.

We spent a day playing the song and came up with some good ideas, but when I arrived on the Tuesday, George and my new engineer, Pete Schwier, had decided that the drums weren't tight enough, so they wanted to program a new rhythm track. I'd thought we could make real drums work but the real drums didn't sound very good. To make matters worse, George's computer decided to take a bit of a dive, so it took eight hours for him to program the drums. Of course, that was the perfect cue for me to get the worst phone call thus far. Lester Bangs, the legendary music journalist, was on the phone – he was penning sleeve notes for the album and there was no time for him to wait until the track was delivered. He had to write his review today. Was there any way I could play him the track down the phone?

'*Definitely not*,' I said.

'Well, what's it like? Can you give me an idea?'

'It's in bits at the moment, I'm sorry to say.'

'Could I hear it tomorrow?'

'Maybe, but it's going to be good,' I said, somewhat half-heartedly, making a mental note not to take that call.

'Okay, I'll give it a great review, but it better be good or you'll be in trouble.'

I don't think he regretted that review.

Next thing, Rob Dickins was on the phone, firing questions at me. 'How's it going? Can I hear it, just a bit of it?' Encouraging as he was, his neck was on the block. The song was his idea and it was costing a lot of money.

Next on the line came Michael Ostin from LA. Michael was the son of Mo Ostin, who was head of Warner US at the time. Mo was one of the best record company executives I've ever worked with. He had a very realistic way of looking at records: he would never schedule an album until it was finished. That might not sound like much, but it makes a difference because

the most common mistake of any artist who's had a successful album is to rush out a sub-standard follow-up just to meet
a record company deadline. Mo avoided all that by not giving them one. Anyway, it was Michael, his son, on the phone,
wanting to know about the song: 'How does it sound? It's very
expensive. We hope it's good. Lester Bangs says he's writing a
great review of it. Can I hear a bit down the phone?'

All this time I had no intro and the drums were still being programmed. I started to get nervous, wondering why I'd agreed to
do this.

———————

I went back into the studio. George De Angelis was still programming the drums, but he'd had an idea and played me
something on a synth that would fit the first verse. It was just a
little bit of fake strings, but it was like somebody had opened a
window. I loved it. George said we'd need a real orchestra and
woodwind to pull it off and I agreed with him. The problem was
that this was Tuesday evening and I was booked on a plane to
LA on Saturday morning. I got back on the phone to Rob, for
whom it must have been nerve-wracking to get a call at home
from a frantic producer, but credit to him, he agreed a budget
for the strings. I hired John Altman to do the arranging and we
organised the session for Thursday evening at Angel Studios in
Islington.

The strings came out beautifully. Putting strings on a record
can be a harrowing experience, but John Altman had done a
beautiful arrangement based on George's ideas – a lovely motif
with plaintive woodwind and soaring strings weaving around

the melody. I sat out in the studio while the orchestra were performing their parts and marvelled at how forty-five people can play so perfectly together.

We finally finished about 7 a.m. on Saturday morning. Almost overwhelmed by tiredness, I nevertheless felt a strange combination of confidence and nerves. After all, Rod hadn't heard our backing track yet but I was fairly sure that he would like it. There was also the fact that I'd never worked in LA before – the closest I'd got was playing at the Spectrum there with Yes.

When you fly to Los Angeles from London you leave at lunchtime and arrive mid-afternoon after eleven hours in the air. Luckily I didn't have to check into a hotel; my buddy Lol Creme had just moved to LA to direct commercials and invited me to stay with him at his house in Laurel Canyon, on a road called Grand View Drive. The view from his house was spectacular, with the whole of LA from Century City to Downtown LA spread out below in a sprawling network of streets, high rises, palm trees, green spaces and swimming pools, all wreathed in a light fuzz of smog.

As it had been absolutely years since I had been anyone's house guest, I felt a little uncomfortable at first, but when I asked Lol about a cup of tea (it was his butler's day off), he gesticulated vaguely in the direction of the kitchen, so I took over and made the tea and organised dinner; once I knew my place, I was fine.

Lol was emphatic about one thing: when you come to LA you must drive, so I rented a Rabbit convertible, which is like an American version of the VW Golf. He also explained that driving in LA is like being on a conveyor belt – just make sure that you're on the right belt and you're dandy.

A&M was a beautiful studio and was in its heyday at the time. It turned out that Rod was already in Studio B recording vocals, while I was based in Studio A. Rod had sent one of the assistants for a copy of the backing track so he could listen in Studio B and I nervously began to set up my little computer while the engineer put up the multi-track. More people came in to greet me, and then Rod rang on the internal phone: 'Fuckin' great backin' track, sounds like the fuckin' *Titanic* going down.' I was so relieved. 'I'll be over to sing it in about 'arf an hour,' he added.

You can't imagine how much better I felt. We set up Rod's preferred vocal mic and waited. He showed up, pumped with enthusiasm. Everything seemed to be going great . . . Right up until the moment that it stopped going great.

The arrangement we'd done began with an orchestra and oboe for five bars, after which Rod was meant to come in with the first verse. Most songs have an intro that is either four or eight bars long, but I'd made this one five bars because the orchestra and oboe played a motif and then paused, hence the five bars. The fifth bar was just the orchestra sustaining the last chord. I'd done this because I have a particular thing about intros – I don't like them to be in the same perfect time as the rest of the song. To me that makes the song sound like someone reading a catalogue. So even though the intro of 'Downtown Train' was perfectly in time, it hung on that last chord for an extra bar and this gave it the appearance of being not in the same time as the song. The opening line was 'outside another yellow moon', which Rod sang, and then stopped.

'Outside another yellow moon . . . fuck it, outside another fuckin' yellow, what the fuck you doing putting a five-bar intro on this song? I'm an R&B singer, I never sing anything with a five-bar intro, this isn't Yes! What the fuck are you doing, Trevor Horn, putting a five-bar intro on song like this?' All this was said good naturedly, but I was starting to get nervous again. Still, he navigated the faux five-bar intro, sang the song through once and then dropped the bomb: 'Great backing track, Trev, but it's in the wrong key.'

I asked him what key he'd like it in, and with me playing the piano he decided on the key of B flat major, three semitones higher than the key of G. I must have been in shock. What could I do about the orchestra? Three semitones make a whole lot of difference. Nowadays we have software that can transpose the pitch of a piece of music without completely ruining it, but this was 1989 – very early days of anything like that. Rod departed, saying he'd send Arnold Stiefel, his manager, to talk to me.

Managers of rock stars come in many different shapes and sizes and are of variable quality. Rod's manager Arnold is a tall, well-built guy and probably the best artist manager (apart from Bob Cavallo) that I'd ever worked with up to that point. Steve MacMillan, Rod's recording engineer at that time, told a story about Arnold that has stuck with me to this day. Steve was hired to record vocals for Rod and spent three difficult days trying to get something decent on tape. He said that Rod was unhappy constantly about the sound of his voice, really putting Steve through the mill. He'd tried different microphones and different pre-amps but still Rod wasn't happy and called in Arnold, who listened for a couple of minutes and then said to Rod, 'It's not Steve, it's you, you're singing badly.' To anyone not used to dealing with stars it's difficult to understand how this kind of honesty is very rare. It would have been so easy for an inexperienced manager to hang the engineer out to dry. It's also a testament to Rod that he could take that kind of input without throwing a complete wobbler. When I look back at all the subsequent work I did with Rod, I don't remember him ever throwing a tantrum – he could be a bit grumpy, but he was never a diva.

So anyway, when Arnold arrived at A&M studios and told me the bad news, 'He won't sing it. It's definitely in the wrong key, what are we going to do? Have you got it in you to fix it? We can help in every way possible because he likes the backing track and still wants to do the song,' I knew that it wasn't just a craven manager agreeing with his client.

I called Rob Dickins in London. He loved the version of the song we'd done in G major and he thought that Rod could be persuaded to stick with, but I knew in my heart that Rod was right. His voice had sounded different this time around and his words from that very first time we'd met rang in my ears. Thus, Monday morning found me in Studio A with a cadre of LA's best session musicians re-recording 'Downtown Train'. It took us all of Monday to record a new backing track, but that still left us the problem with the orchestra. Since LA is the place where most of the major feature films are made, I was sure there must be a device that would change the pitch of the orchestra without destroying the sound quality. Turns out I was right. A French company called Publison made a thing called the Infernal Machine which the movie people used to manipulate dialogue. I rented one, and by Tuesday afternoon we'd managed to pitch most of the orchestra up to B flat. By now the whole multitrack was a bit like a colander, lots of holes in it. It didn't have the magic of the original track in G, but I was working on it with Kevin Savigar, Rod's then-keyboard player (now his producer), filling in bits of the orchestra with synthesisers, so it would have to do for now.

Rod came in to sing the song again, now with me by his side counting in the intro, and the results were so much better. Rod was in great voice and he sang the song five or six times. Apart from a note at the end, I was confident we had it.

This note was in the last chorus and it was a very high note. Rod left this until last and when he'd sung everything else addressed himself to it. He asked for a mike stand to hold, which he referred to as a 'farting post'. We rolled the track and Rod gripped his farting post with both hands then threw his whole body back as he sang the high note. It was a Rod moment I will always treasure.

I spent a couple of hours putting together the best of the different takes and when Rod came back from dinner, he was really pleased with his vocal. I stayed up for the rest of the night sorting out all the little problems in the backing track with a young in-house engineer. We were reclaiming more and more bits of the original version as we learned to work the Infernal Machine better. Steve was going to mix it the next day, so I wanted to give him a good clean multi-track with no choices, just push up the faders and you hear the record. I handed it over to him at 8 a.m. and made my way back up into the hills to Lol's house, where at last, I laid my head down.

I woke up at about 5 p.m. and made my way straight into the studio to a pleasant surprise: Steve MacMillan had the track sounding great. It's very rare that someone mixes a track that I've worked on without me there and, when they do, I generally don't like the mix, but this was the opposite, I loved it. Steve had done some pretty drastic things to the sound of the song in a couple of places: he'd triggered more American-sounding drum samples from George's drums – they sounded fantastic – and the middle, which had been a big problem since we changed the key, now sounded terrific. When I first heard the song, I'd said that the middle was just a bit of 'bashing around' and I'd tried to get Tom to write a middle eight. Well, now the middle eight was a huge bit of 'bashing around' – I'd tried to make it sound like a subway train going through a tunnel and Steve had got that effect by using mega amounts of compression and massive sampled tom toms at the end of it. The finale of the song, where I'd let the English and now the American musicians mess around, lasted about sixty seconds and was really very beautiful.

Michael Ostin and Arnold Stiefel came in to listen to the finished track and they were both thrilled. Rod came in and loved it, too, so it was one of those amazing and very rare moments when everyone liked everything. Or so I thought.

First thing Monday morning, Rob Dickins was on the phone: he didn't like the mix. He didn't really like the version of the song in B flat, but he most definitely didn't like the mix. This was my first real taste of the inter-company rivalry that was endemic in Warner in those days. I think because the Americans were now so happy with 'Downtown Train', Rob may have felt that something had been taken away from him. It's always a bit of a shock to hear your idea in a different country and in a different key so I had some sympathy for him.

In the end, 'Downtown Train' made it to number two in the Billboard top 100 and the $50 anthology boxed set that Warner Bros had expected to sell about 50,000 copies sold 500,000. All in all, not a bad ten days' work.

I didn't realise at the time what a difference this record had made to the power structure at Warners. Mo Ostin invited me to lunch a couple of months later and made a very delicate reference to Rob being very happy with the success of 'his idea'. What I didn't know was that Mo was on the way out and Rob was on the way in – all the way to the top job at Warner Bros in America.

20

'Crazy', Seal (1990)

In which life imitates art

Jill, who often spoke of finding a modern-day Nat King Cole, appeared with a cassette one day and played me 'Crazy' (or it might have been 'Krazy' at that stage) by Seal. It was just a demo and not a very impressive one at that. Although I liked the lyrics, especially the chorus, I couldn't really tell whether Seal was a good singer, not least because somebody had seen fit to put his voice through a phaser.

'Go for it,' I told Jill, who was probably going to go for it anyway, no matter what I said.

As she was trying to sign Seal, 'Killer' was rocketing up the charts – all the way to number one, in fact. Now, under most circumstances, it would be next to impossible for a small label like ZTT to sign someone who had a hit that big. But the majors didn't hear what Jill had heard. In fact, they didn't see Seal as a talent at all; they were focused solely on Adamski. Someone at the record label had offered Seal £10,000 to sign but he protested that they didn't know his music and that it wasn't enough. They threatened to take him off the record and Seal told them to go fuck themselves. (And, of course, they didn't take him off the record.)

Jill loved that. Her ardour increased and so it was arranged for Seal to come into the studio and meet me. At the time I was working on a Terry Reid song called 'Fifth of July', which is a lovely track. Terry's a hell of a singer but difficult to record because of the dynamic range of his voice. So I was mixing this song in Studio Four at SARM, when Jill called from reception and said, 'I'm sending Seal in to meet you. You're gonna love him.'

In he came. Seal is 6 foot 5 and on this occasion wore Cuban-heel boots and his hair in upright, beaded dreads. All in all, there must have been about 7 foot of Seal in the room. It turned out that he knew a good voice when he heard one: 'This guy's great,' he said, meaning Terry Reid. This was an encouraging start. The good artists are confident enough in their own ability that they don't get jealous of other artists. The *really* good ones are happy and secure enough to compliment another's work.

Next, I discovered that we both had the same favourite female singer, Dionne Warwick, in common, by which time I was completely warming to him. 'I've just written this song,' he said. 'I'd love to play it to you. Have you got a cassette player? I've got a backing track on a cassette.'

We went down to the SARM copy room, a tiny space at the back of reception which had multiple cassette decks and a set of small speakers. On came the backing track to what would later become 'Violet' from the first album, *Seal*, and Seal began to sing over the top of it.

Now, I listen to songs all the time, and it's rare for anything to get straight through to me. Sure, there are a few of them in this book, but that's why I've chosen them, and for every one within these pages there are a thousand that left me cold. Don't forget even the demo of 'Crazy' did little for me. But, when Seal sang these two verses from 'Violet', I was struck on three or four different levels. The first thing I thought was, *Fuck me, this guy's got a brilliant voice*, and the second was, *And he can really write*. There was something very moving and poetic about it.

Seal's no mug. He could tell he'd got me. Next, he sang, 'Don't Call Me N-gger, Whitey', which as a Sly Stone fan kind of took my breath away a bit. He continued with more Sly Stone songs, and by now I was in love: I had to get this guy in front of a mic.

Jill began to make moves to sign him. Seal's then-manager had reservations about me producing 'Crazy' and told Seal that if I got my mitts on his music I'd bland it out. Even so, Jill plugged away, fielding various demands, one of which was that Seal wanted 'Crazy' as his first solo single, plus he wanted to work with the guy who had produced the demo, Guy Sigsworth.

By the time that he eventually signed I like to think that Seal had really taken to Jill. I mean, I loved Jill, obviously. She was my wife and the mother of my children. But you had to get to know her. She could be pretty tough but she also could be amazingly charming. I like to think that Seal saw in her what I saw in her.

True to the stipulation, Seal disappeared off to record 'Crazy' with Guy Sigsworth at Beethoven Street Studios in west London. Obviously, I was disappointed that I wasn't working with him right away, but maybe I'd get my chance in the future.

About three weeks into it, Jill told me to swing by Beethoven Street and see how they were getting on, so I bowled up to find Seal sitting around bored stiff and Guy Sigsworth beavering away on the track, but making no real progress. I suggested they listen to what they'd done at SARM, which at that time had far better playback sound than Beethoven Street. Guy was suspicious, I could tell he thought I was making a grab for the track, but still, in they came.

During the playback session I sat down at the desk and did something I hadn't done for ages: I pushed the faders. When Seal was singing the verse, because he was singing quite low, I took the reverb off his voice and pushed him up front quite dry. I'd done something similar with Rod Stewart: I'd put his voice bone dry at the front of the track, with no reverb at all, and it sounded great. You can do that with singers like Seal and Rod, their voices are a full-frequency item. As it was with Rod, so it was with Seal. I kept it dry and then, when it hit the chorus, or when he went up an octave, I pulled his voice back a bit and put reverb on it.

Seal loved it. It was just a way of presenting the voice on the track, but I knew that I'd made inroads and that he wasn't as suspicious of me as he was before.

Meanwhile, Jill wasn't happy with how the record was going and thought we should hire a new producer. Should I step in? Not yet. It wasn't my time. Instead we hired Tim Simenon from Bomb the Bass, who had also produced 'Buffalo Stance' for Neneh Cherry, a huge hit. Tim came on board and right away contributed a great idea, which was the big drum break in the middle of the song. I was very enthused by that, but Tim, for some reason, bailed. I don't know why. He left me with 170 tracks of audio – but no finished song.

I decamped to LA for three months in order to work on a film that Lol Creme was making, *The Lunatic*. I'd rented a house that was meant to be $20,000 a month but they'd had no takers, so I managed to get it for $10,000 a month for three months, which was pretty good.

It was a lovely house. George Clooney lives there now. I freaked the owners by shifting furniture out of the huge ballroom on the very day I moved in. I don't know how they found out, but they turned up with worried looks on their faces, and I had to convince them that I was exercising great care and had even taken Polaroids of the way the furniture had been arranged, so that it could go back in the right place.

Next, I had tons of equipment flown over from England and set up my studio in the ballroom. I was meant to be working on the film but I quit after a couple of weeks because the producer didn't like my style and got stuck into 'Crazy' instead, going through all 170 tracks of Tim's audio, keeping some of it, tidying it up, trying to find order among the chaos. I hired a guy called Mark Mancina, a keyboard and guitar whizz who later ended up writing half of *The Lion King*. Thanks to that, he's as rich as Croesus now, but back then he was just starting out. Together, he and I worked on a new version of 'Crazy'. I was able to do it without Seal because I had the vocals as well as all the stuff that Tim Simenon had done and we got to a point where it was supposedly finished. It was faster than the eventual version, and it was in a different key, but it was still good, recognisably the song you know today.

Shortly after that, I had a visit from Michael Ostin and I played him 'Crazy'. Although his reaction was broadly positive, it wasn't . . . *great*. The thing is that Americans don't mess around with records. Promotion costs them hundreds of thousands of dollars and there's no way they commit that kind of money to a project they doubt. And because there's so much at stake, they tend to really know what they're talking about. So I realised from his lack of enthusiasm that 'Crazy' just wasn't quite good enough.

I started working on another version, this one modelled on productions by Jam & Lewis, especially their work with Janet Jackson. Then I got on the phone to Seal and asked him to come to LA. He wasn't keen on the idea – his manager once again told him that if he came to America, I would suck him into my big machine and bland him out – but Jill, of course, was able to persuade him and he agreed to get on a plane.

Meanwhile, I'd got some new software, SoundTools, that allowed me to load a digital mix into my computer that I could edit myself. Up to that point, the only way that you could ever edit audio was on tape. You marked it with chalk, cut it with a razor blade. This stuff was a revolution and meant I could really attend to the main thing that I had decided was wrong with 'Crazy', which was the arrangement.

Seal finally arrived. He came to the house, and half an hour later, the doorbell rang, I answered, and it was one of the tallest, most beautiful women I'd ever seen. She said, 'Is Henry here?' To a lot of people Seal was called Henry. 'Yes, he's here,' I said. Seal came out, greeted her, they went off into his room and that was it. I hardly saw him for days.

During one of their breaks, I played him this version of 'Crazy' that sounded a bit like Janet Jackson. He listened to it and said, 'Trevor, look at me. Do you think I could move to a track like that?'

I did as asked: I played the track again, looked at him. He looked big and strong, my track sounded weak and poppy. You're right,' I said, shaking my head, 'it's totally wrong.'

Back to square one, where I realised that I wasn't going to get anywhere by making the track more poppy. I had to find another way. In the meantime, I'd hired a Australian Fairlight operator called Mars Lasar for the film. I played him 'Crazy', he dug it, and we started work on a new version.

First, I slowed the song down from 108 bpm to 105, and to make up for it being slower, I took the key up a semitone, going from E-flat to E. There was a section in the old version where the chords changed and Seal ad-libbed some doo-doo thing, so I asked him if he could write a lyric for that bit. He did me proud by coming up with a whole section – 'In a sky full of people, only some want to fly, isn't that crazy?', which I thought was terrific.

I had been working on the arrangement of the song in SoundTools and one night I found a way to add an extra bar to our new middle eight and go back into, 'Ah, but we're never gonna survive. . .', in a really exciting way. We had a climax.

I was jubilant.

We were working on 'Crazy' full time in the ballroom and it was a fun time. Chrissy Shefts, a local guitar player, played my Rickenbacker twelve-string on the track and we would catch Seal coming back from a date at 3 a.m. and get him singing to who-ever he was with, the track blasting out into the California night. I kept all the things that were good about the original version: Guy's great synthesiser programming and Tim Simenon's big wild drum section in the middle.

One night I came back to the house after dinner and there were a bunch of security cars outside, red lights whirling. Entering the house, I saw two security-patrol guys with guns in their hands, Seal spread-eagled on the floor and Mars Lasar standing close by with his hands raised.

I was furious. 'Why have you got this guy on the floor and not him? And why have you got him on the fucking floor anyway? This man is my guest in my house.' They were a bit sheepish about it, and Seal was totally cool, but I was upset for him. Somebody had set off a burglar alarm and they'd come charging in, weapons drawn.

I had to return to England because the rent was up on the house, but when I listened to 'Crazy' at home, it just didn't sound as good. It's a common problem: something that sounds cool in one place doesn't sound so great in another. In my new environment I realised that while 'Crazy' was good, it was sloppy, and this was a fault of the Fairlight, which was a generation 3 Fairlight, notorious for being out of time. We couldn't get anything to lock to the track.

I was in the wars a bit, thinking, *For God's sake, how long is this record going to take?* Until I was saved by a guy called Robin Hancock, who was one of our tape ops at SARM West. He was unusual because he'd already had a career in advertising and was that bit older than our usual tape ops, more like thirties compared to twentysomething.

'We can fix it,' he said. 'We've just got to rebuild it.'

He and I set to work transferring 'Crazy' from analogue to two digital machines, during which time we recreated it and made it all much tighter. It was a long process, like taking a car completely to pieces and reconstructing it, and we did that over a period of about a fortnight.

It still wasn't quite right. Maybe it needed bass? Someone invited me to a session and the bass player was Dougy Wimbish, who was the bassist in the Sugarhill Gang and Living Colour. When the session finished, I drove him to SARM, where he played a lovely bass part on the middle eight.

A musician called Richard Cottle came in and helped me build a new, slightly abstract, intro for the record. Still, 'Crazy' was not quite there. By this time I had about fifty rough mixes of the song at various stages of its incarnation. We had to name all the mixes so by now they were called things like, 'Really Crazy Now', 'Even More Crazy' and the latest one was called simply 'Aaaaaarrrrrgh'. Seal was long gone by now – he'd thought it sounded good weeks ago. But I was so paranoid that in the end, I called in the cavalry: Jill. She came to the studio on a Saturday night and I played her a selection of mixes, ending up with 'Aaaaarrrrrgh'.

'That's the one. Mix that one,' she said, so I did, and during the mix I did the same thing I'd done in Studio One, where we had Seal dry in the verse and then pushed him up and put reverb on him in the chorus.

I summoned Jill. She listened to the new mix: 'Where's his voice? You think I've paid all this money just to hear your fucking backing track? He needs to be louder.'

We pushed him up in the verse and she said, 'Nah, that's not loud enough. Louder than that.'

We pushed up the fader.

'No, louder.'

We pushed more.

'Yes, that's better.'

The mix engineer, Tony Phillips, jumped up from the control board and started pacing around, muttering to himself about amateurs. The thing is that if you put the voice really loud, it weakens the backing track. You have to do something to the backing track or you're left with half a song. I sent Jill home and set to work with Tony to repair the damage.

In the end we used two compressors on the track. A compressor is something that artificially holds the level of something. It doesn't let it go too far up or too far down; it holds it at a constant point. We compressed the backing track and then put Seal's voice on top of that and compressed both of them through an old Fairchild Compressor, which is an old valve compressor from the early 1950s.

In all, we used more compression than I'd ever used on anything else before, but what it meant was that while Seal was singing, his voice dominated the track. The minute he stopped; the compressors pushed the track right back up. I'd used it on 'City of Love' on *90125* and you can hear how the second the band stops playing, the whole track leaps out at you because of the compression. Obviously, it's got its downside. It takes out some of the dynamics of your track and whenever I hear 'Crazy' now, I can hear the compression, particularly in the middle. But overall, the benefits outweigh the negatives – certainly in this case.

I had my record – at last. And it did well. Rob Dickins did a terrific job of marketing and distributing the record, and it practically strolled up the hit parade to number two, its highest position, and spent fifteen weeks in the charts altogether. The subsequent album was a smash – three weeks at number one – and I've made several albums with Seal since. He remains my favourite artist to work with. That year I won Best British Producer for the third time and Seal won Best Male Vocal and Best Album at the BRITs.

The success of Seal cushioned the impact of what was happening with ZTT. By this time we'd lost Art of Noise, Propaganda and Frankie, and even Paul Morley had flown the coop. With him went most of ZTT's unique character. At least I had the comfort of winning a Grammy with Seal for 'Kiss from a Rose' from his second album. Warners had bought half of the label in 1990, but it became pretty apparent to Jill and I that they weren't really going to help us build it up. What they really wanted was to grab whoever was good (for which read 'successful') on the label.

What happened next was loads of infighting at Warners, much of it involving the renegotiation of a deal with Seal. We were caught in the middle so we flew out to LA and talked to the guy running Warner at the time who, it turned out, had never heard of ZTT and thought that Seal was a Warner Brothers artist. Suffice to say, there was a court case that ended with us getting the catalogue back. But they kept Seal.

It was a difficult time. During all of that, we were making Seal's third album, *Human Being*, which was the toughest of the four to make. He and I fell out in the middle of it and I didn't work on it for ten months, but Seal called me and we made up and finished the album together. We never fell out again.

Major record labels have a budget for A&R. Every year they'll spend a certain amount of their turnover on new acts, but they rely on their catalogue and maybe their three or four big artists to make the real money. When you're trying to get a record label going you might have a year before you find anything that's worth doing, and if you've got staff, the temptation to sign something is huge, just to give everybody something to do, which ends up with you spending a load of money. So I guess that's what gradually wore ZTT down and, in the end, it was sold. I sold everything to Universal. The end of an era? I suppose so. But what an era it was.

21

'Can't Fight the Moonlight', LeAnn Rimes (2000)

In which I have my big Hollywood moment

The musical comedy-drama *Coyote Ugly* (2000) was not my first experience of working for Hollywood. That honour goes to the Robin Williams' film *Toys* in 1992, where Hans Zimmer and I collaborated on a whole bunch of songs and I contributed an exclusive Frankie remix. But it remains the one that really sticks in my head. Why?

Coyote Ugly is about a women, Violet, played by Piper Perabo, who dreams of being a successful songwriter while working as a dancer at the eponymous New York bar. The makers needed a producer for the incidental songs which were being written by Diane Warren, but then they also thought that I might be able to write the score, which would later prove more difficult for me. My first twenty or so attempts at orchestrating cues were knocked back. I ended up gaining an even deeper respect for Hans, during that period.

The movie was produced by Jerry Bruckheimer, who produced *Flashdance*, *Beverly Hills Cop* and *Armageddon*, which meant that it was very much a prestige production. Sure enough, one of the first things that happened was that they flew me out to New York, where I was put up in the Trump Tower Hotel. On the day after my arrival, I was ferried up to New Jersey along with a bunch of film executives and Jerry himself. We congregated in a Winnebago to discuss the score and play music. Then, as we were driving back in our people carrier, one of the guys in the van said to me, 'Your plane's tonight at 9 p.m., but I booked you two nights in the Trump Tower so you can go back there.'

I said, 'Oh no, don't worry. I checked out.'

He gave a start. 'Why did you do that?'

'Because I didn't want to waste any money.'

A big New Yorker, built like a line-backer, he looked at me incredulously. His name was Pat Sandston. I didn't know at the time that he was head of post-production for Bruckheimer and therefore Jerry's main hatchet man: 'You were trying to save Bruckheimer money?'

'Yeah.'

'Who taught you that?'

'My wife and I have a company. We never waste money if we can help it.'

'Buddy,' he said, 'put it there.'

He was so pleased that I'd saved his boss from paying extra that he booked me a limo and driver so I could spend a day sightseeing around New York. And, from then on, I became really good friends with him.

As the shoot began, I was on the set the whole time, overseeing musical cues and coaching Piper Perabo in how to mime keyboards and vocals. Whenever you see Piper in the finished movie singing or playing, even when she's up on a roof, what you don't see is me, about 3 feet away from her, conducting her to mime playing the keyboard. That, alone, was an experience.

We recorded four Diane Warren songs with Donna Lewis, a lovely Welsh singer, and they were sounding good. The score was written and recorded in two bedrooms of my house in LA by me, the brilliant keyboard player Jamie Muhoberac, who played on all the Seal albums, and an English guy, Gary Hughes, who was a keyboard player as well as a good writer.

There was an interesting ritual. We would get a scene with temp score on it. We would do something in that vein to replace this temp score, then every couple of days I would go into Bruckheimer Productions and in a room with Bob Badami, the music editor on the film (who I adored), Pat and Jerry and the director of the film, David McNally, we would listen to the results.

Jerry would listen to our score then the temp score (done by Bob using all kinds of suitable score from other films) and then ours again. If he liked it, it was a lock. The director would sometimes try to interject but Pat made sure that if Jerry liked it, that was it. After some earlier failures and nearly being fired off the score, we started to get the hang of it. But I felt as though something was missing from the film.

Jerry was always very approachable. I went in to see him: 'Look, Jerry, I've been watching the film and what's missing is an idea of how moving to New York changes the way she writes. She'd be absorbing all kinds of different styles of music. Hip hop, for a start.'

'How would we show that, Trevor?'

'Well, maybe she could be on the roof. She hears some rap music from across the way. The beat suits one of her songs and she starts to sing the song over the rap music?'

'Record it and let me hear it.'

A month later, I was flown to New York for the shooting of the scene, and I've got to say, it was an incredible night. We were up on a roof in Little Italy, which was meant to be the exterior of the girl's apartment. Piper had her keyboard and a coat on. There were fifty people on that roof and a big balloon above the street with lots of massive lights shining on it. Through a window at the opposite side of the street you could see a guy breakdancing to the rap track. They shot the scene at 4 a.m. and they had to do it a few times. The poor guy dancing in the room across the street was exhausted, he kept flagging and they would shout down the radios, 'Dance! Dance!'

I was standing with one of the producers who was overseeing the whole thing. 'Isn't this costing you a fortune in overtime?' I asked.

'No one on this set is going to charge Bruckheimer overtime,' he said. Very loudly, probably so those fifty people could hear.

So anyway, they finished the film, and we flew down to Phoenix for an audience preview. It was a disaster. The audience didn't hate it, but they laughed where they were meant to cry and vice versa. It was such a disaster, in fact, that the director, who had flown down on the Disney corporate jet, came back with us on normal scheduled airlines. Pat Sandston, the hatchet man who had appreciated my budgeting skills, sat beside me on the flight.

'You don't look worried, Pat,' I said to him. 'I mean, that wasn't a good preview.'

'This is when you're going to see Bruckheimer at his best. You watch us take this turkey of a movie and make it into a successful film,' he told me.

'How are you going to do that?'

He said, 'Watch.'

The people at Disney didn't like Donna Lewis or the end song, 'Fine Now'. To be honest, I'd never liked the song myself but was overruled. In film, you get overruled, you must be a team player. I once said to Hans Zimmer, 'What do you do if you don't like the film you're working on?' to which he'd replied, 'You do everything you can to make the film better, that's all you can do.'

Fortunately, the songwriter who had written the rejected song, the great Dianne Warren, was keen to keep hold of the main song of the movie, and so wrote a much better one called 'Can't Fight the Moonlight'. That was a huge step forward. At this point we were trying to get LeAnn Rimes – a singer I didn't know – to do the lead vocal and be Piper Perabo's singing voice in the film. While that was happening, I decided to go home to see Jill and the kids and was in the Upper Class lounge in LA Airport, booked on to the flight ready to go, when I got one of those, 'Paging, Mr Trevor Horn, paging. . .', which meant I had to find a phone.

It was Kathy Nelson, the music supervisor on the film.

'Where are you?'

'In the airport lounge,' I said. 'I'm going back to London.'

'We've got hold of LeAnn Rimes and she can see you tomorrow.'

My heart sank. It was too important to miss. I had to retrieve my luggage and return my boarding pass. Home would have to wait.

I met LeAnn Rimes at my house. 'Are you going to do all the songs?' I asked her. There were four originals sung by Violet in the film.

'No,' she sniffed. 'I'll just do "Can't Fight the Moonlight". I don't like the other songs.'

I played her my versions of the other three songs: 'They sound better than the versions I heard,' she said.

This was encouraging but what sealed the deal was – amazingly – her boyfriend. Now, under normal circumstances, a female artist's boyfriend is the producer's natural enemy. They tend to get jealous about the influence a producer has over their girlfriend and thus try to undermine him while simultaneously asserting themselves. Not this guy. This was a boyfriend sent from heaven, because just as I was wondering how I could possibly talk her into doing all four songs, he pipes up with, 'Well, I think you're stupid. I'd do all four songs if I were you. I mean, Jerry Bruckheimer's basically spending $80 million doing a video for you.'

So she signed on to do all four songs and was amazing. The first number she sang was 'Can't Fight the Moonlight'. After her first run-through I said to her, 'You look too young. Where the hell did you learn to sing like that?' and she told me that she'd been fronting her own band since she was eleven. She performed it three times then left. I put her vocal together and sent it to her. The next time she arrived, she said, 'I listened to what you did with the three takes. Do you mind if I sing it again?'

LeAnn sang it again. She remembered all the changes and did it in one take. I've got to tell you it is rare in this business that somebody is that sussed. This led on to one of the best moments I ever had in Hollywood. I'm sure everybody who goes and works there has their big moment where they think they've cracked it and here's mine. It involved 'Can't Fight the Moonlight' and it went like this . . .

As she was doing all four songs, LeAnn wanted me to work with her normal guys instead of mine, and her engineer sent us a diagram of the equipment that they used to record her voice. We'd already recorded one song, 'Can't Fight the Moonlight', but this was to record the rest. That session was meant to start at 2 p.m. at a studio in the Valley, but although LeAnn turned up, there was no sign of her people. However, we followed their instructions and set up what we call a vocal chain, which is a whole bunch of equipment for recording her voice. It sounded awful. My engineer Tim was, like, 'What do you want me to do? This is what they've said it's meant to be.'

'We can't use it,' I told him. 'Let's just do what we normally do.'

I've got this piece of gear called an Avalon. I've had it for years. It's like a good mic, pre-amp and compressor all in one. I love it because it's simple, certainly much simpler than the vocal chain LeAnn's team wanted to use, which had two compressors, an EQ and various other bits and pieces. So we started recording her with our Avalon and were about forty-five minutes into that when her team, who were flying up from Texas, burst into the studio: 'I'm so sorry we're late,' they said breathlessly. And 'Oh, and that diagram we sent you was all wrong.'

'We figured that out,' I said, 'so we changed it.'

A situation like this has the potential to go south quickly. You're the big-name producer but they're the team who normally work with the talent. There can be friction. But as it turned out, they were lovely, and they loved the tracks, and once again I was thanking my lucky stars for LeAnn having agreeable associates. I nicknamed them 'The Texas Rangers' and they took up residence in the studio. There was her engineer and her programmer who seemed to be always on his laptop, but they really liked the backing tracks I had done. Everything was going fine.

Meanwhile, Team Bruckheimer had started to re-edit the film. There was a scene between Violet and her father, played by John Goodman, that they redubbed. Jerry always makes his directors shoot lots of coverage, so you take the same scene, but this time you cut to a shot from behind John Goodman and overdub the dialogue. For rewrites they had brought in Paul Schrader, who wrote *Taxi Driver*, and I watched as gradually they turned the film around from something that had left preview audiences yawning to something that was actually almost really good. Still, the working pace was frantic. In the last six weeks of *Coyote Ugly*, I would have regular 4 a.m. meetings, that's how crazy life got. We had to provide new music for the entire end section of the film, about twenty minutes' worth all told, including an as-live performance of 'Can't Fight the Moonlight'. We were working 24-hour days and only sleeping when we were too exhausted to do any more.

It got to the night before the shoot, and I felt like I was going to make the deadline, when I got a call from Jerry at 10 p.m: 'Trevor, I've listened to the sound bed for the shoot tomorrow, and it really needs another gear shift. Is there any way that you can make it move up a gear?'

I ended the call thinking, *How the fuck am I going to get this other gear change out of this song and have it ready for 9 a.m. tomorrow morning?*

They'd given me a direction to have the track start with a band playing live, after which it falters, and she stops, and then it starts again. For this, I had a drummer, Steve Ferrone, booked for 2 a.m. to record the live drums. Steve came in and we made the front bit sound like a live band, but I still didn't know what to do. *Gear change. Gear change.* I was wandering lonely as a cloud in the studio, hoping for inspiration to strike, when I bumped into LeAnn's programmer, who said to me, 'Here, come and look at this.'

To cut a long story short, this guy had a bit of software that I'd never seen before. And to keep the short story even shorter, I was able to use that software to sample my track back onto my main track and give it the gear shift Jerry wanted. I remember thinking that if this guy hadn't been there hanging out, and if we hadn't all been buddies, then I would have been fucked. With everything being done so late at night, I don't know what I would have done. Even having found this gear shift, it took me the rest of the night to finish the cue.

They were shooting on the MGM lot over in the Valley. I was meant to be there by 9 a.m. with the track. In the end, I didn't make it until 9.30 a.m. in a car that had been sent for me. When I arrived, they had people waiting for me at the gate and I was taken straight to the set where they were setting up to shoot – literally ready to shoot to a piece of music that I held in my hand.

It was a tense moment. I had to walk on set, holding the CD as though it were the holy grail, the film crew parting around me in order to let me through. They put the music on a huge rig at the side of the set where Bob Badami had set up for playback. It was exactly what they wanted. I was a hero. That was my big moment, my big Hollywood moment. And then, because I'd been going for thirty-six hours relying purely on coffee, I fell fast asleep mid-conversation with Jerry, slumped off my chair and spilt water down myself, after which they got me in a car and sent me home.

On second thoughts, though, maybe falling asleep mid-conversation with Jerry Bruckheimer was my big Hollywood moment.

22

'All the Things She Said', t.A.T.u. (2002)

In which I'm in serious shit and totally lost

It was being fired from a movie called *Spirit: Stallion of the Cimarron* that led to me working with t.A.T.u. I was actually 'LA fired', where they give you $350,000 in the expectation that you're not going to sue them. Not long after, I was still in LA, kicking my heels a bit, when Jill suggested I go to see Jimmy Iovine, the legendary label executive and producer whose CV includes the likes of Bruce Springsteen, Dire Straits, Tom Petty, Meatloaf and Patti Smith. 'I bet he'll have something for you,' said Jill, and so because I knew Jimmy as a fellow producer – and had worked with him on an oddball Tom Jones album, *The Lead and How to Swing It* – I called him up and arranged a meeting.

As well as his production background, Jimmy had founded Interscope Records, an insanely successful label that dealt mainly with hip hop. Hip hop was blighted by violence and as a result, Jimmy had a lot of protection. I was startled, in fact, by just how much security he had. To get to him, I had to go through at least three different reception areas and even then, his office – palatial, of course – was strategically hidden within the labyrinth of his building. I found him inside reading a copy of *Billboard* magazine open to the album charts.

'Look at this,' he said, virtually by way of greeting. 'All these guys here in the charts, they all love me. Everybody else on the label hates me.'

We talked for an hour or so until Jimmy said, 'Anybody you want to produce?', which in theory sounds like being given the keys to the sweetshop but in practice just doesn't work like that. An artist has got to *want* to work with a producer, and there's no way an American act is going to have an eccentric English producer foisted on them, especially if they don't like his records. So I did what I always do with that sort of question: I avoided it.

Also in the meeting was a guy who Jimmy introduced as Martin Kierszenbaum, his head of marketing. Martin left us, but not without saying to me, 'On your way out, would you mind stopping by my office? I've got something I'd like to show you.' So I ducked into his office and he told me that he had this act: two girls called t.A.T.u., who had sold millions in their home country of Russia, and would I be interested in writing an English lyric for their big hit?

He played me a video of the song, 'All the Things She Said', although it wasn't called that then. The song was about two young girls who have a crush on each other and at one point in the video, they kissed each other, which I knew for certain would cause trouble. Same-sex relationships were hardly a novelty in pop music, but it was rare to actually see one in action, as it were.

Now, although I'd been sacked from the *Stallion* film, the experience hadn't been all bad because at one point during the production I'd been asked to come up with a lyric that every-body ended up really liking enough for Bryan Adams to sing in the finished movie – and I got paid a lot of money. Prior to that, I hadn't written for years. Not since the soundtrack for *Toys* in 1992. But somehow that had put me back in the lyric-writing game and I was feeling confident.

'Yes, I'd like to do it,' I said. 'Is there a multi-track for it?'

They seemed to think there was and that they would get it to me. After that, I didn't hear anything for about three or four months. No doubt they were trying to hire someone cheaper but didn't get what they wanted so eventually came back to me. Same request. Could I write an English lyric and remake the record? The literal translation went, 'Yes, I am mad, she makes me burn, yes, I'm mad, yes, I'm mad, I'm mad, I burn, yes.' Nothing you could make into an English lyric, so it wasn't just a case of port-ing it from one language to another: it needed a whole new song.

Neither was there much of a budget. Nobody had ever redone a Russian track and had a hit before, so they gave me $25,000, which wasn't much for me in those days. The carrot was that for the English lyric, I'd get a share of the publishing royalties from the song.

I started writing an English lyric at 4 a.m. one morning at Hook End, in the garage. The girls – Lena and Julia – were coming over with their manager in three to four days' time and I had to get it done before their arrival. I transcribed the Russian words, writ-ing them down in gibberish. I knew whatever they sang, it would sound like a translation because of their accents, so I wanted to keep it a bit formal. After several goes, I eventually came up with the lines, 'I'm in serious shit, I feel totally lost / If I'm asking for help, it's only because / Being with you has opened my eyes, could

I ever believe such a perfect surprise? / I keep asking myself wondering how / I keep closing my eyes but I can't block you out / Want to fly to a place where it's just you and me / Nobody else so we can be free'. And that was it. I had the beginnings of the lyric, after which, and much to my relief, the rest of the song came. For some reason the Beatles' song 'Things We Said Today' popped into my head. I changed it to 'All the Things She Said' and I had the chorus.

And then they sent me the 'multi-track', a total shambles. In fact, it felt to me as though the people who'd made the original record had deliberately given me something that was unusable, so I really did have to start again. Because I couldn't afford musicians, I had to play everything myself, but as Jill said, 'You've got all this gear, now's the time to use it.'

The girls arrived and, just as I had suspected, were older than they'd looked in the video, possibly something to do with the fact that they'd been dressed as schoolgirls in the video. They were very nice, very funny and courteous and we got on well from the start.

'Not lesbian all the time, we got boyfriends,' they said to me early on, but I quickly discovered that this was just about the only English they knew. That made recording the song in English a bit of a trial, to say the least. The only way to do it was for me to sing, 'I'm in serious shit, I feel totally lost,' and have them copy it. 'I'm in serious sheet, I feel totally lost,' and so on, just trying to get at least one decent take.

It was a long, slow and rather tortuous process. The girls had their manager with them. He and I had taken an instant dislike to each other, and at one point he said to me, 'You're too soft. You're too kind. You must be harder with them.'

'Well, look,' I sighed, tired and hoarse from singing the line over and over again, 'if that's what you think, why don't you go and do it?'

He went into the studio and started yelling at them in Russian. Within five minutes, both girls were in floods of tears, so I kicked him out and started again: 'I'm in serious shit, I feel totally lost,' over and over and over again. I think we spent three days on that first line alone. I was exhausted at the end of it, and we had maybe a third of it that was usable.

I plugged on. And on. I had to go to America and Jimmy wanted the record finished, so they flew t.A.T.u. out as well and they stayed with me at my house in Bel Air for a few days. By this point, I was good friends with the girls. They liked me, and their English had improved. They would say, 'Trevor, Trevor, cigarette. Don't tell manager,' and the three of us would huddle around the side of the building for a crafty cig.

I laboured for days over the lyric for the chorus. Finally, I had a version ready to send to Jimmy and Martin. I still wasn't happy with the chorus but I needed to show them something. They were both disappointed: it wasn't there. By this point the girls had gone, and I was feeling stuck. I decided to go back and listen to the original record to see if I'd missed anything. It's something I often do if I'm at a bit of a loss: listen to the original. Or in most cases, listen to the demo. Try and identify what it was that had caught my attention in the first place. And what I realised was that in the Russian version they'd done the chorus differently. While I'd written a completely new lyric for every line, they had simply repeated parts of the chorus. Mine went something like, 'All the things she said / Going through my head / While I'm lying in my bed'. Theirs had certain lines recurring.

'All the things she said, all the things she said, running through my head, running through my head'.

That was it!

The problem was the girls had gone home and that isn't what they'd sung; they'd sung something completely different. Fortunately – as is so often the case – a new bit of software came to the rescue, allowing me to fix the vocals and move their pitch around, and it made a tremendous difference with my modified chorus. The song went, as we used to say, 'from shit to hit'. Added to that, my engineer Rob Orton came up with a great idea that I'd never tried before, which was to take a straight loop and add a 'swung loop' – a loop that was syncopated in a different way – over the top of it. This made a great deal of difference to the chorus, punching it right up. We took it back to England and I put some power chords on the chorus, played some keyboards on the second verse and Rob did a brilliant mix.

I sent it to Jimmy and Martin and they loved it. That was it, job done. I dusted myself off, went on to my next project, whatever that was, and heard nothing of t.A.T.u for months. Not until somebody called me and said, 'I thought I'd better tell you that your track's coming in at number one next week.'

It was there for a month and ended up going to number one all over the world, pretty much anywhere it was released. The girls went on to make a very successful album, *200 km/h in the Wrong Lane* (I produced two tracks, Rob Orton did the rest). As far as I know, that one song still makes them the most successful Russian pop group ever.

As for me, I received loads of fan mail from people for whom the song meant something. The *Daily Mail*, meanwhile, was up in arms about it and called me a pornographer, which was a bit harsh. True, there was a sexual aspect to a lot of what t.A.T.u did. I'm not sure they'd get away with dressing up in school uniforms these days. The fact that they made a habit of kissing for photographers and maintained – or certainly implied – that they were a real couple didn't exactly do much to dampen the flames of what was a very brief and mild controversy but it wasn't exactly pornography. And anyway, the reason that the song did well is not because of school uniforms or two girls kissing, although that didn't hurt. It's because it's a really good record. Notwithstanding that, my daughter Ally saw the video and said she knew that those two girls were going to snog their way around the world. And that's precisely what they ended up doing.

23

'I'm a Cuckoo', Belle and Sebastian (2003)

In which I don my anorak, my National Health specs and 'go indie'

My daughter, Ally, was a big fan of Belle and Sebastian, an avow-edly indie band in outlook and sound, and often played them in the car. I'd listen politely, and in the time-honoured fashion of dads everywhere, occasionally make cracks about them. The truth was that I didn't really get them at first. I had a lot of time for the notion of indie, of course – after all, ZTT was an indie. But the musical sensibility of an indie? I didn't think I was capable of making an indie-sounding record.

Credit to Ally, though, she persisted, and one day played me a song called 'The Stars of Track and Field' from their 1996 album, *If You're Feeling Sinister*. I loved it. I particularly loved the lyrics. Pop music is such a drivel-ridden business. Ninety-five per cent of all songs that hit big have pretty crap lyrics. But then, just when you've given up hope and you're thinking, *Why do I even like pop music?*, along comes something like 'The Stars of

Track and Field', a song that hooks you and keeps you guessing, that gives you a whole new perspective.

Life goes on, and I was out in LA, where I had a housekeeper called Marianne. One of her jobs when not working for us was fitting out the artist dressing rooms at Coachella, and playing one year were Belle and Sebastian. She got talking to them and, according to her, they were curious about me. The next thing I got a call. Somebody who wanted to know if I'd be interested in producing Belle and Sebastian, so, feeling as though the planets were aligning, I made arrangements to go and see them in Glasgow.

Ally was a bit freaked: 'Daddy, you'd better not spoil Belle and Sebastian. You'd better not over-produce them,' she wailed, possibly regretting ever having introduced them into my life.

'Darling,' I told her, 'I don't even know if I'm going to do it yet.'

But I met them and really liked them. It turned out that they'd tried working with a producer before, but it hadn't worked out and so they'd reverted to producing themselves. The way they recorded was that everything was pretty much live. They were able to achieve this by working everything out very carefully beforehand; they were very, very organised.

What instantly came across about the band was how much of a sealed unit they were. How they were very much on each other's wavelength. They were less like a band and more like a close family. Straight away, I liked that aspect to them very much. They have a hierarchy. The main singer and songwriter, Stuart Murdoch, is the leader. But it's not as pronounced as other bands, and I found that admirable.

We talked for a few hours. They asked me if I would do the album on analogue tape, and I said something that I think they liked: 'When I was a kid,' I said, 'we used to have an outside toilet, and even though there were certain things I liked about outside toilets – you got to leave the house for one thing – I would never dream of building a house with an outside toilet now. The world has moved on to greater luxury. In much the same way, I wouldn't dream of producing a track on analogue tape.'

They liked that, I think, for some hidden Belle and Sebastian reason. In return, I thought they were great, and I really liked the collection of songs that they had gathered for their forthcoming album, their sixth. In fact, I thought they were the best songs I'd heard for ages. I didn't know if any would make hit singles, but all of them were very listenable; three or four of them were *really* good, and there were two, 'Dear Catastrophe Waitress' and 'Piazza, New York Catcher', that I was very fond of indeed.

I went up to Glasgow with a small Pro-Tools rig and recorded the whole album, all the way through, live in their rehearsal rooms, just to see how it might work. I realised that I was going to need a great engineer because the way that Belle and Sebastian performed was quite unusual. The drummer, for instance, played very quietly, much more the way drummers used to play in the 1960s than the way that they play now. To some degree, the way a band play is determined by the volume of the lead singer's voice, which might sound like an odd thing to say, but it makes a huge difference. The Rolling Stones would never be the band they are if Mick Jagger didn't have the surprisingly loud voice that he has. Ditto Led Zeppelin and Robert Plant. But Stuart Murdoch of Belle and Sebastian has a very beautiful, gentle voice, and as a result the band, particularly the drummer, tend to play very quietly.

I got in touch with Julian Mendelsohn, who had been one of the original two SARM engineers back in 1979. By the year 2000 Julian had moved back to Australia, given up producing and was just doing a bit of engineering. He agreed to do the album, which turned out to be a great move because he wasn't at all in in awe of them. That was the thing about Belle and Sebastian: that self-containment. They were all highly intelligent as well. When one member of the band was doing their bit, the others would be sitting in the control room reading books, the room as quiet as a library.

Julian cut through all of that very quickly. The Aussie in him made its presence felt. He'd say, 'Hey, you, singer out there. Sing.' They put up with that, perhaps because they liked his fusspotting. All good engineers are fusspots, always complaining about snare drums being off and so forth. I think Stuart and co. liked that about Julian – it fitted with their ultra-organised ethos.

It's funny, but compared to other records I've produced, I only made a very small musical contribution to the Belle and Sebastian album. Probably my main input was a track called 'Step into My Office, Baby', on which I played some strings and sang some harmonies. The main thing I did was organise them and, frankly, they didn't need a lot of that. The song 'I'm a Cuckoo', for example. They did it in twenty-four takes. For a band to be prepared to play a song that many times to get it right is a rarity. They didn't want to overdub anything and they didn't want to fix anything, so everybody needed to play perfectly. The Beatles might do that many takes of a song, but not most bands. I had wanted to use take nine, that one had it for me. There was one mistake in it, which I said I could fix, but they thought that fixing a mistake was too much like cheating and so they kept playing it until they got it perfect, then we used take nine with the fix in it.

We also decided that we were going to have a string section as well as a horn section on the album, I brought in a brilliant arranger, a lovely guy called Nick Ingman. One evening, Nick called and said, 'They're making me do something in this song and it's wrong. They're making me write stuff that is harmonically wrong. It's discordant.'

I called Mick Cook of the band, who was coming up with all the ideas for the string arrangements: 'Nick's worried you're doing something strange. Why is there this discordance?'

Mick said, 'I was in a club one night and the DJ cross faded an Abba record with a Buddy Rich one and I was trying to get that effect.'

When I explained this to Nick, he calmed down. What an extraordinary idea.

There was another interesting moment when the band went back to Scotland for a week and Julian and I did a set of rough mixes. I remember Julian saying, 'Ah, Trevor, they're going to love this, they're going to love these mixes.'

I said, 'It's a band, Julian. They won't. They'll probably hate them.'

'Nah, they're going to love it, they're going to love it.'

They hated it. In fact, they didn't get back to me for a couple of days about it. They left me hanging, which was not a nice feeling. But you get over those moments. The thing is that when you're dicking around with people's music, they can get pretty upset if they don't like the results. You've got to be careful, you've got to remember that it's not yours and roll with it.

The band programmed one song with drums I didn't like. Most reviews at the time seemed to assume that I had introduced this element to their sound, but it was not the case. By that point I had long since turned my back on techno stuff. In fact, I was just trying to be like an old-school producer on that album, where I got the band in the best environment and made sure we captured the best take.

When the album, *Dear Catastrophe Waitress*, came out, it did well. 'I'm a Cuckoo' was a successful single. I'm pleased to say that Ally liked it, too. They still sounded exactly like Belle and Sebastian to her.

It's funny, but the fact that the world at large expected me to somehow 'do a Trevor Horn' on Belle and Sebastian was I suppose understandable after ABC and then Frankie Goes to Hollywood. However, the truth was that I was always looking for ways *not* to do that kind of thing. Going off to produce Malcolm McLaren after ABC, when I could have worked with any number of bands, says it all – I didn't want to do the same thing and have the same trademark. My thing has always been that the song should decide how the track sounds. Belle and Sebastian knew their songs. They had the music all worked out. What they needed from a producer at that point was somebody to show them how to record something well. Somebody who they could trust to tell them when they played it wrong. They needed somebody to help them make their record.

Epilogue

Produced by Trevor Horn (Prince's Trust) Concert at Wembley Arena (2004) – Part 2

On the afternoon of the concert, we held a full dress rehearsal. The likes of ABC, Belle and Sebastian and Pet Shop Boys were total sweethearts, professionals through and through, ensuring that their slots went well. I'm sure their efforts took at least some of the pressure off me, but it didn't feel like that at the time. By now it had been decided that I should be compère, but I was having problems with the autocue. It's not as easy as you think to read from a screen and not sound like a robot. I was getting jumpy, worrying about my role; worrying about Seal, who still hadn't turned up; worrying about Grace, who was due at the Arena just half an hour before the show started.

Time crept on and there was still no sign of Seal. And then during the afternoon we were running through 'Slave to the Rhythm' as part of the dress rehearsal and it got to the play-out bit when suddenly a voice came on singing, 'To the rhythm, ah to the rhythm, to the rhythm.' For a split second, I thought that somebody had left a track on the multi-track, and then I realised – it was Seal. He'd arrived and picked up a mic. And I don't think I've ever been as pleased to see – or in this case hear – somebody in all my life.

He was wonderful. He was in the best mood ever and was really up for having a good time and enjoying himself. When the Wembley Arena staff had asked me how to assign the dressing rooms, I'd said to them, 'Give the worst dressing rooms to the most secure people and the best dressing rooms to the most insecure people.' I won't tell you who got what, but I will say that Seal and I ended up together in the worst dressing room. Just before Prince Charles arrived, Special Branch with dogs checked the dressing rooms for god knows what. When it came to mine and Seal's dressing room, the dog immediately went over to my bag and buried its nose in it. The Special Branch guy looked in my bag, then said, 'Not today, Fido.'

Great as it was to see Seal, by the time we got to the end of the dress rehearsal, I felt like a condemned man. The autocue was still not working for me, so we had a meeting and I said to the Clear Channel people, 'Take the autocue away. Just have two signs, "keep talking" and "get off", and I'll react to that, it'll be much better.' It was. I waffled a bit, then as soon as I saw the 'get off' card, I would do just that.

Right before the show there was a surreal moment. Jill came and grabbed me: 'You've got to come out and welcome Prince Charles and Camilla to your show.' Already wearing my silver jacket and my in-ear monitors, I followed Jill outside to the back gate of Wembley Arena. Assembled were police with walkie-talkies and we were asked to stand in place to greet the royal pair. At that moment Chris Squire, bass player from Yes, came waddling up, dressed like a psychedelic Yeti.

'What's going on, Trev?'

'Well, I'm just welcoming Charles and Camilla to my concert,' I told him.

Uninvited, Chris and his wife got in line next to Jill and myself. Next thing, a Rolls-Royce swept in and the royal couple disembarked, came over and were introduced first to me, Trevor Horn, star of the show – 'I like your jacket,' said the Prince – then his wife, Jill Sinclair – 'Nice to meet you' – followed by a royal double-take because Chris and his missus weren't on the list. Even so, they introduced themselves and the royal couple swept on into the concert hall.

The gig followed the usual rule, which is that if the rehearsal goes badly, the performance goes well and vice versa. Our rehearsal had gone badly, and sure enough, everyone played their arses off on the show and it went off almost perfectly. I know, because I mixed the DVD with Rob Orton afterwards and we hardly had to change anything. There was one bass note that I got wrong and another I forgot to play, both of which needed fixing. In another instance, I was so impressed with Neil Tennant, thinking, *God, I remember Neil from 1988, now look at him*, before realising that I should have been singing, 'Say goodbye, if I tried. . .', and I had completely forgotten to do it. So I had to overdub that onto the film and make sure I wasn't in shot when it was happening.

My children: Ally, Aaron, Will and Gabriella. And, of course, Jill. To have all those people together in one room was very special indeed, and musically, it was great. Grace arrived twenty minutes or so before she was due on, screaming angrily at somebody for some unknown crime and wearing an amazing, billowing outfit that featured a wonderful headpiece. She was brilliant – 'You're all fucking slaves,' she yelled at the end of her song, and then hung around for ages afterwards, at the side of the stage, watching the show.

Seal was immense, of course. Even though I'd produced so much for him, I'd worried about us sharing a stage for the first time, but I needn't have done. It seemed like the most natural thing in the world, and even though he wasn't certain of the arrangement, we just looked at each other and I cued him. The version of 'Kiss from a Rose' we did was sublime. 'Crazy' and 'Killer' brought the house down, especially when Seal went out into the audience. Others? Well, Belle and Sebastian were great; ABC were slick, sophisticated, literary pop at its best, and I did my backing vocals at the end of 'Look of Love'; both Yes and Lisa Stansfield were brilliant; Propaganda sounded fabulous and 'Dr Mabuse' had all the techno dynamics of the record; Art of Noise still sounded like the future; and Frankie brought the show to a tremendous close with pounding versions of 'Welcome to the Pleasuredome', 'Two Tribes' and 'Relax'.

As for the opening two songs, I wore my silver jacket and the Buggles performed 'Living in the Plastic Age' and, of course, 'Video Killed the Radio Star'. Live for the first time ever with most of the people who played on the original record.

I heard you on the wireless back in '52.

Acknowledgements

I would like to thank Andrew Holmes for putting this together so well and all the people at Nine Eight Books for making it happen.

Thank you to all the artists I've collaborated with over the years, especially the ones talked about in this book – I hope they forgive me.

A special thank you to my partner, Janet Andersen, and my children, Ally, Aaron, Will and Gabriella, as well as my extended family members.

Lastly, a huge thank-you to my friends and the people I've worked with during my life. I'm a very lucky man.

Nine Eight Books would also like to thank Suzanne Deller for her support.